PORSCHE 356

The Story of the Flat-Four Porsches

David G. Styles

The Crowood Press

First published in 1998 by
The Crowood Press Ltd
Ramsbury, Marlborough
Wiltshire SN8 2HR

© 1998 David G Styles

The right of Dr David G Styles to be identified as the Author of this Work is asserted in accordance with the Copyright, Design and Patents Act 1988

All rights reserved. No part of this publication may be reproduced or transmitted in any form or by any means, electronic or mechanical, including photocopy, recording, or any information storage and retrieval system, without permission in writing from the publishers.

British Library Cataloguing in Publication Data
A catalogue record for this book is available from the British Library.

ISBN 1 86126 085 7

Dedication
To my wife Ann, my daughter Emma and my son Philip. They have all endured the the long hours of my sitting at a word processor, or alone in a library somewhere. Without their indulgence and support, I could not write.

Picture Credits
Photographs in this book have been supplied by: Porsche AG, Porsche Cars Great Britain Ltd, the National Motor Museum at Beaulieu, *Road & Track* and the author. Special thanks go to Fiona Loader at Porsche Cars GB Ltd and to Klaus Parr of Porsche AG. Road test data is reproduced by the kind permission of the editors of *Road & Track* and *Autocar and Motor* and drawings are reproduced from the parts and works manuals published by Porsche AG.

Typeset by Florencetype Ltd, Stoodleigh, Devon
Printed and bound in Great Britain by the Bath Press

Contents

	Introduction	4
1	The Early Days of Porsche Design	5
2	Through Conflict to the Cars from Gmünd	17
3	Porsches go into Production	33
4	Developing the Market and Introducing the 1500	50
5	Improving the Breed – Early Competition and Development	59
6	From the Quad-Cam 550 to the Single-Seat Porsches	75
7	The Product Grows – to the 356A and Beyond	98
8	The Mighty Carrera 356	115
9	Towards a New Age – The Carrera GTL, the 356B, 2000GS-GT and the 904GTS	135
10	From T-5 to T-6 and 356B to 356C	152
11	New Kids on the Block – The 912 and the 914	170
12	Enjoying a Flat-Four Porsche and Viewing its Competitors	189
Appendix 1:	The Four-Cylinder Porsche Chassis Numbers	201
Appendix 2:	Porsche Type Numbers	202
Appendix 3:	Porsche Flat-Fours and their Adversaries	205
Index		207

Introduction

There cannot be anyone in the world familiar with the automobile who has not heard the name 'Porsche'. Most people will probably associate the name with one version or another of the immortal 911. Many will recall examples of the 356 with affection or admiration. And some will instinctively think of the Le Mans 24 Hours Race, which has been won more times by Porsches than any other single make of car. There have also been more Porsches across the line at Le Mans ahead of all the others than any other maker has achieved – in one year, twelve Porsches finished ahead of the rest. And, of course, there's the 'young upwardly mobile' fraternity, who probably did more damage to the Porsche reputation than any other group as more and more 911s and other models finished up as repossessions when world recession ushered in the 1990s.

However, none of these things would have happened without that wooden shed in the outer reaches of Austria's Carinthia, in the village of Gmünd, a village which owes its fame to the Porsche family. There was also the resilience of that family who, despite extreme pressure from the Nazi regime in pre-World War II Germany, managed to stay aloof of politics, then after the war found themselves the victims of vested interests during the investigations into their wartime activities. Despite the hardships, the pressures and the close scrutiny under which they laboured, the team of workers under the leadership of Ferry Porsche, son of the founder of the family business dynasty, managed to bring into being the car which would ultimately establish Porsche as a household name in the world of fast cars.

Whilst they never won the Carrera Panamericana, they did win the Targa Florio with Porsche cars that were powered by horizontally opposed four-cylinder air-cooled engines. Porsches also covered themselves in glory at Le Mans, at the Nürburgring 1000 Kilometres Race, the Sebring 12 Hours Race and at Daytona, as well as in many other places where sporting cars gather to do battle. But above all else, Porsche cars are made for people to enjoy. That has always been their hallmark and remains so today. Porsche's first responsibility is to its customers and its first priority is its customers. But it made its name with Flat Fours and built its reputation from Flat Fours.

This book addresses that story in all its aspects, for the Flat Four Porsche story is not just the 356. It is many things – the spaceframe chassis racing cars, the military 4 × 4, the aero engines. Then there was the 912, the 914/4 and the 912E. I hope very much that you, the reader, enjoy this book as much as I have enjoyed writing it. If nothing else, it reminds us of what went before as we celebrate Fifty Glorious Years of Germany's finest automobile, bar none, for it is half a century ago that Project 356 began and 1998 will see fifty years of Porsches on the road. These are milestones in history which cannot go uncelebrated.

David G Styles
Belton 1998

1 The Early Days of Porsche Design

Ferdinand Porsche was born in Maffersdorf, a small village near the town of Reichenberg in Bohemia, on 3 September 1875. He was named after his grandfather and was the third child of Anton and Anna Porsche. Anton was a master tinsmith, having abandoned the family cloth-weaving trade for a future in the new world of industry. He was also deputy mayor of Maffersdorf and a board member of the Maffersdorf Banking Society.

As a boy, Ferdinand was an avid ice skater, but at this early age electricity had already captured his imagination. He once combined these two interests to produce a pair of illuminated skates by fitting a light bulb to each skate and running the wire for their power to a battery in his coat pocket via his trouser legs! He was not yet ten years old when in 1884 Gottlieb Daimler patented his 'Gasmotor' under German Patent Number 28022, and he followed keenly the reports about Carl Benz's automobile a year later. His interest in things mechanical at such an early age was to have a profound effect on his personal destiny and that of the name 'Porsche'.

This was the Porsche family home in Maffersdorf, where young Ferdinand grew up and joined his father to learn the skills of a tinsmith in the workshops behind the house.

The Early Days of Porsche Design

ELECTRICITY AND FERDINAND PORSCHE

By the time he was fourteen years old, Ferdinand Porsche was spending every spare moment in his father's workshop, finding his way about the tools and acquiring the skills of a tinsmith. For now, having lost his elder brother Anton in a workshop accident, Ferdinand found himself expected eventually to take over the family business. Upon the commencement of his formal apprenticeship to the family business, Ferdinand was enrolled in 1890 at the Reichenberg Technical Institute on a course in electro-technology. Even before this he had installed electric bells and, using knowledge acquired from his tutors at the Technical Institute, he provided the family

At the age of thirteen, Ferdinand had equipped the family home with electric lighting. By 1893, when he was still only eighteen, a full electric power system was installed, the first in the district.

home at Maffersdorf with electric lighting, via its own power dynamo. In that same year, 1890, Ferdinand was to join Bela Egger and Company, in Vienna, for further training, away from home, as was then common practice.

By the time he was 22 years old, Ferdinand Porsche had risen to the position of assistant manager at the electrical engineers Vereinigte Elekrizitats AG and had built an electrically powered bicycle for his personal transport. He had examined the internal combustion engine, both petrol fuelled and Rudolf Diesel's new compression ignition oil-fuelled motor, as well as steam power for self-propelled vehicles, and had concluded that electricity was probably a cleaner, quieter and more efficient power source. However, in those days, only very short distances were being covered by automobiles, so battery life for electric propulsion was not yet a problem.

While Ferdinand Porsche was examining alternative power sources for wheeled vehicles, Ludwig Lohner had also followed the same route for a power form to suit the automobile he planned to build. After meeting Porsche, Lohner concluded that, whilst his automobile was a little way off its first road trials, the power unit should now be electrically driven. So he engaged Porsche to design the motors to propel his new car, and in 1900 Porsche began designing and manufacturing cars under the Lohner name. Over ninety-five years later, the design concept of electrically powered hub motors for motor vehicles is considered ultra modern, yet that was exactly the drive mode adopted by Ferdinand Porsche in 1900. In September of that year, Porsche took one of his creations up the Semmering Pass, with the aim of setting a world record over a 10km (6 miles) distance.

On an average 4 per cent gradient, rising some 1,300ft (400m), the car achieved a speed of just under 25mph (40kph) – a pretty startling pace for such a run with any vehicle, but the first internationally significant achievement with an electrically powered one. However, it soon became clear to Porsche that the electrically powered vehicle had far more limitations to its development than the internal combustion engine fuelled by petroleum spirit.

Before leaving the electric car behind, however, the Lohner-Porsche hub motored creation was to carry its most distinguished passenger. Porsche had earlier joined the Austro-Hungarian Army as an infantry reservist and, during a major exercise in western Hungary during 1902, a Lohner-Porsche, driven by its designer, conveyed the Archduke Franz-Ferdinand around his headquarters in Sasvar. Later, the Archduke sent a message of thanks to Porsche to mark his pleasure with the silent automobile.

The last Lohner-Porsches of note were built in 1904, fire-fighting machines built for the City of Vienna. But Ferdinand Porsche's destiny was to lead him to pastures new quite soon. Whilst Porsche and his new bride, Louise, were on their honeymoon in Paris, he met, quite by chance, a man named Emil Jellinek, the man whose financial resources brought the name 'Mercedes' to the cars which the Daimler company built, by naming the car after his daughter. In that meeting, Porsche discovered they had a common interest in motor cars. Almost a year later, in 1905, the two men met again, now on the Semmering Pass. Jellinek's Mercedes had broken down and Porsche came by in his Lohner-Porsche. He set about finding the fault on the Mercedes and got it running again. This resulted in the offer of a post within the newly formed Austrian Daimler company, which Porsche accepted.

The Lohner-Porsche was designed by Ferdinand Porsche and powered by the most advanced concept of electric hub motors. Here, a car shows its potential in an Austrian hill climb at the turn of the century. Inset is the badge of the Lohner System-Porsche.

The Early Days of Porsche Design

Just after the turn of the century, Ferdinand Porsche became an army reservist, joining the young Deutschemeister k.u.k. Regiment. Here, he is seen at the wheel of a Lohner-Porsche, with Archduke Franz-Ferdinand in the passenger seat during manoeuvrs in western Hungary in 1902. Later, the archduke expressed his 'satisfaction in every respect' with both the car and its chauffeur!

PROGRESS WITH AUSTRIAN DAIMLER

Among Porsche's early designs for Austrian Daimler was an electric bus which was exported to Britain under the brand name 'Cedes'. Daimler did not want the name 'Mercedes' used in Great Britain at that time, as the British Daimler company was already well established and there was now no relationship between the British and German companies of the same name. Although Porsche continued work on his electric drive system, he abandoned it for the time being in favour of the internal combustion engine. This was partly because Emil Jellinek had ordered a large quantity of Maja engines for installation in Mercedes cars. These engines were not as successful as had been hoped and Jellinek's business faced serious difficulties for a period.

By 1908, Porsche had created a new car for Austrian Daimler, the 28/36hp. Quickly following it was a lightweight model, the 8/16hp, with an engine of 1,845cc displacement. Both models were offered in chassis-only form for coachbuilders to equip with bodies according to their customers' choice. Soon, Austro-Daimler was exporting cars all over Europe and even to the United States of America, thanks to the results of Porsche's development work.

In the following year, 1909, Porsche briefly returned to mixed power vehicles, using his petrol engined electric hub drive system to power fire engines and other utility vehicles. Then came the 'Taunuswagen', a two-seat sporting vehicle which raced at Brooklands, followed by Porsche's first aero-engine design, a 100hp six cylinder unit. In the same year, Porsche's son Ferry was born and Louis Blèriot made the first-ever crossing of the English Channel by powered fixed-wing aircraft. This was also the year in which an Austro-Daimler first competed in the Prince Henry of Prussia Trial, completing the event with no penalty points.

Ferdinand Porsche had already proved himself an accomplished driver in competition, so it came as no surprise that he entered a team for the 1910 Prince Henry of Prussia Trial. A new 86hp four-cylinder

The Early Days of Porsche Design

The 1910 Prince Henry of Prussia Trial saw a Porsche-designed Austro-Daimler, entered and driven by its designer, win the event. It was a great achievement for Ferdinand Porsche and his company.

engined car was developed, with a tulip-type body and English Riley detachable wire-spoked road wheels. The car proved capable of an amazing 140kph (88mph) and the team of three cars, driven by Porsche, Count Schonfeld and Herr Fischer (a director of Austro Daimler) won a thoroughly deserved outright victory.

The year 1911 was a momentous year for Austro Daimler: Emil Jellinek was replaced as Director-General by Baron Skoda and the company separated from its original parent, Daimler AG in Stuttgart. Ferdinand Porsche's stature grew in the new company and a new 9/20hp model was introduced to appeal to the lower end of the expanding market for smaller cars. Capable of 45mph (72kph), this new torpedo-bodied tourer, fitted with Riley detachable wheels as standard equipment, did much to establish the profitability of the newly reorganized company.

Aero engines and military vehicles became the main focus of Porsche's attention in 1914. In particular, his M12 motor tractor, an 80hp machine designed to tow the 30.5cm (12in) Skoda gun, was noted for its reliability in the early part of World War I. Once again, petrol electric vehicles returned to Porsche's drawing board, as he produced a new vehicle called a 'Landwehr-Train', a very early road rail machine. The tractor part of the ten-trailer combination was powered by a 100hp engine, driving a 300volt/270 ampere dynamo. For his technical achievements, Porsche was awarded the Officer's Cross, First Class, of the Order of Franz Josef in 1916.

Military equipment kept Daimler busy until the war ended, then Porsche's artillery tractor found itself replacing horses in agriculture. Many thousands of horses had been lost on the battlefields of France during that terrible conflict – so many, in fact, that a civilianized version of the tractor continued in production post-war until Austro Daimler was able to resume the manufacture of cars.

Meanwhile, Ferdinand Porsche found himself replacing Baron Skoda as Director General of Austro-Daimler. It was now up to him to find work for some six and a half thousand workers at Wiener-Neustadt. In

The Early Days of Porsche Design

In 1915, with his country at war, Ferdinand Porsche turned his mind to the problems of bulk transport. One of his many creations was the 'Landwehr', or 'Land Train', yet another concept thought of as modern in the last quarter of the twentieth century. This picture shows an example, which was adaptable to road or rail (again a 'modern' concept) parked in the yard of Austro-Daimler's works at Wiener-Neustadt. A six-cylinder engine powered a 300 volt/270 amp dynamo to drive the petrol/electric vehicle.

As war receded and the opportunity to manufacture motor vehicles for peaceful use returned, Porsche designed the Austro-Daimler AD617, out of which was developed the 'Sascha' sports car for Count Kolowrat. Four Saschas took part in the 1922 Targa Florio and swept the board in the Voiturette Class, with Alfred Neuebauer (a name destined to become world famous in later years) driving the leading Austro-Daimler.

order to use many of the stockpiled car components that had been put to one side in 1914, he put into production the remaining parts essential to completing motor cars and set his workers to the task of assembling the 35hp Austro-Daimler Double Phaeton to create new car sales while he developed a completely new model, the AD617.

Perhaps one of Dr Porsche's most momentous designs of the period was Austro-Daimler's first 'People's Car', the 'Sascha'. This new small car was to be the basis of a racing team entered for the 1923 Targa Florio race around Sicily. Its reliability brought victory in the voiturette class, the first car of the team being driven by a man whose name would, in a few years, become synonymous with the Three Pointed Star. That man was Alfred Neubauer who would twice lead his team to world supremacy in Grand Prix racing. The 'People's Car' concept would, of course, occupy Ferdinand Porsche's thinking again in the next decade.

PORSCHE GOES TO STUTTGART

Producing a car that could withstand the rigours of the Targa Florio had considerable appeal for Ferdinand Porsche, so it should come as no surprise that one of his first designs for Daimler in Stuttgart was a sporting 2-litre, which was entered for the 1924 Sicilian event. Two cars, one driven by Christian Werner and Karl Sailer, the other driven by Christian Lautenschlager and Alfred Neubauer, went to do battle with such notable adversaries as Antonio Ascari and his Alfa Romeo.

The Mercedes team won the race convincingly, with Werner and Sailer crossing the line five and a half minutes ahead of Ascari's Alfa. In that same year, Porsche received an honorary doctorate from Stuttgart Technical Institute, which mentioned the Targa Florio victory in the citation of his achievements in automobile engineering.

The Porsche-designed 2-litre Mercedes cars were entered for the 1924 Targa Florio. One was driven by Christian Werner and Karl Sailer, the other by Alfred Neuebauer and Christian Lautenschlager. The Werner/Sailer car won the race, beating Antonio Ascari's Alfa-Romeo to the line by eight and a half minutes, whilst Neuebauer and Lautenschlager finished fifteenth.

The Early Days of Porsche Design

The 1928 Mercedes-Benz SSK (Daimler and Benz had merged two years earlier) was a sporting titan. Here, Rudolf Caracciola, one of Germany's all-time great racing drivers, charges up the Semmering hill to win his event.

More distinctions followed, and in 1925 the king of Italy made him a Knight of the Crown. During this time he was working on developing the big supercharged models for which Mercedes was soon to become internationally famous.

For the companies of Daimler and Benz, the year 1926 was probably the most significant in their twin histories and one of the most momentous in the history of the world's motor industry. This was the year in which these two great companies became one. Having witnessed the merger, and the birth of a new name in motoring, 'Mercedes-Benz', Ferdinand Porsche saw his Mercedes SSK reach the pinnacle of sporting success. Daimler and Benz experienced giant management upheavals following the merger and Porsche decided to leave Daimler Benz to return to Austria and join Steyr. This move was clearly not the success he had hoped for, because in 1930 Porsche returned to Stuttgart to establish his own design office. Hard times ensued, as Germany saw six million of its workforce unemployed, and its quality cars found fewer and fewer markets. Porsche's company almost perished in that same great recession.

By 1933, one of the most significant designs in automotive history had taken its embryo form. Porsche had already experimented with a 'People's Car', but in 1932 one of Germany's leading motorcycle manufacturers, Zundapp, had commissioned such a car to be designed and built. The commission resulted in the Porsche Type 12, a small car intended to be powered by a small radial motor. NSU, another leading motorcycle maker, also decided that a 'Volks-Wagen' would be a useful adjunct to their product range, and so the Porsche Type 32 came into being, taking on what is today a very familiar shape and being powered by a horizontally opposed four-cylinder air-cooled engine mounted at the rear end of the car. So was born the forerunner of one of the best known cars in the world.

Cheap motoring was absolutely essential if any manufacturer was to reach the mass market in the 1930s, and as a result the motorcycle came back into fashion. Both NSU and Zundapp returned to and concen-

The Early Days of Porsche Design

In more down-to-earth mode, Ferdinand Porsche was determined to produce a 'people's car' and this 1932 design for motorcycle manufacturer Zundapp, the Type 12, was an early attempt. Zundapp thought highly of the design, but decided the economic climate better suited motorcycles, so they stuck to them for the time being.

trated their whole attention upon the volume production of two-wheelers and abandoned their 'Volks-Wagen' projects for the time being. As far as Porsche Design was concerned, the abandonment of his two designs was nothing more than a minor setback, for, with the political changes taking place in Germany at that time, supremacy of the Fatherland would be all important and motor racing would be one avenue of demonstrating that supremacy.

DEUTSCHLAND ÜBER ALLES

The year 1933 was momentous for both Germany and Dr Ferdinand Porsche. The country was to change dramatically as President von Hindenburg summoned Adolf Hitler to the Chancellery to form the government that was to become the Third Reich. Hitler's first target was to restore Germany's pride in itself and to make the country a top achiever in all things. Sport was high on the agenda, and this is where Ferdinand Porsche had a role to play. An early objective was to ensure that a German car should win the German Grand Prix and then become the supreme racing car of Europe. Porsche's contribution was the Auto-Union Grand Prix single seater, a revolutionary vee-sixteen rear-engined racing car that was to sweep the board of international Grand Prix racing.

In the Auto-Union's debut year, 1934, Hans Stuck won his national Grand Prix, as well as the Swiss Grand Prix and the Masaryk Race in Czechoslovakia. He also led that year's French Grand Prix for the first thirty of its forty laps, when he retired with a cooling system fault. Stuck was declared 'the Most Successful Driver of the Year' and the Auto-Union was reckoned to be the car to beat.

1934 was also the year in which construction work began on Germany's autobahns, a network of high speed motor routes linking the major German cities. It was also the year in which Ferdinand Porsche returned to the Volks-Wagen theme. The Porsche Type 60 was announced to an eager mass market, and formed the basis of the most popular car ever built in Germany, with

The Early Days of Porsche Design

Finally, the development of the 'People's Car' was taken seriously and government orders were given for its advancement, with Daimler-Benz instructed to build the first thirty cars for evaluation. The upper picture shows a Type 30, with its rear view grilles extending above the engine compartment, whilst the lower is a Type 60, the definitive version of the Volkswagen.

The Auto-Union V-16 P-Wagen ('Porsche-Wagen' – Porsche Design Type 22) became Germany's motor racing flagship. Hans Stuck, partnered by Ernst von Delius, took this car, Number 12, to fifth place in the 1936 Hungarian Grand Prix. Bernt Rosemeyer, in a similar car, won the race. These cars were the true forerunners of today's Grand Prix machines.

The Early Days of Porsche Design

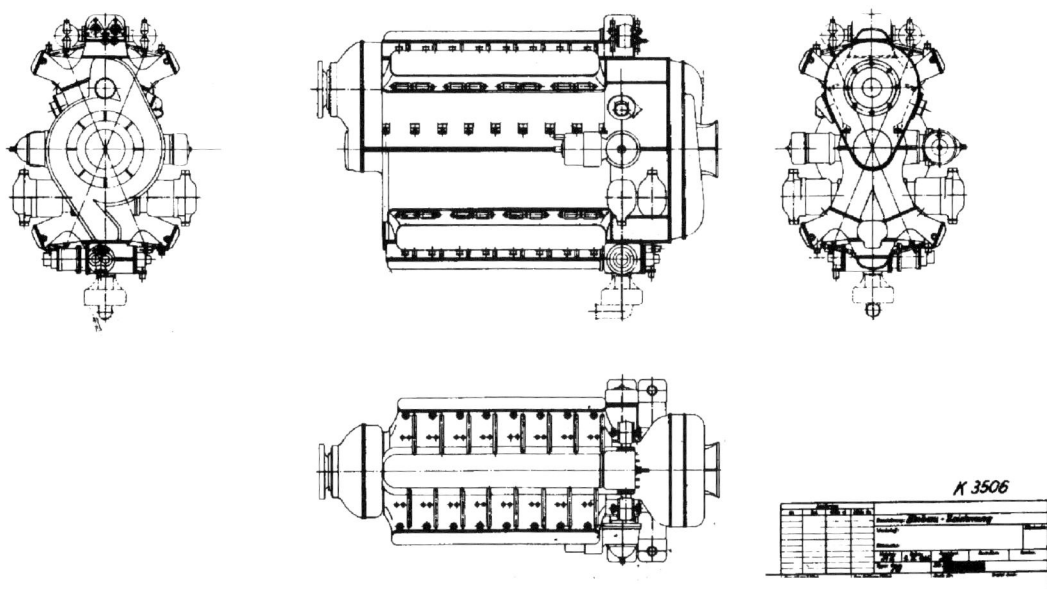

Ferdinand Porsche retained a fascination with aero engines and, after he had completed his work on the Auto-Union, produced this 32-cylinder 'X' form power unit, which embodied his other fascination, for opposed cylinder arrangements. The Type 70 eliminated the need for the twin crankshafts of 'H' form engines (such as Britain's Napier Dagger) and was thought more reliable, whilst the centrifugal turbo-supercharger provided a power boost. This concept was later pursued by Wifredo Ricart at Alfa Romeo in Milan.

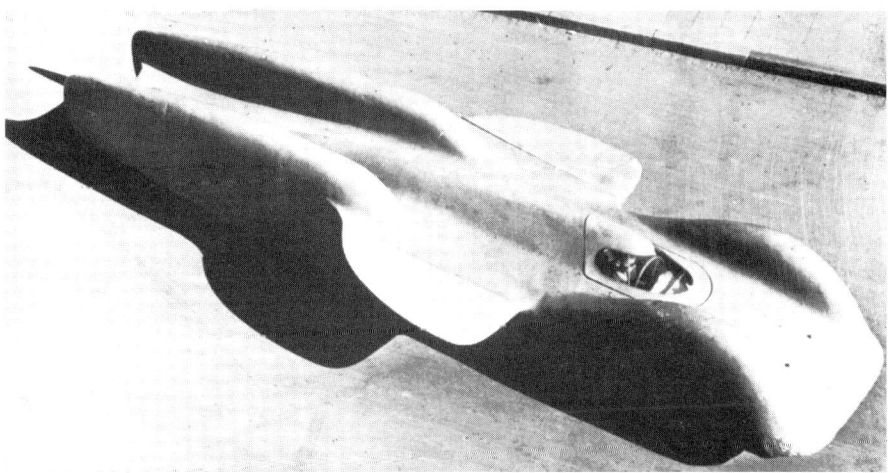

Aero engines came into use again here, with the Daimler-Benz DB603, introduced in 1937, to power the Mercedes-Benz Land Speed Record car, Porsche's Design Type 80. This overhead view shows the six-wheeled car with its twin aerofoils, one each side, to create downforce and improve the car's adhesion. With the onset of World War II, the car never turned a wheel under its own power, but again a Porsche design pointed the way for things to come.

some sixteen and a half million vehicles produced in Germany alone. The 'Beetle' is, of course, still being manufactured in South America, over sixty years later!

While the black American athlete, Jesse Owens, was setting new Olympic records in Berlin in 1936, Ferdinand Porsche was overseeing plans for the manufacture of the first thirty production-standard Volkswagens in Daimler Benz's Stuttgart factory. These cars would undergo extensive road testing ahead of the final version being created during 1937 for production a year later. At the same time, development of the Auto-Union continued apace and Berndt Rosemeyer took a fully streamlined car on to the Frankfurt–Darmstadt autobahn and achieved a speed of over 250mph (400kph) on four wheels for the first time ever.

In Great Britain, the Donington Grand Prix races saw Auto-Union and Mercedes-Benz involved in spectacular battles for supremacy in motor racing. Their only real competition came from Alfa Romeo, as Mussolini had the same aspirations for Italy as Hitler had for Germany when it came to beating the world on four wheels. The 1938 Donington Grand Prix was the most memorable of these races, and it was in that same year that construction work began on the Volkswagen factory. The 'People's Car' was to be manufactured for a planned selling price of less than one thousand Reichmarks. 1938 was also the year in which design work began on the car which was to be the very foundation of Ferdinand Porsche's own car manufacturing business. That car was the Volkswagen Type 64 Coupé.

2 Through Conflict to the Cars from Gmünd

The development of the basic Volkswagen (VW) was complete by 1938 and the construction of the Wolfsburg factory, where the new car for the masses was to built, was finally under way. The Auto-Union racing car had now developed into a 3-litre V-12 and Professor Porsche was able for a time to turn his attention to road-going sports cars.

As he was examining design ideas for a two to three-seat sporting coupé, Porsche was confronted with a design requirement for a lightweight sports racer to take part in the planned Berlin–Rome–Berlin road race. The Type 64 Coupé was the opportune product of this requirement, since Porsche already had the bones of the design on his drawing board. It was to be a car based on the floorpan and mechanical components of the Volkswagen, but developed to a level where it would have true competitive potential.

FORERUNNER OF THE REAR-ENGINED PORSCHE

The Type 64 Coupé was the true forerunner of the classic flat-four rear-engined Porsche sports cars. However, there seems to be quite a lot of confusion about how this fasci-

The Porsche Design Type 64 came from the Type 114 and was initially labelled 60-K-10. It was the amalgamation of the VW chassis and Type 114 body to make a car suitable for the Berlin–Rome–Berlin road race that never took place.

Model: Porsche/VW Type 60K10(T64) – 1939

Construction	Volkswagen Type 60 pressed/fabricated steel platform chassis with aluminium alloy bodywork
ENGINE	Modified Volkswagen Type 60, rear-mounted
Crankcase	Light alloy crankcase with individual cylinders
Cylinder head	Light alloy with inserted valve guides and seats
Cyls/Type	Four, horizontally opposed
Compression	8.0:1
Cooling system	Air, with finned cylinder barrels and belt-driven fan
Bore & Stroke	73mm × 64mm (2.85 × 2.5in)
Capacity	1,071.5cc (65.36cu in)
Main bearings	Four, three light alloy bush and one shell-type
Valves	Two overhead per cylinder, pushrod actuation
Fuel supply	Diaphragm type mechanical pump and two Solex carburettors
Power output	40bhp @ 4,000 rpm
Ignition system	Coil and distributor with auto and manual advance/retard
Lubrication	Wet sump, bevel drive pump and oil cooling
BRAKES	
Type	Drum front and rear with cable actuation
TRANSMISSION	
Clutch type	Single dry plate
Gearbox	Modified four-speed Volkswagen
Final drive ratio	Integral with gearbox, driving rear wheels
SUSPENSION/STEERING	
Front suspension	Transverse torsion bars with trailing parallel links
Rear suspension	Transverse torsion bars with leading parallel links
Steering type	VW type worm and peg with unequal arms
Wheels	Pressed steel 3.0D × 16
Tyres	5.00 × 16 cross-ply
DIMENSIONS	
Wheelbase	2,400mm (93.6in)
Track (front)	1,290mm (50.3in)
Track (rear)	1,250mm (48.8in)
MODELS AVAILABLE	Coupé (three only built)
TOP SPEED	90mph (144kph)

nating little car came about, so it seems logical to give a little time and space here to putting the record straight.

The body line of this coupé has its roots in a potentially much more exciting project numbered Type 114, which was meant to be anything but the flat-four Volkswagen based design. The Porsche Type 114 was, for its time, a very adventurous and advanced small sports car concept, which was to be powered by a V-10 mid-mounted engine of 1,500cc displacement. Originally, the body was to accommodate three people, the single rear passenger sitting across the car, behind the driver and front passenger who were in the orthodox side-by-side position. After closer examination of the aerodynamics, Porsche decided that the alternative body line of a narrower two-seat body would be more practical.

The result of these aerodynamic improvements was that the seats had to be positioned very close together. There was no room even to move the passenger seat back a little to create extra space, as the engine and gearbox assembly was already a very tight fit. The chassis was to be a tubular ladder frame design, housing the engine ahead of the gearbox, rather than behind as in the VW designs. Torsion bar suspension already featured in Porsche designs and the potential of this magnificent little car seemed tremendous.

The 72-degree V-10 engine was to have been a four-cam unit and, despite being only 1.5 litres, mounted ahead of the transmission and rear axle, with a fire wall between the front of the engine and the passenger compartment, it was a very tight fit. This was why the ultimate design was for a two-

---

Erwin Komenda

Imagine what the world would be like today if it had not experienced the shape of Volkswagen's immortal 'Beetle' or the 'bathtub' form of Porsche's 356. Whilst someone would certainly have come up with substitutes for both of these, the world would surely have been a poorer place without them.

Aerodynamic efficiency and ease of manufacture were two bywords in the vocabulary of Erwin Komenda. It was he who made a major contribution to the shape of the 'Beetle' and, as anyone who has even a scant awareness of the process of press tooling will confirm, the ease with which that car could be manufactured was demonstrated in its shape. It happened also to be aerodynamically efficient at a time when drag co-efficients were not the fashionable topic of conversation that they became in the last quarter of the twentieth century.

Practicality, of course, had also to be considered in the VW design and so it didn't quite demonstrate the flair that Komenda possessed for creating the best line for the job. But the Porsche 356 was a classic demonstration of form and function. The functional bit was the chassis, with its unorthodox rear engine position. The form was the product of Komenda's styling ingenuity, which created a car that was formidable, functional and fast. The rest is a matter of record.

Erwin Komenda was born in Jauern, a small Austrian town, on 6 April 1904. Educated at the State Trade School at Steyr, to the north of the country, he first worked with the Wiener Karosserienfabriken as a designer, moving to the Steyr company as his experience and skills grew. Leaving Steyr, he went to work at the body plant of Daimler-Benz in Sindelfingen, where his path crossed that of Dr Porsche, whose design studio he joined in 1931.

Komenda was extensively involved in the Auto-Union project, which equipped him well to play a major part in the design work for Piero Dusio's ill-fated Cisitalia Grand Prix car. As the Porsche 356 was being evolved, Erwin Komenda was drawn into the project to make his contribution, which was to give the car a 'look'. His success was confirmed by over 76,000 sales.

There were differences of opinion between Erwin Komenda and Ferry Porsche, but these apart, Porsche appointed him Chief Engineer in 1955, with control of the Body Department, where he remained until his death in 1966.

seater. All this was created at the behest of KdfWagen Werke, who also paid the design and development bill. They wanted a sports racing car and Porsche was commissioned to produce the design.

However, political tensions were building up in Germany at the beginning of 1939, and as a result the Type 114 did not reach production. Development and production costs were another major factor, for it did not take long for the Volkswagen board to realise that the cost of creating this sports/racing car would be prohibitive when set against the allocated budget. But all was not lost, as the body design, a product of the talent of Erwin Komenda, was to find its way on to the chassis platform of a Volkswagen, to become the Volkswagen Type 64.

The VW engine was enlarged from its original 985cc to 1,100cc and the power raised from a meagre 25bhp to a slightly more than modest 40bhp. Testament to Komenda's styling and comprehension of aerodynamics, together with his ability to translate the results of wind tunnel testing into metal, was the fact that the VW Type 64 was capable of almost 90mph (144kph). This may not seem much today, but it was pretty awesome in its time. This was the car intended to take part in the Berlin–Rome–Berlin race. Three cars were built and Porsche awaited formal confirmation of the date for the event. But, sadly, it never came, as the onset of World War II intervened and the race was cancelled. However, the lessons of the car were saved for the day when the conflict would end.

Only one of these attractive little coupés survives to this day, but after the beginning of World War II, Professor Porsche used one as his everyday transport and frequently drove long distances, confirming the car's reliability. What was more, on the very lightly populated roads of those early wartime days, he was often able to average journey times between Stuttgart and Berlin of more than 80mph (130kph) with quite modest fuel consumption. All this was useful development data for the day when peace would return and Porsche could commence the manufacture of cars which would carry his own name.

TO THE TOOLS OF WAR

When Hitler's storm troops advanced into Poland at the beginning of September 1939, the British government declared war on Germany. So began the greatest conflict of the twentieth century, the Second World War. The Wolfsburg Volkswagenwerke, built to manufacture the 'People's Car', was now tasked to manufacture a utilitarian adaptation of the VW for war use.

The military Volkswagen Type 62 used the same floorpan, suspension and running gear as the original car design, though the bodywork was a very basic open type with four doors, fold-flat windscreen, racks for tools and a front mounted spare wheel laid on top of the sloping front panel. The doors and the panelwork were ribbed to give rigidity and strength and the ground clearance was substantially increased from the original road car.

This little vehicle quickly developed into the two-wheel-drive Type 82, then the 4×4 Types 86 and 87. The original Type 82 was modified for use in the Western Desert campaign as the Type 82A, with tropicalized ignition system and electric wiring, larger tyres for use on sand and other modifications. It started life with the original 985cc engine of the 'Beetle', but by 1943, a slightly larger and more powerful engine of 1,130cc had been developed to propel the 80-Series vehicles.

Through Conflict to the Cars from Gmünd

These two views show the development of the Type 62 low-chassis 'Kübelwagen'. The one on the left has soft side curtains to protect the occupants from road dirt, whereas the second version has doors corrugated to improve the strength of otherwise quite flimsy metalwork.

The Type 82A, with its improved electrics and sand tyres, was a highly successful utility vehicle in the North African Desert and quite a few changed hands between German and Allied forces as they charged to and fro across the deserts of Egypt and Libya in a fight which culminated in the Battle of El Alamein. Many Allied troops who drove this odd-looking German vehicle found it preferable to the Willys Jeep, with its longer wheelbase, better enclosure of its occupants and sometimes more reliable air-cooled engine. The 82A was ultimately joined in service by four-wheel-drive versions, as the Germans found themselves ploughing through the notorious Italian mud.

Many lessons were learned by Porsche from the development and production of the 80-Series 'Kübelwagen', as it was called. The weatherproofing of electrics was vital to the smooth running of the horizontally

The tropicalized Kübelwagen, the T82A, featured sand tyres, tropicalized electrics, sand filters and tropical equipment for the crew, including the ubiquitous sand shovel! This was an extremely successful vehicle on the battlefields of the Western Desert.

opposed, air-cooled rear-mounted engine of a vehicle whose power unit was so exposed to the elements. This and the occasional transmission problems were all sorted out in the name of military progress and even an amphibious variant, labelled the Type 128, was produced. The prototype 'Schwimmwagen' was built at the Porsche works in Zuffenhausen and was tested locally. About thirty examples of this early version were built before the Type 166 evolved from it. Some 15,500 production examples of the Schwimmwagen were built, alongside more than 200,000 Kübelwagens.

This versatile and remarkable little vehicle did not even stop at the standard-version Kübelwagen and Schwimmwagen. The Kübelwagen found itself adapted to the roles of service car, light gun tractor, mobile air raid warning unit and half-track. Then there was a version with a mock-up body that made it look like a battle tank! One variant of the Schwimmwagen was equipped with paddle wheels to help propel it through snow, though only a few examples went into service. There were even generator gas-powered versions of these robust little vehicles, produced to compensate for the drastic shortage of petroleum spirit. All in all, the military Volkswagens gave Professor Porsche and his team a wealth of development experience, which would prove to be of tremendous value in the design of the flat-four Porsches.

As the conflict wore on, all the European protagonists suffered increasing shortages of all commodities. Electric power was a major problem in Germany, so Porsche turned his thoughts back to electricity and set about creating a wind generator under Porsche Design Number 136. This wind vane drove a generator to give 736 watts of electricity and the prototype was installed in Hohenheim, near Stuttgart. Shortly after that project was completed, in 1943, attention focused again on the Volkswagen engine, now modified to power a light barge for military use in river and canal transport.

Porsche's largest contributions physically to the German war effort included work on the *Tiger* and *Leopard* battle tanks. Because he disliked firearms of any kind, he used his lack of knowledge about guns to excuse himself from being involved in the firearms aspect of tanks. His expertise was applied to the hull and running gear of tanks, with

Through Conflict to the Cars from Gmünd

This idyllic scene could just as easily be a picture of a lone fisherman enjoying a break on the river. In fact, it was taken during the test programme for the Type 174 KdF engine used in cross-river landing barges employed by the Wehrmacht.

The 'Ferdinand' was an anti-tank cannon mounted on to the hull of Ferdinand Porsche's Tiger tank. It is seen here on trial, with its designer seated at the right in front, with Supplies Minister Albert Speer just behind him.

the result that, for example, the *Tiger*, Types 101 and 103, was a highly successful exercise in mobility. The assault cannon *Ferdinand* was another Porsche tracked vehicle design, as was the Type 205 *Maus*.

Allied air supremacy in 1944 caused Porsche considerable concern, as he felt the Zuffenhausen plant was now a sitting target. As a result, he had all drawings reproduced with two extra copies made – one set was kept in the Stuttgart works, another was stored at an old flying school site at Zell-am-See, whilst the third was taken to the tiny Austrian village of Gmünd

This is the unimposing entrance to the Gmünd sawmill which was home to the Porsche family firm from 1944–50.

in Carinthia. This was a relatively safe place and was, of course, to become the first home of the now internationally renowned Porsche product. The whole Porsche activity moved to Gmünd in late 1944.

As the winter of 1944–5 eased, it became clear that Hitler's war was coming to an end and the Porsche family was compelled to begin considering both its future and the future of its business. The Porsches had never supported Hitler's regime politically, but a natural sense of patriotism had brought them, like so many ordinary Germans and Austrians, to support the defence of their homeland. After all, the population of Germany was told that Britain had declared war on them! In view of Ferdinand Porsche's work in the war effort, he would find himself vulnerable to the efforts of war crimes investigators, some of whom would be bent on prosecution at almost any cost. The Porsche family's worst nightmares would soon become reality.

PEACE AND THE REVIVAL OF PORSCHE DESIGN

Shortly after the Allied occupation of Germany and Austria, Ferdinand Porsche met an American officer with whom he had first become acquainted in 1936 during a trip to the United States. Major Frenssen and he discussed all kinds of topics, mostly connected with the professor's engineering work during the war. In July, he was arrested and interned for three months under further investigation for war crimes, his crimes being the design and development of the weapons of war – given that his designs had been wheeled and tracked vehicles, with others designing the firepower.

Professor Porsche's freedom was short-lived, however, as very soon after his release by the Americans, with no charges brought against him, a French officer visited him at Zell-am-See to discuss producing the

Volkswagen in France. The two went to Baden-Baden, in the French zone of Germany. Whilst there, it appears that people connected with a rival industrial group engineered Porsche's re-arrest on charges connected with the treatment of prisoners of war. Professor Porsche, Anton Piech and Ferry Porsche were all interned. Ferry Porsche was released after six months, but the two older men were detained for a further fourteen months in sometimes quite appalling conditions.

It seems ironic that, during the time that Ferdinand Porsche was interned, the Renault company sought his help in the development of the post-war Renault R4. Typical of the man, even though he stood accused of using slave labour in the Peugeot factory during the war – when he had actually protested against it – he still gave his help, even to his captors, in the interests of reconstructing a war-torn Europe.

During these very difficult times, Louise Piech, Professor Porsche's daughter, drew together all the artefacts and materials of the family business and registered Porsche Design in Austria in 1946. Ferry Porsche had returned to Gmünd by this time and so

---

Professor Dr Ferdinand Porsche

Ferdinand Porsche's meteoric rise to fame is covered at length elsewhere in this book. His love affair with electricity took him to Lohner, where he created a vehicle which had the same method of power that was used in the lunar rover vehicle built by NASA for the expedition to the Moon by astronauts Scott and Irwin in 1971. But no-one ever thought to give Ferdinand Porsche his due credit! Yet his propulsion idea predated the NASA project by seventy-one years.

Porsche's designs were almost always well ahead of his contemporaries. Everyone thought he was mad when he set about designing a Grand Prix car with the engine behind the driver. His massive World Land Speed Record contender was ridiculed by some when they saw the aerofoil 'wing stubs' on the sides of the T80 project, a car designed from the outset to take John Cobb's 370mph (595kph) record, yet a little over thirty years later we saw aerofoils on Grand Prix cars in order to give them extra surface adhesion. Again, Professor Porsche was not credited with the original idea, though it was a Porsche enthusiast, Michael May, who fitted one to a Porsche car (though he was banned from using it).

The 'People's Car' *was* credited to Professor Porsche and he lived long enough to see it reach production and recognition, as he also saw his only son's creation, the Porsche 356, reach production, too. During World War II, Ferdinand Porsche was given charge of the Tank Commission by the German government. During this time, Germany didn't really have a decent battle tank, and so the Russian T34 was closely examined. It was discovered that the T34 used Porsche torsion bar suspension and American-designed running gear. Porsche's *Tiger* design was to be the answer to the need for a 40-ton tank, though Porsche was never involved in the design of turrets or firepower.

The design for which Ferdinand Porsche will be best remembered must be the Volkswagen, and especially its wartime utility derivative, the *Kübelwagen* in its various forms. With Hitler's armies fighting on so many fronts, if the Porsche-designed *Kübelwagen* in 4×2, 4×4 and amphibious forms could prove to be reliable, then the post-war future of the Volkswagen was assured, even despite such names of the motor industry as Rootes and Ford deciding it wasn't worth development. They had reckoned without the millions of miles the VW platform had covered in the most arduous of conditions, to say nothing of the tenacity of Ferdinand Porsche!

Through Conflict to the Cars from Gmünd

Professor Ferdinand Porsche

had Karl Rabe. Together, they set about creating a car manufacturing workshop out of the old sawmill in the little Carinthian village. From the beginning, they took in all kinds of mechanical repair work to pay their way. By 1947, an Italian industrialist, Piero Dusio, had expressed a desire to build a Grand Prix racing car. Among his acquaintances were Carlo Abarth, later world famous for his sports car exhaust systems and his adaptations of the Fiat 500, and Rudolf Hruska, the man who later created the immortal Alfasud. They both had known and worked with Porsche and so recommended that Porsche Design be given the task of creating the Cisitalia.

Now, into the midst of these discussions came the world's all-time greatest racing driver up to that time – Tazio Nuvolari. He had been contacted by Carlo Abarth, who knew Nuvolari was looking for a suitable car to race at Grand Prix level now that the war was over and motor sport was reviving.

Nuvolari was enthusiastic about the Porsche idea, as he had driven Ferdinand Porsche's pre-war piece of genius, the Auto-Union, with great success. And if Piero Dusio needed any further persuasion to proceed, Piero Taruffi, a close friend of Dusio and rival of Nuvolari on the track, supported the idea wholeheartedly.

So it was that the 1,500cc supercharged Grand Prix Cisitalia went to the drawing board as Type 360. The logistics of just completing a design in those days were horrific, as each individual piece of work had to be approved by the occupying officials to ensure that neither Germany nor Austria were creating any new weapon of war. A little ironic, perhaps, when the only 'battles' that the Porsche family was interested in were those on the Grand Prix circuits of Europe.

This highly ingenious car was developed from the outset to be different. Certainly, Alfa Romeo had pioneered a flat-twelve supercharged-engined Grand Prix car in 1940 – the Tipo 512 – and three examples had been built, but never raced. The Cisitalia took the flat-twelve concept one step further, introducing air cooling and four-wheel drive into the equation, with a Porsche synchromesh gearbox and side-mounted fuel tanks in the style of a much later age. Sadly, while the Cisitalia did make it from drawing board to construction, the project died from shortage of cash before it could make any kind of name for itself other than for the ingenuity of its design. This part-time four-by-four survives in two places: the original is in the Porsche Museum at Stuttgart whilst a second, built up from spare parts acquired in the early 1970s, sits in the Donington Collection, a fine museum of racing machinery at the Donington Park Circuit in the English Midlands. Donington Park was, of course,

Through Conflict to the Cars from Gmünd

The Cisitalia 'in the metal'. Like another historically famous flat-twelve supercharged Grand Prix car, the Alfa Romeo 512, it never turned a wheel in anger.

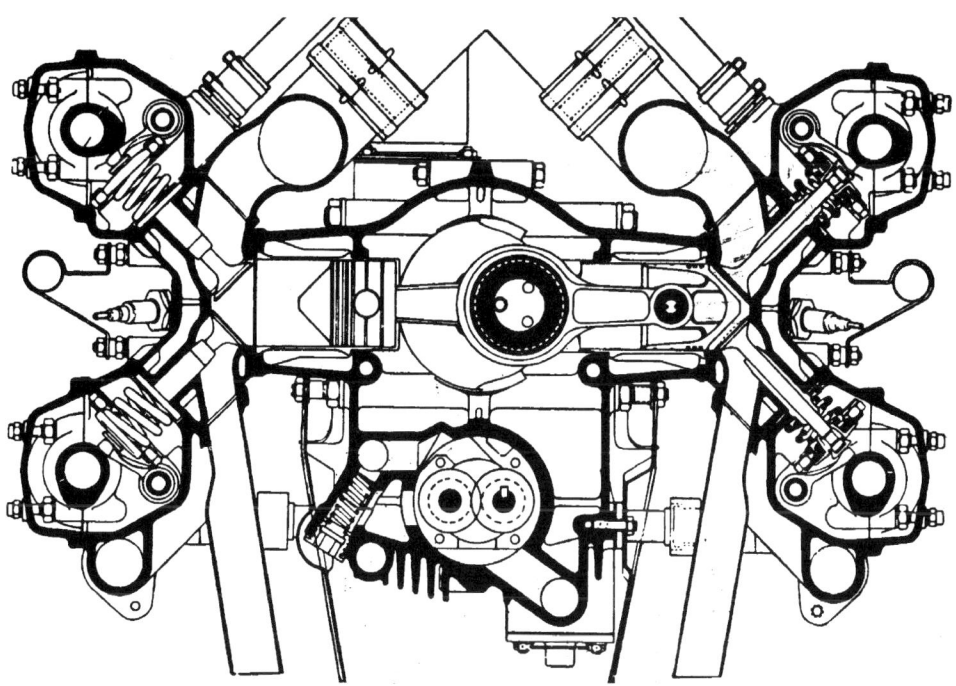

This cross-section of the Cisitalia engine shows a line of design thinking which would be revived by Porsche in later years for its own racing engines.

famous in its pre-war days for some of the mightiest battles between Auto-Union and Mercedes-Benz.

AT LAST – THE FIRST 356

Design work on the first car to be built by Porsche under their own name began in 1947. A drawing of the prototype, dated 17 July 1947, shows a small two-seater, with the engine positioned ahead of the rear wheels and gearbox. The bodywork was to be of aluminium alloy, attached to a tubular spaceframe chassis, the whole car being built at Gmünd, using several Volkswagen components. This then, was Porsche Type 356 Number 356.001.

Those Volkswagen parts focused, of course, on the engine and gearbox, primarily, though suspension components were also transferred form the VW to Porsche's first car. The trailing arm front suspension was used in its entirety, though the rear suspension assembly did not go into 356.001 exactly as it left Wolfsburg, for it was turned round, so that the original trailing arms running from the torsion bars became leading arms on the Porsche. The power output for this first engine was 35bhp which, from an 1,100cc unit of the time, was reasonable, but it seemed hardly enough to propel the car at 80mph (130kph), though, amazingly, it did.

Looking at the 356 and the pre-war Volkswagen Type 64, several aspects of common thought can be seen in both designs. Aerodynamics were considered important to both, as in each case the engine was really quite small and of limited power output. Bearing in mind that Porsche was already involved in wind tunnel testing of models to determine their shape and efficiency of penetration through the air, long before drag co-efficients became a talking point, it is hardly surprising that there should be a distinct relationship in the lines of the two cars, save that the Type 64 was a coupé and the 356 was initially a roadster, though its coupé variant soon followed.

Taking the engine which was used as a barge power unit as the benchmark, Porsche now went to work to create a power unit of 1,131cc capacity. The angled exhaust valves of this new Type 369 engine were, very cleverly, operated by rocker arms which had been positioned at 90 degrees from the inlet valve rockers, allowing them to be positioned as they were without relocating the pushrods from their straight-line position parallel to the inlet pushrods. This kept down production costs, for the original Volkswagen cylinder barrels and crankcase were retained.

There was a deal done between Heinz Nordhoff, of Volkswagen, and Ferry Porsche in which engine, gearbox and running gear parts were to be supplied to Porsche and Volkswagen would promote the new car through its dealers. However, this distribution arrangement did not take place until later, for the problems of moving goods between Germany and Austria were still huge and, in any case, the prototype had yet to be built and proven. This prototype differed from the early production variants of the 356 in a number of ways, not least in its mid-engined configuration, which proved impractical for volume production and operational maintenance.

The way in which the engine and gearbox were installed into that first Porsche is quite novel. It is explained by the fact that the Gmünd workshops were not equipped for the major re-engineering of any of the car's components. In consequence of this, the Volkswagen engine/transmission/suspension subframe was installed virtually as it left Wolfsburg. With the engine positioned ahead of the gearbox, the normally

Model: Porsche Type 356 Gmünd Prototype (356-001)

Construction	Tubular spaceframe chassis with aluminium alloy roadster bodywork
ENGINE	Volkswagen/Porsche Type 369, mid-mounted
Crankcase	Light alloy crankcase with individual cylinders
Cylinder head	Light alloy with inserted valve guides and seats
Cyls/Type	Four, horizontally opposed
Compression	7.0:1
Cooling system	Air, with finned cylinder barrels and belt-driven fan
Bore & stroke	74mm × 64mm (2.89 × 2.5in)
Capacity	1,131cc (70cu in)
Main bearings	Four, three light alloy bush and one shell-type
Valves	Two overhead per cylinder, pushrod actuation
Fuel supply	Diaphragm type mechanical pump and one Solex carburettor
Power output	35bhp @ 4,000 rpm
Ignition system	Coil and distributor with auto and manual advance/retard
Lubrication	Wet sump, bevel drive pump and oil cooling
BRAKES	
Type	Drum front and rear with cable actuation
TRANSMISSION	
Clutch type	Single dry plate
Gear ratios	1 = 15.95:1, 2 = 9.17:1, 3 = 5.54:1, 4 = 3.54:1. R = 29.23:1
Final drive ratio	4.43:1
SUSPENSION/STEERING	
Front suspension	Transverse torsion bars with trailing parallel links
Rear suspension	Transverse torsion bars with leading parallel links
Steering type	VW type worm and peg with unequal arms
Wheels	Pressed steel 3.0D × 16
Tyres	5.00 × 16 cross-ply
DIMENSIONS	
Overall length	3,860mm (150in)
Overall width	1,670mm (65in)
Overall height	1,250mm (48.8in)
Track (front)	1,290mm (50in)
Track (rear)	1,250mm (48.8in)
MODELS AVAILABLE	Roadster (one only built)
TOP SPEED	84mph (135kph)

Through Conflict to the Cars from Gmünd

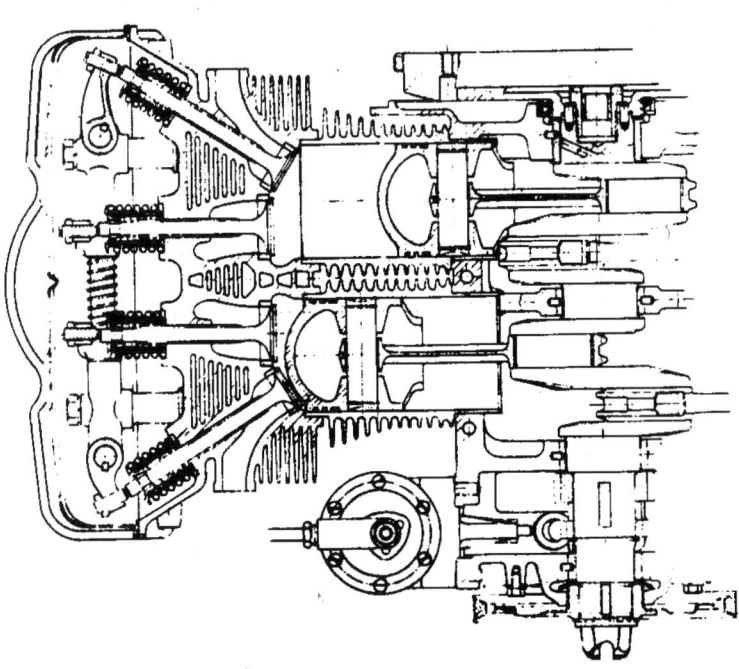

This part-section drawing depicts the top end of the Type 369 engine for the first Porsches. Note the valve angles and the ingenious positioning of the rockers.

trailing arm suspension became leading arm, which led to quite a few handling problems and a pronounced toe-out under cornering.

DEVELOPING THE CONCEPT

Whilst Porsche's ideal concept for this new car was mid-engined, the practicalities of the situation were such that the standard VW type of layout was essential to the commercial success of the car.

Recalling that Gmünd could not undertake any major machining work, the fabrication was done there, while the machined mechanical and running gear parts were brought in and fitted as built, and so the prototype remained the only mid-engined Porsche of the time. The chassis design was not carried over to production either, as Professor Porsche contended that it would take up too much space and would be too expensive to produce.

Even so, the car went ahead and the body panels, designed to be as aerodynamically clean as they could be, consistent with simplicity for the panel beaters, were beaten and fitted at Gmünd. Testing, however, began in March 1948, before the body was created and fitted. The panels were created by a Viennese genius named Friedrich Weber, who was reputed to have a bit of a problem with drink, but not the slightest problem with either the tools or materials of his trade. So Weber had a complete body on this little flyer by the summer of 1948.

Right: These two drawings show the tubular chassis design for the first Porsche sports car, Number 356-001, and the body which was to envelop it, hand-crafted by Porsche employee Friedrich Weber.

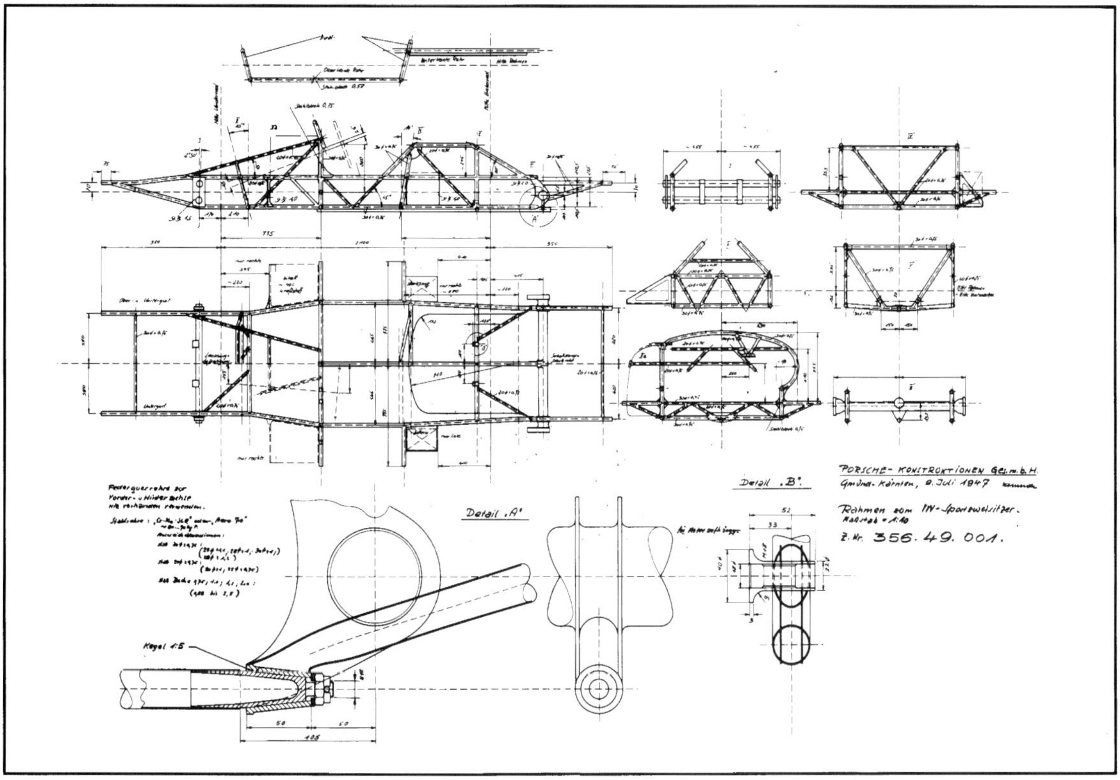

Through Conflict to the Cars from Gmünd

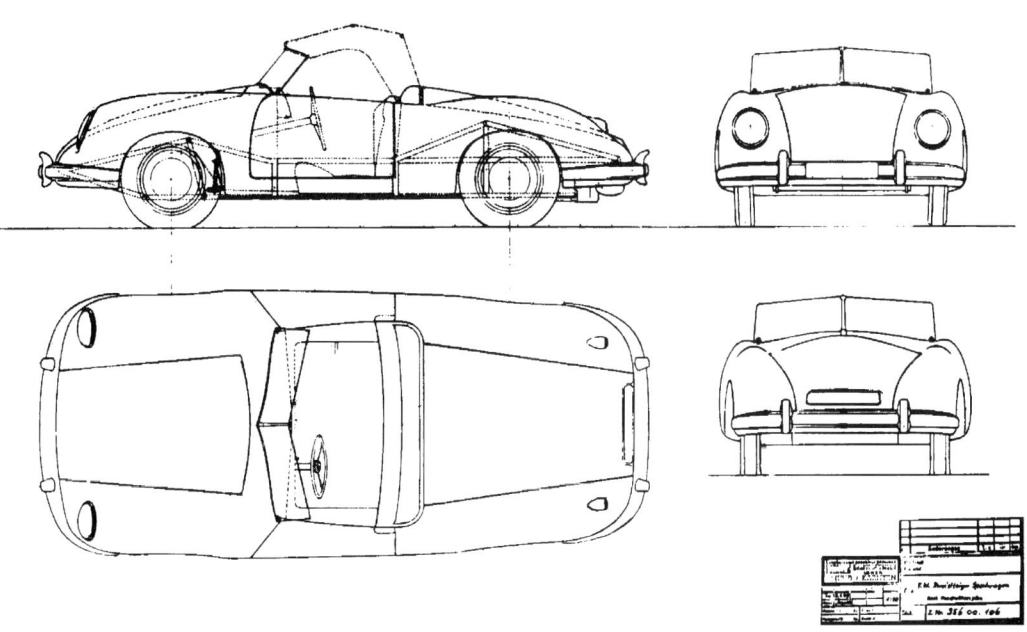

It then went about an exhaustive further test programme, suffering its only failure on theGrossglockner Pass. A bent suspension member was reinforced with a piece of angle iron which is still on the car today!

It was during the March testing, and before the body was mounted on the prototype, that a Swiss sports car enthusiast named Rupprecht von Senger took a keen interest in the Gmünd project and placed an order for the first four cars to be built. Already, the design intentions for the production version, the 356/2, had progressed to a sheet steel chassis, in recognition of Professor Porsche's observations about production costs, as well as in realization of the limitations of the Gmünd facility. The installation of the standard Volkswagen engine/gearbox/rear suspension assembly was also taken account of in the production design.

So, before the body was finally mounted to the prototype 356, the welded platform chassis of the first of the /2 Series was already completed. This first production car was to be a 'Limousin', as described by Porsche, and its panelwork was again the product of Friedrich Weber's skills. The future of Porsche was gradually becoming assured. The first sales order had been placed by the Swiss VW distributor and contacts were now being made for the spread of a dealer network. The Porsches, father and son, had no idea then, in the spring of 1948, that over 76,000 examples of the various models of 356 would be produced. The name 'Porsche' was now on the road to becoming a major force in the world of sporting cars.

3 Porsches go into Production

Accepting an order for a Porsche car in 1948 was potentially a tricky business, as a manufacturing permit had not been issued by the authorities at the time that Rupprecht von Senger's Swiss Volkswagen distributorship, AMAG, had confirmed its requirement for the four vehicles ordered by von Senger. That order, however, was to prove invaluable in the process of Porsche achieving the permit, as it served to confirm that export business was available for the product and, of course, it helped to show that the Porsche business was not seeking to manufacture any kind of armaments.

Gmünd was in the Austrian province of Carinthia, and the provincial administration had been re-constituted by the occupying Allied forces with the specific objective of ensuring that there were no former Nazi party officials in positions of influence. The other very important factor in the eyes of the occupiers was that no company in Germany or Austria should be able to manufacture tools of war under the guise of the product that they were applying for a permit to produce. Third behind these two considerations was the simple question of material shortages. Raw materials of any

This very famous picture has been published many times, but merits reproduction here as it represents the very cornerstone of the Porsche company and the continuity from father to son. It is the first Porsche car, Number 356-001, with Ferry Porsche and his father alongside it. The car would at this time have received its approval certificate and was almost certainly now sold to Rupprecht von Senger.

kind were in such short supply throughout Europe after World War II, even among the winning powers, that the value of any commodity in terms of economic reconstruction, together with its potential to earn foreign currency, weighed heavily in the decision to issue manufacturing permits.

APPROVAL AND FIRST BUILD

The permit system meant that Porsche had to have approval in order to put its new car into any kind of serious production. Having an order from a vehicle dealership was one thing, but the fact that the dealership in question was a prominent Swiss VW dealer added great value to the infant Porsche business's application. This order, for four vehicles from a hitherto untried manufacturer, meant that jobs could be created in an area where there was no new industry, that the sale would bring in foreign currency to Austria and that, of course, the product had no resemblance to anything military.

When finally Permit Number 4328 was issued, on 8 June 1948, the prototype Porsche 356 had been examined and the permit was approved with no special restrictions. The car, Number 356-001, had a Volkswagen engine, numbered 356-2-034969, a VW gearbox and suspension, and was registered with the now famous licence plate K45 286. Porsche was now in business, though it was to be the welded, fabricated steel chassis of the second design that was to be the basis of that business, not the tubular frame of the prototype. The business was now to make cars for sale to whatever public could be won.

Ferdinand Porsche's many years of experience in the motor industry had made him a wily old fox and much of that valuable experience was invested in his son, Ferry.

The result was that both were, each in their own way, well aware of the need for salesmanship and both were capable of giving good account of themselves. So, when the 356 was ready to be shown to the world, they went out and showed it. They took 356-001 to Berne in Switzerland, the venue of the Swiss Grand Prix that year. The German magazine *Motor und Sport* described the little sports car as 'A cross between an Auto-Union and a Volkswagen' (an apt description in the circumstances), praising the Porsche and welcoming it to the new motor sporting scene.

About a month later, 356-001 made another public outing, this time in a race through the streets of Innsbruck. It was 11 July and the driver was Herbert Kaes, Ferry Porsche's cousin. The event was the Runt um den Hofgarten and Herbert Kaes won his class. Bearing in mind the diminutive size of the Porsche company then, its very limited resources and the problems attached to building a new sports car in early post-war Austria, that was no mean achievement. Porsche was now established in the business of producing winning sports cars.

Even before this first car was completed, and with the pressed/welded sheet steel chassis platform still under construction for the definitive 356 variant, it had been decided that a coupé, or 'Limousin' as Porsche chose to call it, should be the standard body design to follow. The kind of customer perceived for this newcomer from Austria was one who wanted the comfort of a closed car combined with the performance of a true sports car. This is what the Porsche company would deliver.

Only three cars left the Gmünd factory in 1948, one of which was the prototype, 356-001. That car went to von Senger's AMAG company in Switzerland during August. AMAG also took delivery of the first

Model: Porsche Type 356 Gmünd Production – 1949

Construction	Pressed steel fabricated and welded box-section chassis with unitary steel coupé ('Limousin') or roadster bodywork
ENGINE	VW/Porsche Type 369, rear-mounted
Crankcase	Light alloy crankcase with individual cylinders
Cylinder head	Light alloy with inserted valve guides and seats
Cyls/Type	Four, horizontally opposed
Compression	7.0:1
Cooling system	Air, with finned cylinder barrels and belt-driven fan
Bore & Stroke	73.5mm × 64mm (2.87 × 2.5in)
Capacity	1,131cc (70cu in)
Main bearings	Four main journals
Valves	Two overhead per cylinder, pushrod actuation
Fuel supply	Diaphragm mechanical pump and two Solex 32PBI carburettors
Power output	40bhp @ 4,000 rpm
Ignition system	Coil and distributor with auto advance/retard
Lubrication	Wet sump, gear pump and oil cooling
BRAKES	
Type	Drum front and rear with cable actuation
TRANSMISSION	Four-speed gearbox mounted ahead of the engine – rear wheel drive
Clutch type	Single dry plate
Gear ratios	1 = 15.95:1, 2 = 9.17:1, 3 = 5.54:1, 4 = 3.54:1. R = 29.23:1
Final drive ratio	4.43:1
SUSPENSION/STEERING	
Front suspension	Transverse torsion bars/trailing parallel links/telescopic shocks
Rear suspension	Transverse torsion bars/trailing parallel links/lever arm shocks
Steering type	VW type worm and peg with unequal arms
Wheels	Pressed steel 3.0D × 16
Tyres	5.00 × 16 cross-ply

DIMENSIONS	**Cabriolet:**	**Coupé:**
Overall length	3,880mm	3,880mm (151.3in)
Overall width	1,666mm	1,666mm (64.9in)
Overall height	1,300mm	1,300mm (50.7in)
Wheelbase	2,100mm	2,100mm (81.9in)
Track (front)	1,290mm	1,290mm (50.3in)
Track (rear)	1,250mm	1,250mm (48.7in)
MODELS AVAILABLE	Cabriolet/coupé	
TOP SPEED	87mph (140kph)	

Porsches go into Production

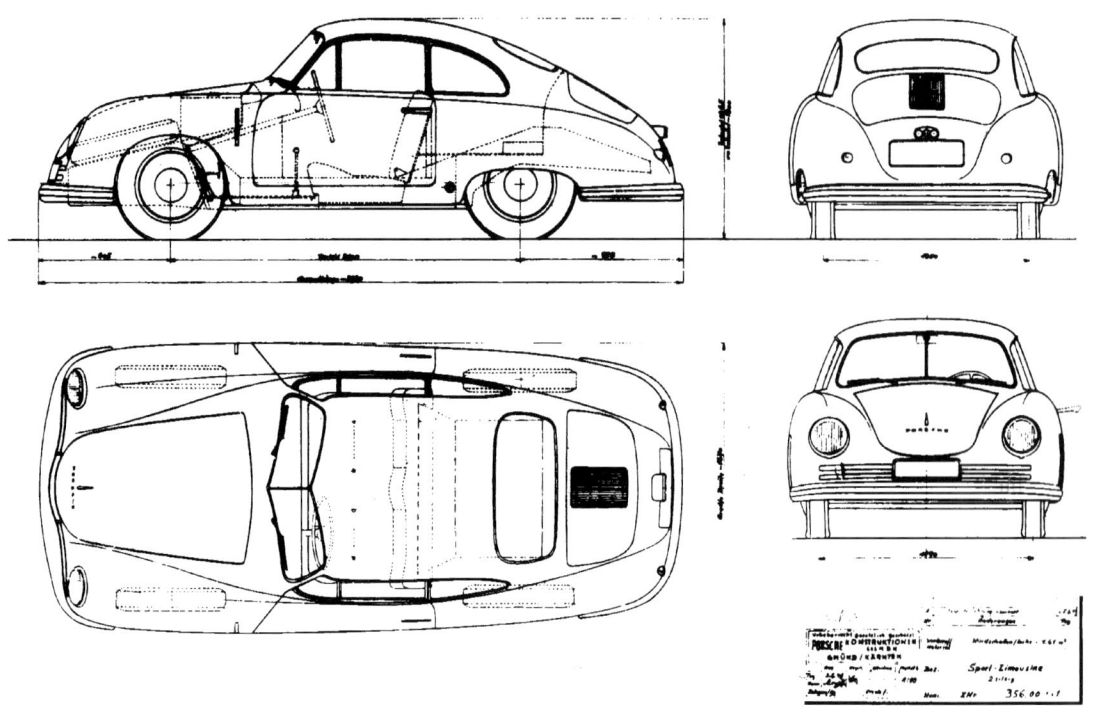

Above and below are the definitive general arrangement drawings for the body designs of the production Type 356 Coupe and Cabriolet models which were to be built at Gmünd.

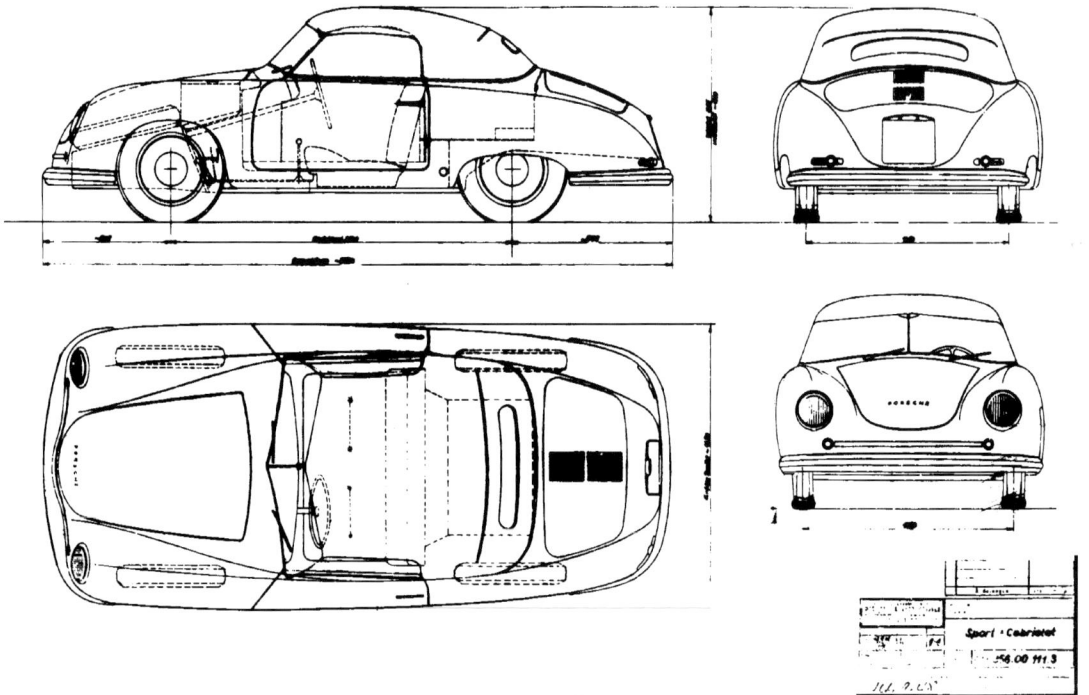

'2' Series 356, the prototype 'Limousin' and Car Number 356/2-002, which was delivered as a chassis for coachwork to be fitted by Beutler in Switzerland. That was the sum total of Porsche's car sales in 1948 – 100 per cent export in their first year!

1949 saw an increase in the number of Porsche cars leaving Gmünd, though it was fortunate that there was quite a lot of general engineering work to keep the workers busy and earn the bulk of the company's income, while the Porsches, father and son, built on the initial success of the 356. In fact, an eightfold increase in car production took place in 1949, with the cars' new owners being so impressed that word was soon about that Porsche cars were excellent value and good fun to drive. The question before the Porsche family now was whether there was profit to be had from making cars, for there had been no cash gain from that activity in 1949.

Among the early customers for the cars from Gmünd was Ing. Rudolf Hruschka, an Austrian expatriate who was to settle in Italy and who had worked with Porsche for almost ten years. He now worked with the Italian government organization Finmeccanica and would make his name almost a quarter of a century later with Alfa Romeo, as the man behind another highly successful flat-four engined car, the immortal Alfasud. It was he who, using much of what he gained from the lessons of Porsche, created not only the car, but the whole manufacturing facility at Pomigliano d'Arco. Dr Ernst Henschel, whose name had been famous for aeroplanes in pre-war Germany and later for heavy trucks, was another early Porsche buyer, as was the world-renowned racing driver Rudolf Caracciola.

There were fifty cars built at Gmünd, including the prototype, so production there could never really be described as serious, though the effort that went into their manufacture certainly was. Twenty-five of these cars left the wooden sheds in 1949, another nineteen in the following year and the last three in 1951. Austria faced continuing problems with dire material shortages in those early post-war years, having to import most of what was needed to manufacture any kind of goods.

Shortage of supplies of components and raw materials was one thing, though. The Allies' restrictions on Austria at that time seemed to be even tighter than those on Germany, despite the fact that Austria had so much less political significance. Restrictions were eased more quickly in Germany, perhaps because there were so many more people there and so much more industry to reconstruct. As a result, the Porsche family took the decision to seek authority for their return to Stuttgart.

BACK TO ZUFFENHAUSEN

It was not just a case of getting more raw materials and components that brought the Porsches back to Germany. They owned a large house and workshops in Zuffenhausen, a suburb of Stuttgart. Once they had returned, they made application to the occupying US authorities for the restitution of the works to Porsche possession. After a long struggle through the carefully laid red tape, they finally gained approval for the repossession of the premises, which were being used by the US Army as a vehicle pool. Now the only problem was to lever the Army out. Delay followed delay and when Professor Porsche visited the works with a request to examine the premises, the American commander, General Funk, refused even to meet him. The Porsche company was forced to rent production space elsewhere until they finally recovered tenure of the old workshops.

Porsches go into Production

A Gmünd Coupé at the 1950 Geneva Motor Show, showing well the frontal aspect, the split windscreen and VW wheels of the early models.

In the process of creating the 356 Coupé, contacts had been established with the Stuttgart coachbuilder, Reutter. Reutter's were only a short walk away from the old Porsche works and they were very sympathetic to the Porsche family's problems in re-establishing themselves in Stuttgart. In fact, Reutter's were so confident of the 356's potential that they prepared press tooling for the volume production of the bodies, the majority of which they would manufacture once Porsche had set up their chassis shop in Stuttgart. For their part, Porsche, having despatched Albert Prinzing on a sales drive to Volkswagen dealers, were able to give Reutter an order for 500 bodies, after estimating sales expectations out of show reactions and Prinzing's success with the VW dealers.

Setting up the chassis erecting shop actually meant that Porsche had to rent 5,000 square feet (465 square metres) of space

This Gmünd Coupé has become famous as one of the cars which was used extensively in competition and proudly displays its "battle honours" on the door panel. The lowered roof line is apparent in this view of a car which is today in the Porsche Museum collection.

Porsches go into Production

This factory drawing from the driver's handbook of the period, shows clearly the positioning of everything in the car, including its occupants, but also gives a very clear indication of the raised rear quarter of the Reutter-built body

Albert Prinzing

A school friend of Ferry Porsche from Bad Cannstatt, Albert Prinzing was born in February 1911. A brilliant academic from an early age, he studied economics and became one of the youngest professors of his subject in pre-war Germany. By the time World War II began, he had been lecturing in his field at the University of Berlin and was recognized as a suitable candidate to be appointed economic adviser to the cultural attaché at the German embassy in Rome. He acted as an intermediary to Benito Mussolini during the war years and then returned to internment until 1948.

It was Albert Prinzing who established the contacts essential to recovering possession of the Porsche properties in Stuttgart. He set up an office in the Porsche family villa in Feuerbacher Weg, with the support of engineer Hans Klauser, administrator Karl Kirn and a secretary, and kept the pressure on to secure the release of the Porsche workshops in Zuffenhausen. This took a long time, but his tenacity was ultimately rewarded as he saw the plant return to its rightful owners.

When the Porsche company moved production from Gmünd to Stuttgart, it was Albert Prinzing who laid the plans for the transfer, and who suggested that the pre-Stuttgart production development work be carried out in the garage at Feuerbacher Weg, so as to provide a tax loss to offset the royalties from Porsche design work. He also was the man who secured an early major order (thirty-seven cars was a lot to Porsche then!) during a dealer conference at Wolfsburg.

Such was the trust that Ferry Porsche felt for his old school chum that it was Albert Prinzing who went to head up Porsche Diesel Motorenbau GmbH when Mannesmann funded the establishment of the Friedrichshafen factory. Eight years later, in 1964, Prinzing moved away from the Porsche businesses to take up a board appointment with AEG, then later he went to Osram, where he was chairman of the board until his retirement in 1975. Even then, and after his retirement, Albert Prinzing maintained his friendship with Professor Ferry Porsche and his contacts with 'the old firm'.

in Reutter's factory. Before that, the old Porsche villa in Stuttgart was where the 356 design was reworked prior to production. The objective here was to make the car easier to manufacture in volume, paying particular attention to refining the body line so that it looked better than the original, but was also suitable for production in steel from press tools rather than hand-beaten aluminium on wooden bucks. This decision was taken on the grounds that Reutter's craftsmen had little experience of producing aluminium alloy bodies, and steel would in any event be less expensive.

The early Stuttgart 356 acquired a wider interior than the original Gmünd model, as well as a higher waistline running into more rounded flanks at the rear. At the front, the bonnet line was raised a little and the roof was made to flow more smoothly down to the rear bumper, whilst the quarter lights in the doors disappeared. Inside, the instrumentation was still a bit spartan, with just a speedometer, an oil temperature gauge (very important to an air-cooled engine) and a clock.

On the mechanical front, the short engine was still basically the VW unit, with alloy cylinder heads manufactured by Karl Schmidt in Neckarsulm. The non-synchromesh gearbox, the steering box and the export-type braking system made by ATE all came from the Volkswagen parts inventory. As with the VW Beetle, there was no fuel gauge, the level being determined by a filler mounted dipstick. The carburettors used to deliver fuel to the engine were Solex Type 32PBJ and, on a compression ratio of 7:1, the engine produced a reasonably respectable 40bhp.

In March 1950, the first Stuttgart-built Porsche rolled out of the assembly shop. It was a coupé, painted pale grey and named 'Windhund'. This vehicle became Ferry Porsche's personal transport and demon-

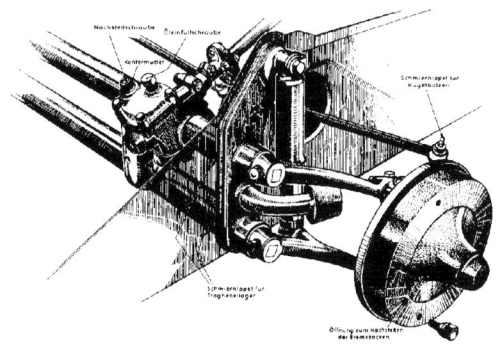

The front suspension and brakes of the early model 356 came straight out of Volkswagen parts bins. This was the VW export specification brake assembly.

strator and started the line of one of the finest sports cars of its time. It was the first of those 500 Reutter bodies ordered in November 1949, for which Reutter produced the press tools at a cost to Porsche of DM200,000. That figure could not have been half the true cost of the tooling, but clearly Reutter's anticipated that it would not take as long as Porsche expected to sell those first 500 cars (and many more), so amortizing the tool costs over a relatively short period.

There were just sixty Porsche people at Augustenstrasse 82, Reutter's body plant, when operations began there, but the manpower level soon rose as serious production got under way. By the end of 1950, some 298 Porsche cars had been built, producing an income from sales of an amazing DM3.58 million. Now, the cost of production time was being examined and in this context it is interesting to observe that Beutler, in Switzerland, took 450 hours to convert a Porsche chassis into a finished cabriolet, while Reutter took 550 hours to complete a coupé. For this reason, Porsche considered at one stage the prospect of splitting production, but the prospect of handling the

Porsches go into Production

1950 Porsche Typ 356 'Ferdinand' in 'Windhund-Look'.

Austrian Tatra built a number of Gmünd cabriolets in Vienna. They produced good quality work, but the prime reason for Austrian coachbuilders being employed at that time was economics and logistics, rather than style.

taxes and the problems and costs of transport soon killed the idea. So, the five-hundredth Porsche to roll out of Stuttgart's workshops was a Reutter bodied car.

VIENNA, SWEDEN AND SWITZERLAND

We have to go back to Gmünd for this part of the story, because some of the early Porsche chassis were despatched from there to Vienna to be bodied, as well as to Beutler of Thun, in Switzerland. Once the prototype cars had been built and the design settled upon for both the cabriolet and the coupé, coachbuilders were approached for prices to produce the bodywork on a bare chassis. In fact, after the first few, some panelwork was actually produced in a semi or unfinished state and shipped with the completed chassis. The dashboards were seldom finished, because bodywork was to be attached to them and so chassis left Gmünd in varying states of completion.

Three coachbuilders were used in those early days: Kastenhofer, Keibl and Tatra (the same Tatra that produced one of Czechoslovakia's most famous cars). Kastenhofer and Keibl were established Viennese companies, whilst Tatra had set up a division in the Simmering district of Vienna in 1921, as Austro-Tatra GMBH. The original function of Austro-Tatra was the provision of an additional assembly plant for Tatra cars and a distribution centre for the Austrian market. After World War II, Austrian Tatra was registered as an independent company from the original Czech parent and occupied itself with vehicle servicing, repairs and coachwork.

The incentive for Porsche to use coachbuilders in Vienna was the avoidance of import and transfer taxes which would have resulted from the purchase of bodies outside Austria. All three Austrian coachworks worked to Porsche designs and, in reality, they only produced and assembled the components that were outside of the Gmünd factory's capabilities. Of course, once the company moved to Stuttgart, the need to produce any panelwork pre-coachwork was eliminated, as Reutter initially produced a wooden buck upon which panelwork was hand beaten prior to the construction and use of press tools for volume production.

Apart from the Porsche family's desire to recover possession of their property in Stuttgart, there was one other, quite major, factor which increased the pressure upon them to move out of Gmünd and so leave Austria. This was the decision by the Swedish truck maker, Scania-Vabis, to place orders for Porsche cars. Scania-Vabis had taken on the Volkswagen concession for Sweden in the very early post-war years, as they saw it as an opportunity to fill a gap in the Swedish car market which their own manufacturing facilities could not meet.

Sweden had never been an easy market for foreign car makers to penetrate, not least because it was a large expanse of thinly populated land. The Swedes already had Volvo, and then SAAB, the aeroplane maker, had decided to enter the car business and was making its mark on the home market. But locally made cars were not cheap, so Scania-Vabis's move to import VW was something of a master stroke. The German cars were well made, were very capable of withstanding and running in Swedish winters as they had no anti-freeze problems and they were not expensive. What was more, they were very economical, immensely reliable and took the many unmade Swedish roads in their stride. As a result, many a Swedish motorist has cut his or her motoring teeth on a Volkswagen Beetle.

With a continuing eye to profitable trading, the Scania-Vabis sales team saw another opportunity in the new Porsche sports cars. The fact that Porsche had been responsible for the original VW design and that many Volkswagen components were used in the Porsche could only be advantageous as the Swedes saw it, so they decided to invest in the cars from Zuffenhausen. Here, then, was a major motivation for the family to exert maximum pressure on the American authorities to release the old Porsche works. Clearly, with the Scania-Vabis connection now made in Sweden and the AMAG in Switzerland, Porsche's future was becoming ever more assured.

Before moving our story on, it is worth dwelling for a moment or two on what this author considers to be one of the most attractive versions of the open Porsche 356 ever built. These were the cars built by Beuttler of Thun in Switzerland. There were not many of them, but the line and style of this Swiss body design merits mention because of its near agelessness. The body hugged the chassis more closely than Porsche's own design and so the wheels were nearer to the outside line. In many ways, this cabriolet pre-empted Porsche's own Speedster and was a prettier car. It is believed that Chassis Number 356/2–003 is the only survivor of Beuttler's art on a Porsche and was the subject of a ground-up restoration in 1989, whilst owned by a Swiss Porsche enthusiast.

EXPANDING THE RANGE

By the end of 1950, it was pretty apparent to the whole Porsche management team that the rented space at Reutter's would not be adequate for the planned expansion of production, nor would it allow for the exploitation of new overseas markets with a view to earning valuable foreign currency.

The Swiss coachbuilder Beutler of Thun was to feature in Porsche history more than once, but this beautiful cabriolet must stand as one the finest examples of the coachbuilder's art, being totally in sympathy with the chassis, a very snug fit and still clearly identifiable as a Porsche. Beutler, however, was somewhat expensive so, unfortunately, very few were built.

Model: Porsche Type 356 1100cc and 1300cc – 1951

Construction	Pressed steel fabricated & welded box-section chassis with unitary steel coupé or cabriolet bodywork
ENGINE	Porsche Type 369 (1100) or Type 506 (1300), rear-mounted
Crankcase	Light alloy crankcase with individual cylinders
Cylinder head	Light alloy with inserted valve guides and seats
Cyls/Type	Four, horizontally opposed
Compression	1100 = 7.0:1, 1300 = 6.5:1
Cooling system	Air, with finned cylinder barrels and belt-driven fan
Bore & Stroke	73.5mm × 64mm/80mm × 64mm (2.9 × 2.5in/3.1 × 2.5in)
Capacity	1,086cc/1,286cc (66.2/78.4cu in)
Main bearings	Four main journals
Valves	Two overhead per cylinder, pushrod actuation
Fuel supply	Diaphragm mechanical pump and two Solex 32PBI carburettors
Power output	40bhp/44bhp @ 4,200 rpm
Ignition system	Coil and distributor with auto advance/retard
Lubrication	Wet sump, gear pump and oil cooling
BRAKES	
Type	Drum front and rear with hydraulic actuation
TRANSMISSION	Four-speed gearbox mounted ahead of the engine – rear wheel drive
Clutch type	Single dry plate
Gear ratios	1 = 15.95:1, 2 = 9.17:1, 3 = 5.54:1, 4 = 3.54:1. R = 29.23:1
Final drive ratio	4.43:1
SUSPENSION/STEERING	
Front suspension	Transverse torsion bars/trailing parallel links/telescopic shocks
Rear suspension	Transverse torsion bars/trailing parallel links/telescopic shocks
Steering type	VW type worm and peg with unequal arms
Wheels	Pressed steel 3.0D or 3.25D × 16
Tyres	5.00 × 16 cross-ply

DIMENSIONS	**Cabriolet:**	**Coupé:**
Overall length	3,860mm	3,860mm (150.5in)
Overall width	1,660mm	1,660mm (64.7in)
Overall height	1,300mm	1,300mm (50.7in)
Wheelbase	2,100mm	2,100mm (81.9in)
Track (front)	1,290mm	1,290mm (50.3in)
Track (rear)	1,250mm	1,250mm (48.7in)
MODELS AVAILABLE	Cabriolet/coupé	
TOP SPEED	87mph (140kph)	

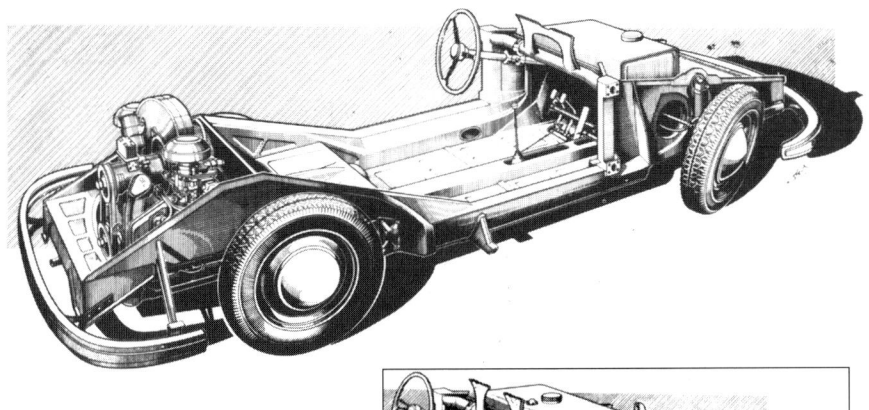

The production 356 chassis of pressed and formed sheet steel was much easier to build and lighter that 356-001. Inset is the modified design for 1952, showing the revised heater vents to the windscreen and floor, the steering wheel and fuel tank with level sender unit.

Further representations were therefore made to the US Army for the repossession of their own factory. At the same time, a decision was made to commence design and development work to make the Porsche car acceptable to the American and British markets.

The American market was obviously the prime target market, but the psychological benefit of gaining acceptance in Great Britain, even in small numbers, would, Porsche reasoned, persuade more American sports car enthusiasts to take a second look at the 356. Why? Because as far as many Americans at that time were concerned, Great Britain was the home of the sports car and if the Porsche could appeal to British connoisseurs, then it had to be a good car.

Because it was proving so difficult to move the Americans out of the old Porsche works, the company went ahead in 1951 and bought land behind the old factory. Here, they planned to build a new and modern plant capable of producing cars in sufficient numbers to meet the now growing demand and to feed the new markets into which they intended to expand. Construction work did not begin immediately, but typical of Ferry Porsche's management team was the logic of planning well ahead.

The 1951 production programme was to see an expansion of the model range, with the 356 now being offered in 1,100cc and 1,300cc versions. Further, the 1,300 model was to be available with single carburettor and twin carburettor engines. Then there would be a 1,500cc engine to follow, though this demanded a little more design work, as we shall see later. With North America featuring so high in the priorities of Porsche marketing, the 1,500 engine was to be of great importance, but the immediate aim was to double the 1950 production volume and reach four figures for the first time.

Quality control was now becoming ever more important to Porsche in the preparation for a successful launch into the US market, so now each car was very carefully checked before being placed into the

Porsches go into Production

All Porsche engines were hand-built at Zuffenhausen. Each of the eight engine assemblers built an average of one engine a day, which was then run on a dynamometer for about two hours before installation in a car. The assemblers stamped their initials on their handiwork before it left them, so an engine could always be traced back to the man who built it.

delivery hall. Road tests of each car were carried out to ensure there were no mechanical faults, the nearby Solitude race track being frequently used for this purpose. There was also now an increasing need to secure sufficient raw materials and components in order to keep the company fully occupied and growing. Export sales were a major key to securing incoming supplies. For Germany, it was a matter of earning enough foreign currency to rebuild the country's fragile economy. For Porsche, it was the need to move ahead so as to avoid stagnation. History tells us that both the country and the company were successful in their goals.

THE EARLY 1,300 AND TEETHING TROUBLES

The new 1,300 engine was designated Type 506. Its actual displacement was 1,286cc, though it looked scarcely altered from the original Type 369 1,100cc unit. Inside, however, it was a different story. Now, pistons designed specifically for the job were installed, with the objective of giving 45bhp at 4,400rpm and a flatter torque curve to provide pulling power over a greater range of engine speeds. However, the Mahle pistons, designed with a wedge on the crown at the inlet side, gave quite a few problems in service.

The wedge design was intended to direct gases towards the exhaust valve after combustion, but as the piston was pushed down on the combustion stroke, it rocked on the gudgeon pin, there being greater weight on the wedge side of the crown. As the pistons rocked, they pumped oil and so created a very smoky engine. Mahle put the fault down to the wedge-shaped crown throwing the weight distribution out, so causing rocking action. A tighter limit on the piston ring gaps did little to help, as the skirt length of

Porsches go into Production

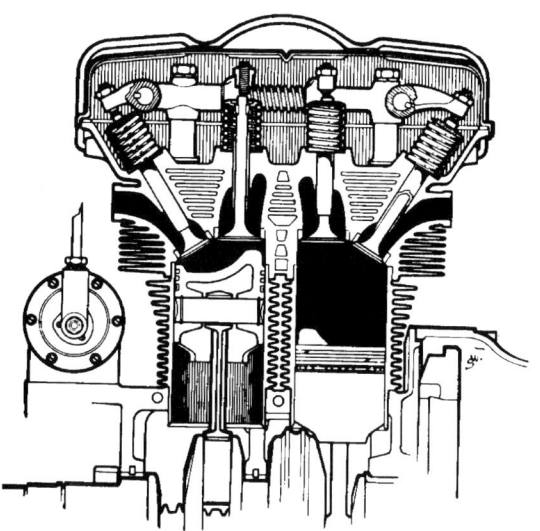

This drawing shows the wedge-crowned Mahle pistons in the 1,300 engine, which were fine in theory, but rocked on the gudgeon pins.

the pistons was not long enough to restrict the movement. Interestingly, the problem did not arise with every 1,300 engine, but enough to justify an investigation which confirmed the fault and its cause.

Despite this running fault, the 1,300 engine continued in production, the primary advantage being its increased power, and, whilst the piston problem was known to be there, not every customer fell victim to it and the prospect of losing sales as the result of discontinuing the larger engine was beyond contemplation. The reality of the situation was that the warranty costs of replacing pistons in engines where the problem manifested itself were probably significantly lower than the lost revenues which would have resulted in not having a 1,300 engine at all. And there were other teething troubles to be addressed in any case.

Karl-Peter Rabe

Karl Rabe was born in the last decade of the nineteenth century at Pottendorf, in southern Austria. Graduating with honours in Vienna during 1913, he started his career in the motor industry at Austrian Daimler in Wiener Neustadt and soon came to the attention of the director of Austro-Daimler, Dr Ferdinand Porsche.

The quality of his work, and his commitment to the company, earned Rabe quick promotion so that, by 1919, Dr Porsche was ready to make him a director of the passenger car division. He repaid the faith placed in him by producing the Austro-Daimler 'Sascha' (which won the 1922 Targa Florio), as well as guiding other models into successful production. When Dr Porsche left Austro-Daimler for Stuttgart, Rabe remained in Vienna, but took up a new post in 1927 with Steyr, as their acting chief design engineer.

Within twelve months of Karl Rabe's move to Steyr, he was back under the direction of his old boss, as Dr Porsche was appointed technical director of that company. But Porsche's fertile mind was becoming ever more difficult to harness and in 1930 he set up Porsche Design and lured Karl Rabe away from Steyr to join him as chief designer, where his solid engineering prowess earned his employer much respect. His work on all aspects of Porsche design was highly thought of and, many years after his most innovative ideas were converted into metal, Karl Rabe was rewarded by the Stuttgart Technical Institute with the title of honorary senator.

Retiring from the Porsche firm in 1965, Karl Rabe was not the kind of man who could just stop what he had been doing for many years, so he remained in contact with the company during his very short retirement and was often consulted for advice. However, at the age of 73, in 1968, he died, leaving a legacy of fine engineering for younger Porsches to follow.

Porsches go into Production

Professor Dr Ferdinand Anton Ernst 'Ferry' Porsche

Ferry Porsche was born in Wiener-Neustadt, a small town about 30km (19 miles) to the south of Vienna, Austria's capital city. His father was then technical director of Austrian Daimler and was already making his name in the world of the automobile.

That Ferry should be thoroughly indoctrinated with the motor car was inevitable. His tenth birthday present was a car built by his father. At eleven, he competed in his first sporting event, with the Vienna Automobil Club. When he was fourteen, the family moved to southern Germany, to Stuttgart-Unterturkheim, where Ferdinand Porsche was to work with Daimler Motoren AG. Young Ferry went to school at the Gottlieb Daimler School in Bad Cannstatt, then began an apprenticeship with Robert Bosch in Stuttgart.

A modern photo, taken in 1989 during his eightieth year, showing Professor Ferry Porsche with one his creations, a 356, and one of his eldest son's (Ferdinand 'Butzi' Porsche), the 911.

Joining Porsche Design, Ferry was initially given work on detail design on the forebears of the Volkswagen, work on NSU, Wanderer and Zundapp. So the horizontally opposed engine type was ingrained in his thinking from a very early stage of his career. Small wonder, then, that he should be enthusiastic about the Porsche-VW Type 64 and the 356 from its inception. It was Ferry Porsche, in fact, who led the design of the 356 and brought it to production; but he had a war to go through first.

World War II was not an easy time for any of the Porsche family. They were not Nazi party members, but were known to those in power for the achievements of Porsche Design, not least of which were the V-16 Auto-Union and the immortal Volkswagen. Ferry was given charge of the Porsche works in Zuffenhausen at the beginning of the war, and after it, when the Americans occupied those workshops, he faced the gruelling experience of internment. The first of the family to be freed, he then spent over a year working for the release of his father and brother-in-law, Dr Anton Piech. They were released on bail of one million francs each, the money being raised from Ferry Porsche's design commission from Piero Dusio for the Cisitalia Grand Prix racing car.

Emerging from the shadow of his genius father, Ferry Porsche led the family firm to success after success, creating a sports car that people wanted to buy, and taking that car, and derivatives of the experience gained from it, to racing and rallying success. Honour after honour has been bestowed upon Professor Dr Ferdinand Anton Ernst Porsche, whose contribution to the world of the automobile is as far beyond calculation as that of his father.

Porsches go into Production

Every car ever manufactured throughout the history of the automobile has encountered teething troubles of one kind or another, even when a car may be perceived as the most perfect machine possible, built in the most ideal conditions. Now the Porsche 356, as we have already witnessed, was a bundle of compromises from the beginning, built in some of the worst manufacturing conditions imaginable. Developed in the wake of the most ravaging war in history, in a cluster of sheds totally unsuited to their purpose and at a time when material shortages were crippling, to say nothing of the prolonged internment of two of the company's principals, it is actually surprising that the 356 did not disappear under the myriad restrictions and regulations that would have thwarted many a lesser organization.

But the 356 did not disappear and it did manifest teething problems, but, to the immense credit of the Porsche company, the car survived those troubles to emerge a highly desirable and successful sporting car. Much of that was due to the company's attitude to its customers, facing up to and dealing with complaints instead of pretending that they did not exist. Most of the problems were solved quickly and every complaint, however feeble it may have seemed, was investigated and acted upon where action was called for. That's how Porsche achieved repeat sales.

One of the early problems in the wake of the larger engine was the original gearbox, for it was quickly realized that almost double the power was going through the transmission than was ever originally intended from the 985cc Volkswagen engine. Road tester Paul Pietsch observed that, to effect clean gear changes, the driver had to double declutch on both up and down changes and even then, ugly transmission noises still occurred until the gearbox was run in. Quite clearly, Pietsch was recommending a development in the transmission area that was not yet there. Of course, Karl Rabe had already picked up this problem for himself and a synchromesh gearbox was to be the solution, but that would take a little while longer yet.

Other revisions to the car included improved heating ducts for interior comfort, improved brakes with 19.05mm cylinders to all four wheels and bevelled shoes all round. Then the rear shock absorbers were changed from the early lever-action type of the standard VW Beetle to telescopics, though Porsche had to await the manufacturing convenience of Volkswagen before they could implement this modification. Body resonance was another problem to be addressed and, after a lot of testing and calculations, was significantly improved upon. The car inevitably had lots of modifications still to be made, but it was making progress, it was in production and it was ready to take on the world.

4 Developing the Market and Introducing the 1500

The 1950 Paris Motor Show was a very significant event for Porsche, for this was where some of the most important links between the Zuffenhausen firm and some of its international markets were made. It was also the public event at which Porsche chose to mark the fiftieth anniversary of its involvement in automobile design, progressing from the Lohner-Porsche to the 356 in half a century. However, Porsche's stand at that motor show was very small, being only just big enough to display two cars – a coupé and a cabriolet.

In that same year, Ferdinand Porsche celebrated his seventy-fifth birthday. A great party was laid on at Schloss Solitude to mark the occasion and many celebrities who owned Porsche cars came from far and wide to wish the old man 'Happy Birthday'. Rudolf Caracciola, the famous racing driver, was among those celebrities and Ferry Porsche, unbeknown to his father, had had a special car laid down as a birthday present, which was now presented to him at the party. The car was a 'stretched' version of a 356, built as a four-seater, but still with two doors. How the car's manufacture was kept from the old man is an interesting question, for he had a tendency to wander about the factory, taking note of what was happening.

Sadly, a little over three months later, on 30 January 1951, Professor Ferdinand Porsche died, and his body was quietly laid to rest at the family's country home at Zell-am-See. The company now had to survive and move on without its founder, but his son, Dr Ferry Porsche, proved to possess sufficient of those qualities of the leader, mediator and planner to take the company forward to new heights, including, not within the scope of this book, more outright wins at the Le Mans 24 Hours Race than any other car manufacturer in history.

PORSCHE CROSSES THE ATLANTIC

The year 1941 was unwittingly one of great significance for the family and company of Porsche, as it was when a young fellow Austrian managed to gain entry into the United States of America. His name was Maximilian Edwin Hoffman and his aim in life was to import European sports cars into the New World. Of course, World War II had thwarted his early plans and he had to find an alternative way to earn a living for a few years.

With no idea how long the war would last, nor whether his enterprise was likely to succeed, Hoffman borrowed the princely sum of $300 and set himself up in the plated plastic jewellery business. One thing which may have helped his progress was the fact that many New Yorkers regarded his limited English vocabulary as 'quaint' and his activity as 'novel', two characteristics which would attract interest and support.

He worked long and hard to make ends meet and improve his English.

Even though the United States was extensively involved in World War II, firstly providing huge quantities of armaments to Great Britain and the allies up to 1941, then taking a major active part in the Orient and Europe after Pearl Harbor, the effect on the domestic economy was minimal. Hoffman was therefore able to develop his business apace once he had gained acceptance. As a result, he was able to build quite a market for his products and generate a substantial capital base. When the war was over, he went back to Europe and explored the prospects for his original business idea – importing European cars into the United States.

It took a long time to establish a motor business, not least because there was such a limited range available, for in 1945 few European car makers had returned to the business of producing cars. Undeterred, Hoffman set about establishing a showroom in New York, on Park Avenue of all places, which goes to show that his amassed capital – and the value of his contacts in New York City – was not inconsiderable. By 1947, the new Hoffman showroom was open, with a single Delahaye 135 gracing the display space! Soon, though, Max Hoffman had three more cars in his inventory: Healey, Jaguar and Citroën.

The Jaguar XK120 was quickly the flagship of Hoffman's product range, with buyers queuing out of the door to buy the new British sports car. The downside to this was a rapidly growing list of warranty claims and breakdowns – so bad that at one time Hoffman had to get an unlisted telephone number at his home in order to avoid calls from irate customers at the most unsociable of hours. As if he had not had enough problems with the Jaguars, he took delivery of twenty Volkswagens in July 1950 and spent the next three years trying to sell them! This was really down to two factors: the first was that Hoffman had made a rare miscalculation of his market, in that he had failed to realize that many Americans would perceive themselves as 'buying from the enemy' if they bought a VW, and secondly, the car was radically different from anything most Americans had seen before.

The Jaguar XK120 was the flagship of Hoffman Motor Company's sports car importing business in New York, though its reliability left something to be desired and Porsche was not long in taking its place.

Developing the Market and Introducing the 1500

The Type 530 was a two-door, four-seat extension of the 356, produced during the period when Porsche was working on a car for Studebaker.

Hoffman persevered, however, and by the late summer of 1950, he had seen previews of the Alfa Romeo 1900 and the Porsche 356. Impressed by the sleek lines of the 356 and knowing the reputation of Professor Ferdinand Porsche, Hoffman ordered three cars and a small inventory of spare parts. The cars were displayed at a *concours d'élégance* at Watkins Glen race track and among the early buyers of note from the world of American sporting cars was Briggs Cunningham, who was most enthusiastic about the handling and performance of this new German import. The name 'Porsche' was now launched in the US and inside a few years Hoffman's sales figures were to grow from 32 cars in 1951 to almost one-third of Zuffenhausen's total production.

Max Hoffman also opened up other business opportunities for the Porsche company. For example, he introduced Ferry Porsche to the Studebaker Corporation, who had an interest in developing a small sports car, designed in Europe for sale in the United States. That the project came to nothing is a matter of record, but not before Porsche had produced the Type 530, a four-seat, two-door extension of the 356. The Porsche design ideas earned a tidy sum before Studebaker merged with Packard in 1954, and their fees made a substantial contribution to the cost of building the new Porsche plant at Zuffenhausen on the site bought in 1951.

Hoffman was a flamboyant and aggressive marketeer, and opened a number of other doors for Ferry Porsche in the process of promoting the association between them. One result was the meeting between Porsche and the Mid American Research Corporation to discuss the prospect of designing and developing a lightweight military jeep-like vehicle for American Airborne forces along the lines of the VW Kübelwagen. That idea came to nothing, but another military project did materialize, in prototype form at least, although it did not reach volume production.

Gyrodyne Corporation of New York had been awarded a development contract by the Navy Department for a one-man lightweight helicopter for use by the US Marine Corps. This was intended to be used as an observation platform, with no panelling or glazing to enclose any part of the machine, either mechanical components or the pilot. It was as 'utility' as the classification 'UH' (utility helicopter) could get. The Porsche part of this machine was the engine, essentially a Porsche car engine modified for aviation use and adapted to a helicopter drive train. The Gyrodyne did not reach volume production, but it did pave the way for the development of the ultra-lightweight military helicopter, a slot filled later by the Hughes Corporation.

While Max Hoffman was promoting Porsche on the east coast of America, on the west coast a man named Johnny van Neumann set up a little workshop in North Hollywood to service mostly European cars for the small but growing band of sports car enthusiasts. That was in 1948, and by the mid 1950s, Competition Motors had become something of a Mecca for sports car fans. The company also acquired a Porsche and Volkswagen dealership, so moving into new car sales too.

One personality in the public eye who put the name of Porsche on the map among the Hollywood fraternity was film actor James Dean. He had bought from Competition Motors a white Speedster, which he raced at club level with no mean success. Dean shot to fame as the star of the film *Rebel Without a Cause*, taking his Porsche to stardom with him. From the day he took delivery of his Speedster, he had become a passionate fan of Porsche cars and went on to buy a 550 Spyder, which he also raced, driving it to and from the events in which he took part, seemingly at hair-raising speeds. It was this car in which he died, in a horrifying crash with a Ford convertible which had jumped a red light, whilst on the way to a race.

PORSCHE REACHES BRITISH SHORES

The 1951 Earl's Court Motor Show in London saw the 356's British debut, where it was exhibited for the first time. Apart from vehicles shipped into the country for official government purposes, and they were precious few, the import of motor vehicles to Great Britain was banned until 1953, eight years after the end of the war. This had little to do with any reluctance to allow the import of German cars to Britain, as the ruling embraced all foreign vehicles, even from former allies. The objective was the promotion of anything exportable in order to pay off the huge war debt which had been built up. Finally, the government succumbed, realizing that the inflow of limited imports might help smooth the outward path of British exports.

Czech-born Charles Meisl is probably the one man who did more to bring Porsche to its British customers than anyone else. He was working with Connaught Cars as a salesman and returned from the 1950 Geneva Motor Show, where he had seen the 356 for the first time. So enthusiastic was he, that he managed to persuade his employers to sponsor the special import of two cars for display at the 1951 Earl's Court Motor Show. A third car was shipped to Britain as a demonstration model.

However, Connaught was not sufficiently enthusiastic to follow up an agency agreement, and Meisl was very frustrated that his first attempt at creating a British outlet for Porsche had failed. He left Connaught as a result, such was his conviction that this was a product which had a place in the British market. His new employer was John Colbourne-Baber, a Volkswagen dealer who, because of the link between the two products, viewed the Porsche with more favour. He was already gaining more Volkswagen sales by the month, as British servicemen brought home their 'Beetles' and extolled their virtues. That the two products were 'related' was one of Meisl's selling points.

Before Colbourne-Baber had reached the stage of crystallizing his long-term plans and moved to formalize any arrangement

Developing the Market and Introducing the 1500

The RAC Rally was one of the most gruelling road events around for road-equipped sports and touring cars and a Porsche performed well in the 1952 event, prior to the product's establishment in the British market.

with Porsche to become its official importer, another 'name' of the British motor business, Bill Aldington, was contemplating a future for Porsche cars, having also seen and admired them at Geneva. Aldington not only had experience of importing German cars to Britain, having been BMW's distributor before the war, but his company, AFN Ltd, also had experience of car manufacture. The letters 'AFN' were the initials of Archie Frazer-Nash and Frazer-Nash cars were still being produced as a very low volume hand-built sports car which had a tremendous rallying and racing pedigree.

The Aldington brothers, Bill and Harold, were convinced that Porsche was for them. Now they had to persuade Ferry Porsche and Albert Prinzing (the finance director of the Porsche company) that they were the best prospect for Porsche in Great Britain. Porsche's public relations and competitions director was Baron Huschke von Hanstein, who had been a close friend of the Aldingtons before the war, when they were all involved in racing BMWs. This link was to

prove very valuable to the Aldingtons in their negotiations, as was their knowledge of car manufacture. In addition, Aldingtons suggested that they should employ Charles Meisl as their sales manager. The result was that AFN Ltd became the first official British importer of Porsche cars.

The first car, a Reutter cabriolet Chassis Number 60277, arrived in late 1953. It took until January 1954 to sell it and another four months for the next sale to take place AFN persevered with the Porsche brand, despite such a pitifully slow start and within three years was enjoying some success. There is no doubt that the established link between Volkswagen and Porsche, though becoming more tenuous by the year in design terms, was a positive factor in winning acceptance in a market which was still resistant to German imports. The growing reputation of Volkswagen, combined with an increasing list of Porsche competition successes, was to win over hesitant customers.

Another factor which helped Porsche get established in the British market was

Developing the Market and Introducing the 1500

A 1953 cabriolet of the type imported as AFN Limited's first Porsche.

AFN's standard of customer care. As a car maker in its own right, Frazer-Nashes still being built in limited numbers, AFN knew how important it was to keep customers and, perhaps much more importantly, knew how fickle sports car buyers could be. Like the Porsche company, AFN wanted its reputation for customer care to spread, for that was one major route to increased sales. A measure of their success in this direction was the decline in other AFN activities in favour of Porsche. Sales of motorcycles and sidecars, BMW Isettas, DKW cars and even Frazer-Nashes receded as Porsche sales grew and a small dealership network was fostered too, under AFN's leadership. Porsche was now established in what it saw as its two key markets for international success. Things could only get better.

MAKING THE 356 A RIGHT-HAND DRIVE CAR

We go back to 16 May 1951 for the decision to produce a right-hand drive version of the Porsche 356. It was on this date that Ferry Porsche issued the instruction for the cars that were to be shipped to England for the Earl's Court Motor Show to be fitted with their steering wheels on the 'wrong side'. Apart from creating a better opportunity for sales to be generated in Great Britain, it also opened up the prospect of sales being made in better numbers in Australia, the right-hand drive African countries and even Japan and India.

One factor, of course, which had to be considered in producing a right-hand drive option was that its cost had to be economical, which really meant that it had to have a selling price which the customer would be prepared to pay. Initially, the cost estimate for a 'one-off' conversion was reckoned to be around DM1,000 which was a fair portion of the price of the car, when marked up from cost to selling figures. Ferry Porsche's conclusion was that the cost had to be much lower than this for the car to sell profitably.

After a lot more work on the drawing boards of Porsche and Reutter, a 'production' variation of the right-hand drive conversion was completed in June 1951, with the cost being reduced to about half of the

Developing the Market and Introducing the 1500

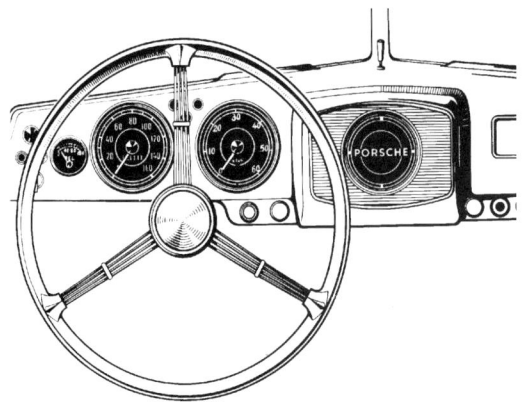

This is the dashboard layout of the original left-hand drive Porsche 356 before the adoption of the amalgamated Wurttemburg and Stuttgart city emblems to create the now world-famous Porsche house badge.

'one-off' original. The conversion was not easy to implement, as it turned out, for there were no less than ten body and chassis modifications to be carried out to accommodate the relocation of the steering wheel.

The right-hand drive car firstly required a new and different pedal cluster, a new handbrake mechanism and, of course, a revised steering mechanism, because the existing steering gear could not simply be inverted so as to put the steering wheel on the other side. The chassis also had to undergo a number of modifications. For example, the battery had to be moved from the right to the left-hand side, then the mounting holes for the steering gear had to be relocated to the other side, the instrument panel had be reversed from the home market version of the car, as did the hole for the fuel cock, the tube for the clutch cable and the fusebox, not forgetting the windscreen wiper motor.

The carpet shaping had to be reversed and the floorboards underneath made to fit. Headlamps which dipped the opposite way were also required. It has to be said that the early cars modified to right-hand drive could not possibly have been an economical proposition, but AFN's confidence in being able to sell the 356 in enough numbers to make it economical convinced Porsche to carry the production costs of the early right-hand drive cars. The reward to both was the sales they had hoped for. Now for the bigger engine.

DEVELOPMENT OF THE 1,500 ENGINE

A limiting factor in Porsche's marketing success was seen by Ferry Porsche and others at Stuttgart as being engine size, or more particularly power and performance. So a larger engine than the 1,300 had to be developed, so as to provide a performance improvement. But there were restricting factors to enlarging the existing Porsche engine, such as the Volkswagen crankcase, which was at the very core of the Porsche's mechanical specification. However, as the 1,300 proved still inadequate to meet customer demand, there was a need to increase the power output even more. This meant, in those days, increasing the size of the engine. The immediate problem was that the cylinder barrels of the original engine were already on their limit at 80mm (3.1in) bore. What was more, it was felt that the over-square characteristic of the 1,300 engine's 64mm × 80mm (2.5in × 3.1in) was over-square enough, so an increase in stroke was what was needed here.

Having now decided there was need for an increase in the stroke, the problem was how to achieve it. It would not be easy, for there was a strong desire to retain the Volkswagen crankcase, for the time being at least, but a longer throw crankshaft would bring about a meeting of metals, for there were things in the way, such as the

Developing the Market and Introducing the 1500

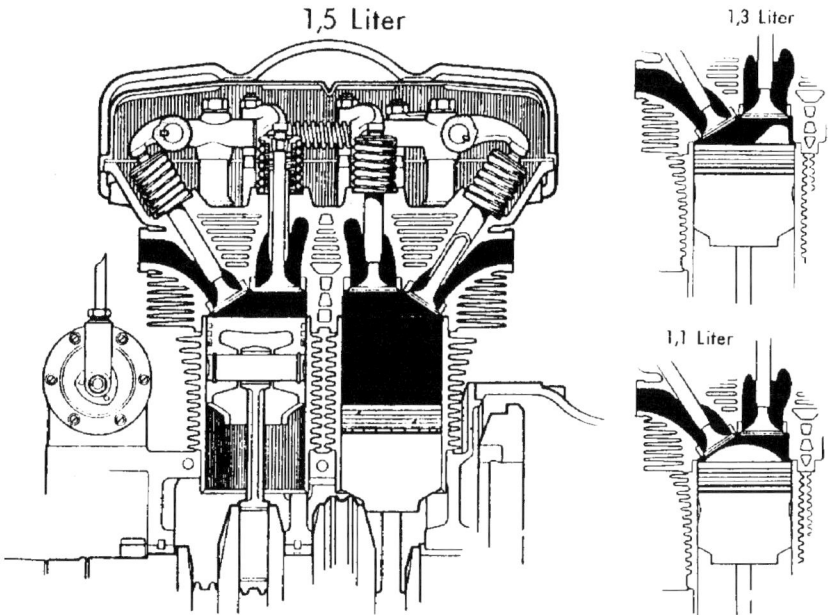

This drawing shows the differences between the pistons of the 1,100cc Porsche engine, the 1,300 (with its troublesome wedge-shaped crown) and the longer stroke 1,500 unit.

camshaft at the bottom of the engine. A quick check of dimensions revealed that the big end bolt bosses on the connecting rods would be brought into contact with the camshaft if the stroke was increased by 10mm (0.4in). So the first problem was to examine the possibility of reducing the size of those bosses and in turn the big end bolts. The notion of four-bolt big ends was quickly discarded, because there was not enough metal in the rods to accommodate that idea. It was also decided that bolts small enough to provide the clearance needed would not hold the big ends together, so where next?

There was really only one solution if the combination of a larger engine displacement and the retention of the Volkswagen crankcase was to be the way ahead – not to use big end bolts at all, but to move to roller bearings in the bottom ends of the connecting rods. However, this demanded a different design of crankshaft. A multi-piece crankshaft was the only way that roller bearing big ends could be used, but Porsche did not have the machining facilities to make such a crankshaft. Nonetheless, the Type 502 engine went to the drawing board.

The new engine was to retain the cylinder bore of 80mm (3.1in) and the Volkswagen crankcase, but the stroke was to increase to 74mm (2.9in) to give a displacement of 1,488cc. To achieve this, a multi-piece crankshaft was designed with the help of a company named Albert Hirth. Hirth had worked with Porsche on the Cisitalia flat-twelve engine, which had roller big ends for a different reason, so knew the Porsche's philosophy and way of working. But even with the decision to abandon big end bolts, there were still a few design bridges to be crossed. The roller bearing to be used had to give equal or better performance than the plain bearing. Careful thought had to be given to its lubrication and, perhaps most important of all, the crankshaft had to be capable of being assembled and dismantled in a dealer's workshop without any compromise to reliability.

Developing the Market and Introducing the 1500

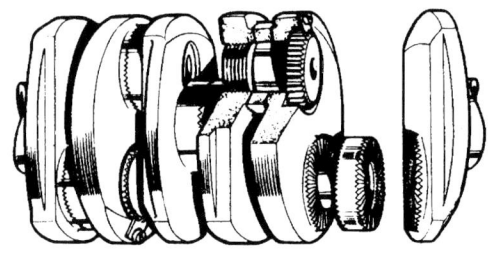

The roller-bearing split crankshaft was an expensive way to solve the problem of achieving 1,500cc, but was still less expensive to Porsche than the castings for a new crankcase.

Having worked together on the design and development of the crankshaft for the new 1,500 engine, Hirth and Porsche now followed separate paths in the life of the crankshaft. Hirth was entrusted with the task of manufacturing the crank and delivering it to Porsche, and handling major service work including repairs, whilst Porsche dealt with the weighing, balancing and fitment of the connecting rods, together with the fitment of the bearings into the con rods.

Of course, the required clearance between crankshaft and camshaft resulting from the 10mm (0.4in) increase in stroke was achieved with ease, but the Porsche engine shop was still anxious to assemble and bench run the engines prior to installation, just to ensure there were no problems. The roller bearing rods gave the major benefit of much lower friction at high engine speeds, but the counter to this was rougher running at low speeds. Lubrication was another problem, as the use of clean oil was vital, so regular oil and filter changes became a very important part of regular engine maintenance. The engine also had to be carefully tuned and warming up was essential before prolonged high speed running.

Only sixty-six Type 502 engines were built before it was superseded by the Type 527. This new engine had no major internal modifications over the 502, though the Solex Type 32PBI carburettors were replaced with a pair of 40PBICs. These were chosen to enable the engine to increase by 500rpm to the new maximum of 5,000rpm, whilst the power output increased from 55bhp to 60bhp. For competition use, the throttle bodies were interchangeable and even the carburettors themselves, for certain requirements, could be exchanged for the 32PBI, with throttle venturi to suit. The Porsche 356 would now be acceptable to a much wider market and, as a result, sales would increase.

5 Improving the Breed – Early Competition and Development

From his earliest days, Ferdinand Porsche was committed to the principle that motor sport improved the breed. He first proved this with the Lohner-Porsche at the beginning of the twentieth century, then in his superb drive in the Prince Henry of Prussia Trial in 1910 aboard a tulip-bodied Austro-Daimler. His personal achievements in both spoke volumes for his skill and the level of his commitment.

Porsche's enthusiasm remained with him as he created the mighty SSK Mercedes for Daimler-Benz and on into his period with Auto-Union, where he was responsible for producing Germany's quantum leap into first-class motor racing in the form of the V-16 'P' Type, first launched in 1934 and leaving in its wake a string of Grand Prix wins, hill climb and outright speed records. It has been said that Porsche Design earned 300,000 Reichsmarks from this project. The 'P' Type was then followed by the 3-litre V-12 'D' Type and Germany reigned supreme.

It is hardly surprising then, that the old gentleman was keenly enthusiastic to support Herbert Kaes in the first competitive event in a Porsche car, the 'cross between an Auto-Union and a Volkswagen' as *Motor und Sport* had described it in 1948. Other people quickly saw the potential of the 356 and Porsche entrants were soon to be featured in a variety of sporting events.

THE LONG ROAD TO RECOGNITION

Auguste Veuillet was a French quality-car dealer who raced cars as a pastime. He saw the two Porsches on display at the 1950 Paris Auto Salon and was immediately entranced by them. Veuillet had already heard about the Volkswagen-based sports car and was interested in taking up the rights for their distribution in France. He was also keen to see Porsche cars do well on the international sporting scene. It was Auguste Veuillet who introduced Ferdinand and Ferry Porsche to Charles Faroux, one of the originators of the Le Mans 24 Hours Race and long-time Clerk of the Course of that greatest of sports car races.

Faroux examined the specification of this exciting little sporting car, then looked at a car 'in the metal' and immediately suggested that the Porsches might like to enter a car in the 1951 event. Professor Porsche thought it was a challenge worth taking up and persuaded his son to enter. Sadly, whilst the old man lived to see his 'People's Car', the Volkswagen, reach production in volume at Wolfsburg, he died before the car bearing his family name took part in the first of many Le Mans Races, the event which Porsche was ultimately to win more times than any other motor manufacturer in the world.

Improving the Breed – Early Competition and Development

In those early days of competition, Porsche used Gmünd-built coupés, primarily because they were lighter in weight than the Zuffenhausen-produced cars, but also because repair of these cars was easier if they were damaged in competition. Among early international events entered successfully was the 1950 Swedish Midnight Sun Rally, in which an 1,100cc coupé scored a class win.

Preparations for the 1951 Le Mans 24 Hours Race began in the winter of 1950. It was a gigantic undertaking for the tiny company which had only recently sustained the cost of relocation from Gmünd to Zuffenhausen. But Professor Porsche's view, that press reports of success in competition were far more effective than paid advertising, was constantly borne in mind as precious capital was spent preparing three Gmünd-built coupés for the world's most prestigious sports car race. In order to achieve homologation and acceptance of the entry of these three cars into the prototype class of the race, a brochure was published by Porsche offering the 356SL, a production car with all the modifications that were featured in the Le Mans vehicles.

Firstly, a new camshaft designed by a young engineer recruit to Porsche named Ernst Fuhrmann raised the power output of the 1,100cc engine to 46bhp and improved torque so that higher gearing could be used. This enabled the cars to achieve a top speed of around 100mph (160kph). Wheel spats covered the road wheels for improved aerodynamic performance and an external fuel filler eliminated the need to lift any panels in refuelling pit stops. Extra lamps were fitted to cope with the night section of the race and there were several other minor modifications. The weight of the car was 1,400lb (635kg), and now the three were taken to the Sarthe circuit for testing.

Whilst three cars arrived to take part in the Le Mans event, Fate seemed to conspire against the tiny team. Firstly, in the process

Much-modified – with wraparound front and rear valances, wheel spats and external fuel fillers immediately marking them out from production road cars – after a series of mishaps reduced the entry from three cars, these two Gmünd-built 356s finally made the entry list of the 1951 Le Mans 24 Hours Race.

Improving the Breed – Early Competition and Development

Here, the two 1951 coupés are running nose-to-tail around the Sarthe circuit. This is clearly a practice session, however, not the race, as only the car of Auguste Veuillet and Edmond Mouche actually made the start of the race, the second vehicle being wrecked during a rainstorm.

of avoiding a cyclist on the circuit during early testing, one car was damaged. No sooner was it back in the workshops for repair than a second car was totally wrecked in a crash with another car on an autobahn. The best bits of the two were combined with another Gmünd coupé to create a replacement. There were now only two cars in preparation for the race, until one of them was damaged beyond repair in a rainstorm during another practice session. The last Porsche hopes were pinned on Auguste Veuillet and Edmond Mouche driving the sole survivor.

Despite all the problems of getting a car to the start of that first Le Mans for Porsche, which many people began to think was jinxed, Veuillet and Mouche drove a model race to finish an amazing twentieth overall, winning the 1,100cc Class along the way at a race average speed of 73mph (117kph). Whilst the old professor would have been proud to have seen his car finish where it did, his son went one better. He stayed in the pits throughout the 24 hours to monitor the car's performance and supervise the pit crew. He was overjoyed at the result and vowed to return with the same car the following year, as its performance had entitled it to do.

Also in June 1950, the Baden-Baden Rally was staged, featuring the competition debut of the 1,300 engine, with three coupés running in that event, two works entries and a private entrant, all running on works test licence plates to allow them on the special high speed road stages to go in excess of the contemporary 80kph (50mph) autobahn speed limit. All three averaged over 120kph (75mph) on those stages and ran the thirty-hour duration without a single mechanical fault. This demonstration quickly put the 1,300 on the map and sales of Porsche cars grew apace, especially the new 1,300 model.

SUCCESS BEGETS SUCCESS

Having achieved significant success in both the Baden-Baden and Le Mans races in 1951, Porsche was ready to do battle in the Liège–Rome–Liège Rally, which took place in August. This was another gruelling test,

Improving the Breed – Early Competition and Development

Guillaume and von der Mühle entered a 1,300, but their car was actually a 1,500 prototype with which they took the 1,500cc Class win and third overall in the 1951 Liège–Rome–Liège Rally. Here, von der Mühle stands by his car (front), whilst Huschke von Hanstein and Peter-Max Müller stand alongside their 1,100cc car.

the route of which passed over alpine mountain roads (in reality sometimes little more than mountain tracks), and two Porsche cars were brought to the start. One was an 1,100cc car, driven by Peter-Max Müller and Huschke von Hanstein; the other was listed as being a 1,300 driven by Paul Guillaume, with Count von der Mühle. The first car finished second in its class, after a brilliant drive, whilst the second, which actually turned out to be a 1,500cc prototype, won the 1,500cc Class and finished third overall, despite the car suffering transmission problems. Porsche was now 'on a high'.

Barely had the team returned to Stuttgart than Auguste Veuillet was pursuing Ferry Porsche again. This time, the quest was time and distance records at Montlhery Track, France's Brooklands. Veuillet persuaded Porsche to prepare an 1,100cc car and a 1,500cc car for a run at several records. The cars, once again, were Gmünd-built coupés and the driving team was to consist of Veuillet, Peter-Max Müller (who had already set a number of records at Montlhery with his home-built VW special in 1950), Huschke von Hanstein (who was, by this time, Porsche's public relations and competitions manager), Richard von Frankenberg, Hermann Ramelow and Walter Glöckler. Glöckler had had his own roadster body built on to a Porsche chassis, which had the appearance of a hybrid between the Swiss Beutler cabriolet and the factory's own Speedster of later days, and he brought that roadster to the track for a run at some of its own records.

During the last week of September, Ferry Porsche and his support team set up camp at Montlhery. The first Gmünd coupé went out and was soon taking the first of three new records set on that day. By the end of

Improving the Breed – Early Competition and Development

its run, it had put up new 500-mile (800km) and 1,000km (625-mile) records, as well as the six hours duration for the 1,100cc Class. Walter Glöckler's car was next out and, fitted with a 1,500cc engine, it took three short-distance records and set up a new fastest lap at over 120mph (192kph). With a bag of records to its credit already, the team now prepared for the final record-breaking assault of its visit to Montlhèry.

On 30 September the 1,500cc coupé embarked on an attempt at the absolute record for a 72-hour run, which had been set by a 3-litre Citroën before the war. The target was to better 80mph (128kph) for the three-day marathon, picking up any other records along the way. Two days into the run, the car had averaged 99mph (158kph) and looked set to send the Citroën's record into oblivion, when crisis overtook it. Pulling into the pits for a refuelling stop, the hose was directed into the under-bonnet filler neck and when the valve was opened – nothing: not a drop came out. An onlooker fortunately had a reserve can of fuel. As the clock ticked away, he brought it to the car and poured its couple of gallons in, so that the car could continue its run until the valve in the pit refuelling hose was repaired.

Walter Glöckler's 1,500 roadster special set up a new fastest lap at Montlhery at over 120mph (192kph).

Then came another crisis, which almost put paid to the whole record attempt. In the early hours of day three, the car rolled into the pit with a broken gearbox. After a period of frantic fiddling and tweaking, third gear was recovered, though none of the others was able to be used. After some rapid arithmetic, it was decided that a new record was still possible, so the car was pushed back on to the track to finish its run. Despite the much higher engine speeds and higher fuel consumption, bringing the engine close to expiry, a new 72-hour record was achieved, along with ten other class records. The car was then taken to the 1951 Paris Salon where it had pride of place – still covered in dirt, bugs and oil – on the Porsche stand.

Early in the new season, another Gmünd-built car went to the 1952 Liège–Rome–Liège Rally, in the hope of achieving some of the previous year's success. This car had a 1,500cc engine and was the only works entry, to be driven by Helmut Polenski and Walter Schlueter. There were several private entrants, too, all driving Zuffenhausen-built 1,500cc-engined production models (though doubtless tuned with a little help!). Beyond their wildest dreams, the magnificent drive put up by Polenski and Schlueter brought them an outright win, whilst third, fourth, ninth and tenth places fell to the privateers. Now for the big one – the Mille Miglia.

Going for Broke

Once again, a single works entry, a Gmünd coupé, was prepared for the 1952 Mille Miglia, Porsche's first venture into this car-breaking classic road race, the nineteenth in the series, marking the 25th anniversary of the first time this Italian classic was run. The coupé was pitched against such veteran Mille Miglia competitors as the amazing eleven times winners Alfa Romeo,

Improving the Breed – Early Competition and Development

four times winners Ferrari, Mercedes-Benz, Lancia, OSCA, Jaguar, Aston Martin and other experienced runners. It was expected that the works-entered Porsche, driven by Italian Count Giovanni ('Johnny') Lurani and German Count Constantin von Berckheim, would bring in its wake a number of private-entrant Zuffenhausen cars, and it certainly did.

At the top end of the scale, Ferrari did battle with Mercedes-Benz. In the middle, the 2-litre Grand Touring category was fought over by Lancia and Alfa Romeo. Porsche had to battle against these odds, in the clear and honest expectation that they would be very lucky to win anything. The Lurani/Berckheim car was joined by Polenski/Mijorini in a 1,500, Prince Metternich and Count Einseidel in an 1,100, Della Favera/Artusi in another 1,500 and Dinca Levis/E. Facca, also in a 1,500. Other entrants in the 1,500cc Class, competing against the Porsches, were Siatas, Cisitalias and Maseratis. The Lurani/Berchkeim Porsche started last in its class at 3.27am. By Rome, it was fifteen minutes ahead of the first Cisitalia, driven by the Musitelli brothers.

Just after Florence, the leading Porsche lost top gear and continued with the remaining three, Lurani punishing the clutch in the process of extracting a maximum 88mph (140kph), but leading his Class by Bologna. The Porsche stayed ahead of the Musitelli Cisitalia, despite having no top gear, and went on to win the 1,500cc Class at a race average speed of 66mph (105kph). Dalla Favera and Artusi were second in their Class, whilst Dinca Levis and Facca made it a Class hat-trick. In the 1,100cc Sports Car category, Prince Metternich and Einsiedel took the win ahead of a brace of Fiats.

There is an amusing story attached to the Polenski/Mijorini Porsche's quest for success in the Mille Miglia. Polenski misunderstood an instruction from his Italian co-driver (given in French), and went straight on at a curve, rolling the car in the process. With no space to sit upright in the car after the incident, a rather substantially built spectator climbed in and pushed the kink out of the roof with his back, so making adequate headroom for the crew. It turned out to be in vain though, for the car retired with mechanical difficulties.

Prince Paul von Metternich drove this 356 cabriolet to an eighth place finish in the gruelling 1952 Carrera Panamericana race.

In June, it was back to Teloche, the Porsche Le Mans HQ, with two Gmünd coupés, both fitted with 1,100cc engines. Veuillet and Mouche, class winners the previous year, were now joined by Huschke von Hanstein and Peter-Max Müller. A long hard race ensued, in which the von Hanstein/Müller car was unable to stay the course, leaving the prospect of an 1,100cc Class prize in the trust of Veuillet and Mouche. To the absolute delight of Ferry Porsche and all those who had supported the gallant venture, the French pair did it again and walked away with the 1,100cc victory. However, the privately entered 1,500 was disqualified whilst in a strong position, because the drivers changed over before switching off the engine. It was a disappointment, but took nothing from Porsche's great success – and its last competition event with the Gmünd-built cars.

Probably one of the most gruelling road races ever, even considering the awesome Mille Miglia, was next on Porsche's 'Giant Killer's Calendar'. This event was the 1952 Carrera Panamericana in Mexico, run in November. Two cars, a cabriolet driven by Prince Paul von Metternich and a coupé driven by Count Constantin von Berckheim, were imported into Mexico for the event by Prince Alfons von Hohenlohe. Such was the financial shoestring upon which the Porsches were run, that the Mercedes-Benz team, who had nothing to fear from the diminutive Zuffenhausen cars, carried Porsche's consignment of spare parts throughout the race.

After four days of driving between Tuxtla Guitterez and Ciudad Juarez, over roads that could often barely even be described as respectable tracks, let alone roads, the von Metternich car finished eighth overall, but von Berckheim was forced to retire with a broken transmission. This was the race which gave the name to a succession of top-of-the-range Porsche models which continues to this day.

DEVELOPING THE PRODUCT

Whilst these early competitive events were taking place, Porsche was seeking to improve its products by embodying into them the experiences of the rigours the cars had endured. An early example is the development of the 1,500 engine, which was commenced in late 1950, at about the same time that one of Porsche's suppliers, Heinrich Sauter, pressed for the creation of an out-and-out sports two-seat roadster. Sauter had raced a 356 Coupé in 1950 and decided he could do better with a lighter-weight,

The 540 America Roadster was the ultimate result of Heinrich Sauter's design experiment.

open car for his future competition. So he bought a 356 chassis and took it to a friend, Hans Klenk, for him to build an open two-seater body upon it in steel.

By the time this car had been built, in the spring of 1951, Max Hoffman had been consulted in New York as to the saleability of such a vehicle, whilst the factory design team took a strong interest in the project, consulting Sauter as the car was being created. Once built, a prototype 1,500 engine was installed and the vehicle found itself being used as a testbed for the new engine. The car finally became a Porsche catalogue model and was to be called the America Roadster, after Heinrich Sauter had sold it back to the factory. Whilst in his ownership, the car had been fielded in the Nürburgring 1,000 Kilometres Race and the Liège–Rome–Liège Rally. Next came the development work essential to creating a production model from a prototype in order to create a car for sale to the public – most of that public being in the United States.

By the spring of 1952, Max Hoffman had persuaded Ferry Porsche that the America Roadster was a worthwhile proposition, and so an order for an aluminium alloy bodied version of the Sauter design was placed with Glaser coachworks in Munich. Four such cars were built initially and sent to New York for Max Hoffman to offer to his public. Cabriolet chassis were sent by road from Zuffenhausen, the bodies being assembled and fitted before the mechanical components were installed. This made production a cumbersome business, which perhaps helps to explain why the car did not go into volume production, some estimates being that about 100 cars were built, while others, probably more realistically, suggest that only a dozen over the original four were produced. Glaser was in financial difficulties as that dozen cars were being built, casting doubts on a high production figure being likely. In any case, the Speedster would appear in just over a year's time – another product inspired by Max Hoffman.

During this same time of great excitement in the world of competition and record-breaking, the company was also spending time and money on improvements that the customer (and competitor) would not necessarily see, but would certainly feel in benefits conferred upon the car. For example, Porsches in competition had suffered from the weakness of the Volkswagen transmission. At last, synchromesh was to be incorporated into a new, Type 519, Porsche gearbox, using split-ring synchronizers of the type which first appeared in the Cisitalia gearbox designed by Porsche back in 1947–8. The Porsche synchromesh design was to achieve international fame for its durability and reliability and was incorporated into the gearboxes of many other makes of cars worldwide.

Originally, this pioneer Porsche synchromesh design was offered to Volkswagen, in the hope that Wolfsburg would manufacture the whole gearbox. After all, even lower priced cars were moving towards a need for synchromesh in order to beat off the competition. The idea was to offer VW the benefit of the design and to buy gearboxes from VW for the continuing range of Porsches, so helping to keep Porsche costs down, because the gears and synchronizers would all fit into the existing VW casing. There was a cost benefit to both companies, but Heinz Nordhoff, the Chief Executive of Volkswagen, was sceptical, as was his chief engineer (both of whom, incidentally, were ex-Opel men), so they decided to opt for what they saw as a tried and tested design from Borg-Warner. So Porsche went to Getrag, who were mainly heavy equipment transmission engineers. As a result, Porsche no longer had to rely on VW for supply, and so was able to develop a whole new range of

Model: PorscheType 540 America 1500cc – 1952

Construction	Pressed steel fabricated and welded box-section chassis with unitary steel coupé or cabriolet bodywork
ENGINE	Porsche Type 528 (1500)
Crankcase	Light alloy crankcase with individual cylinders
Cylinder head	Light alloy with inserted valve guides and seats
Cyls/Type	Four, horizontally opposed
Compression	1500 = 8.2:1
Cooling system	Air, with finned cylinder barrels and belt-driven fan
Bore & Stroke	80mm × 74mm (3.3in × 2.9in)
Capacity	1,488cc (90.1cu in)
Main bearings	Four main journals/roller bearing big ends on composite crank
Valves	Two overhead per cylinder, pushrod actuation
Fuel supply	Diaphragm mechanical pump/two Solex 40PBIC carburettors
Power output	70bhp @ 5,500rpm
Ignition system	Coil and distributor with auto advance/retard
Lubrication	Wet sump, gear pump and oil cooling (magnetic filter)
BRAKES	
Type	Drum front and rear with hydraulic actuation
TRANSMISSION	Porsche Type 519/2 synchromesh four-speed plus reverse
Clutch type	Single dry plate
Gear ratios	1 = 15.94:1, 2 = 9.17:1, 3 = 6.53:1, 4 = 3.54:1. R = 15.575:1
Final drive ratio	4.375:1
SUSPENSION/STEERING	
Front suspension	Transverse torsion bars/trailing parallel links/telescopic shocks
Rear suspension	Transverse torsion bars/trailing parallel links/telescopic shocks
Steering type	Worm and peg with unequal arms
Wheels	Pressed steel 3.25D × 16
Tyres	5.00 × 16 cross-ply
DIMENSIONS	
Overall length	3,880mm (151.3in)
Overall width	1,600mm (62.4in)
Overall height	1,100mm (42.9in)
Wheelbase	2,100mm (81.9in)
Track (front)	1,306mm (50.9in)
Track (rear)	1,272mm (49.6in)
Lubrication	Wet sump, gear pump & oil cooling (magnetic filter)
MODELS AVAILABLE	Roadster
TOP SPEED	109mph (176kph)

Model: Porsche Type 356 1100/1300/1500 – 1952

Construction	Pressed steel fabricated and welded box-section chassis with unitary steel coupé or cabriolet bodywork
ENGINE	Type 369 (1100)/506 (1300)/546 (1500), rear-mounted
Crankcase	Light alloy crankcase with individual cylinders
Cylinder head	Light alloy with inserted valve guides and seats
Cyls/Type	Four, horizontally opposed
Compression	1100 = 7.0:1, 1300 = 6.5:1, 1500 = 7.0:1
Cooling system	Air, with finned cylinder barrels and belt-driven fan
Bore & Stroke	73.5mm × 64mm/80mm (2.86 × 2.5/3.1in) × 64mm/80mm × 74mm (2.5/3.1 × 2.88in)
Capacity	1,086cc/1,286cc/1,488cc (66.2/78.4/90.8cu in)
Main bearings	Four main journals (roller big ends/composite crank in 1,500)
Valves	Two overhead per cylinder, pushrod actuation
Fuel supply	Mechanical pump/two Solex 32PBI (1,100/1,300) or 40PBIC (1,500)
Power output	40bhp/44bhp @ 4,200 rpm/55bhp @ 4,400rpm
Ignition system	Coil and distributor with auto advance/retard
Lubrication	Wet sump, gear pump and oil cooling
BRAKES	
Type	Drum front and rear with hydraulic actuation
TRANSMISSION	Four-speed gearbox mounted ahead of the engine – rear wheel drive
Clutch type	Single dry plate
Gear ratios	1 = 13.91:1, 2 = 7.70:1, 3 = 4.94:1, 4 = 3.5 7:1. R = 15.575:1
Final drive ratio	4.375:1
SUSPENSION/STEERING	
Front suspension	Transverse torsion bars/trailing parallel links/telescopic shocks
Rear suspension	Transverse torsion bars/trailing parallel links/telescopic shocks
Steering type	VW type worm and peg with unequal arms
Wheels	Pressed steel 3.25D × 16
Tyres	5.00 × 16 cross-ply sports

DIMENSIONS	**Cabriolet:**	**Coupé:**
Overall length	3,950mm	3,950mm (151.1in)
Overall width	1,660mm	1,660mm (64.7in)
Overall height	1,300mm	1,300mm (50.7in)
Wheelbase	2,100mm	2,100mm (81.9in)
Track (front)	1,290mm	1,290mm (50.3in)
Track (rear)	1,250mm	1,250mm (48.7in)

MODELS AVAILABLE	Cabriolet/coupé
TOP SPEED	1,100/87mph (140kph), 1,300/90mph (145kph), 1,500/100mph (160kph)

Improving the Breed – Early Competition and Development

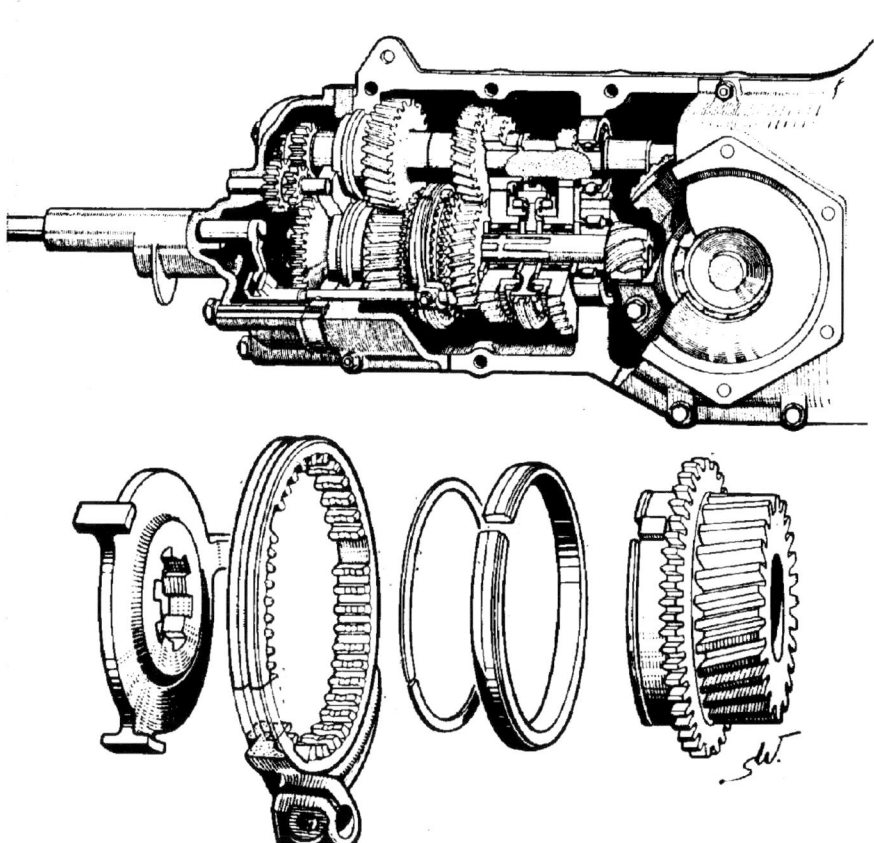

The Porsche Type 519 split-ring synchromesh gearbox was a major advance in making gear changes easier for the everyday motorist.

gear and final drive ratios which were distinctly marketable options.

Braking was another area with which Ferry Porsche was dissatisfied, for as performance improved with the 1,300 engine, then the 1,500, it became apparent that the stopping power was not keeping pace with developments elsewhere in the 356 line, so a decision was made to switch to Lockheed two-leading shoe brakes of larger diameter, the efficiency of which was to be further aided by the use of aluminium-finned brake drums. Otherwise, the front axle remained exactly as before, though the rear end of the car was changing as the transaxle switched from Volkswagen to the Getrag-built assembly.

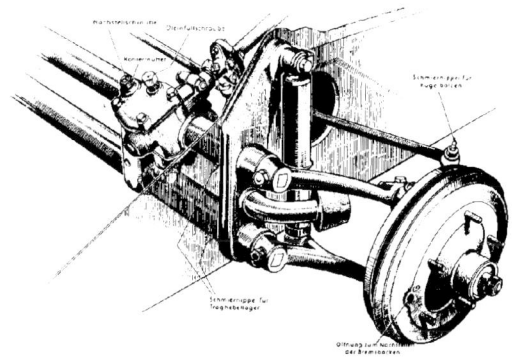

The revised front axle/suspension assembly now featured finned brake drums and Lockheed's two leading shoe brakes, though retained the VW torsion bar suspension.

Model: Porsche Type 356S 1300cc/1500cc – 1953

Construction	Pressed steel fabricated and welded box-section chassis with unitary steel coupé or cabriolet bodywork
ENGINE	Porsche Type 589 (1300)/Type 528 (1500)
Crankcase	Light alloy crankcase with individual cylinders
Cylinder head	Light alloy with inserted valve guides and seats
Cyls/Type	Four, horizontally opposed
Compression	1300 = 8.2:1, 1500 = 7.0:1
Cooling system	Air, with finned cylinder barrels and belt-driven fan
Bore & Stroke	1,300 = 74.5mm × 74mm (2.9 × 2.88in), 1,500 = 80mm × 74mm (3.1 × 2.88in)
Capacity	1,300 = 1,290cc(78.7cu in), 1,500 = 1,488cc (90.8cu in)
Main bearings	Four main journals/roller bearing big ends on composite crank
Valves	Two overhead per cylinder, pushrod actuation
Fuel supply	Diaphragm mechanical pump/two Solex 40PBIC carburettors
Power output	1,300 = 60bhp @ 5,500 rpm, 1,500 = 70bhp @ 5,000rpm
Ignition system	Coil and distributor with auto advance/retard
Lubrication	Wet sump, gear pump and oil cooling (magnetic filter)
BRAKES	
Type	Drum front and rear with hydraulic actuation
TRANSMISSION	Porsche Type 519/2 synchromesh four-speed plus reverse
Clutch type	Single dry plate
Gear ratios	1 = 13.91:1, 2 = 7.7:1, 3 = 4.94:1, 4 = 3.57:1. R = 15.575:1
Final drive ratio	4.375:1
SUSPENSION/STEERING	
Front suspension	Transverse torsion bars/trailing parallel links/telescopic shocks
Rear suspension	Transverse torsion bars/trailing parallel links/telescopic shocks
Steering type	Spindle, with divided unequal length arms
Wheels	Pressed steel 3.25D × 16
Tyres	5.00 × 16 cross-ply
DIMENSIONS	**Cabriolet**: / **Coupé**:
Overall length	3,950mm / 3,950mm (151.1in)
Overall width	1,660mm / 1,660mm (64.7in)
Overall height	1,300mm / 1,300mm (50.7in)
Wheelbase	2,100mm / 2,100mm (81.9in)
Track (front)	1,290mm / 1,290mm (50.3in)
Track (rear)	1,250mm / 1,250mm (48.7in)
MODELS AVAILABLE	Cabriolet/Speedster
TOP SPEED	100mph (160kph)

Improving the Breed – Early Competition and Development

The Type 546 1,500cc engine now had plain bearings and a lower compression ratio, becoming known as the 'Dame' engine. The short cast manifold illustrated here was an easy identifier of the 546 unit.

Leading into the 1953 model year, engines were, of course, a very important area for development at Zuffenhausen. The first of Porsche's engines to receive attention was the Type 527 1,500cc unit. The roller-bearing crankshaft was retained, but the camshaft was redesigned to give an extra millimetre of lift and the dwell was extended. With improvements in post-war fuels, it was possible now to increase the compression ratio and give a true performance benefit, so it was raised to 8.2:1. This resulted in the roller-bearing engine acquiring a new Type Number – 528. This new engine, combined with the Type 519 synchromesh gearbox, made the Porsche 1500S a very desirable little car, with 70bhp at its disposal through a much quicker and smoother gear change.

There were, of course, potential Porsche owners who did not require that level of performance, and for them the Type 546 1,500cc engine was developed, the key benefit of which was the lower production cost, for Karl Rabe had now found a way to produce a two-bolt big end cap that would not collide with the camshaft, so allowing a return to plain bearings for the bottom end of the engine. He had eliminated big end bolts and resorted to the use of studs, threaded integrally into the cap, so allowing the bottom corners to be removed, leaving an oval shape to pass by the camshaft. It was essentially a plain-bearing version of the Type 527, though with a milder cam form, smaller carburettors and a 7.0:1 compression ratio. This came to be known as the 'Dame' engine, in the days when the female of our species was still regarded as less aggressive, but capable of appreciating the finer things in life.

So the 1953 model year was approached with a positive optimism. Porsche had made numerous innovations in the new range and was bringing to the world of motoring in general ideas that would be taken up, and earn royalties on patents, by many much longer established car makers. Also, by the end of 1952, Porsches were rolling out of the assembly hall of Werke II, the new factory built to the rear of the old Porsche workshops. Interestingly, the building was originally planned to be a single-storey unit, but, as construction commenced, the decision to go to two floors was made, and before the second deck was roofed another floor was added to house every department of the now rapidly expanding company that had risen from the ashes of war-torn Europe less than a decade before.

THE FIRST PURPOSE-BUILT SPORTS RACER – THE 550

Having proved itself in action at the world's major races, using not tuned versions of production models but obsolete Gmünd coupés, Porsche decided by the end of 1952 that it was time to create a dedicated competition vehicle. Inspired by the creations of Walter Glöckler, a committed Porsche enthusiast who had had his own body designs fitted to Porsche chassis, the factory now embarked on its most serious sporting venture yet.

Glöckler had enjoyed factory support for the creation of his little sports-racing two-seaters, because in those early days anyone willing to fly the Porsche flag at his own expense had to be welcome. What was more, in return for the factory support, Glöckler fielded his own car at the Montlhery record run. His second special creation, bodied, like the first, by Weidenhausen of Frankfurt, used a factory-supplied 1,500 engine and carried, with approval, the Porsche script on the nose, being described officially as a Glöckler-Porsche. With the results of this co-operation in mind, Ferry Porsche was persuaded by Huschke von Hanstein and Karl Rabe to use the Glöckler car as the

Walter Glöckler's second special roadster also featured a 1,500cc Porsche engine and was built with much factory support, evidence of which is the Porsche script on the nose.

Improving the Breed – Early Competition and Development

The 550 was to introduce a whole new era to Porsche sports car racing, for this signified the factory's seriousness of intent to embark on a winning path.

At Le Mans in 1953 Richard von Frankenberg and Paul Frere were timed down the Mulsanne Straight at 124mph (198kph), setting a new 1,500cc Class record and finishing fifteenth overall in this 550.

starting point for their new works creation, which was to be labelled the Type 550.

Design work on the 550 began in early 1953. The chassis was a ladder frame type, with the rear suspension at the extreme tail end of the car and the engine ahead of the gearbox in mid-location, like the original 356-001 and the Glöckler cars. Telescopic dampers were used to control the vertical movement of the rear suspension, whilst an odd 'rubber band' ran from a pulley on the underside of the centre of the chassis to front and rear suspensions to aid the control of suspension movement. The running gear for the new car was largely from the production line, though a ZF limited slip

Improving the Breed – Early Competition and Development

Hans Herrmann drove the Fletcher Aviation 550 in the 1953 Carrera Panamericana, bringing to an illustrious end the brief career of the pushrod-engined 550 and paving the way for the quad-cam 550RS.

differential was incorporated into the transmission, whilst a hydraulic clutch was thought advisable for this application and the oil cooler was fitted at the front of the car.

The engine in the early 550s was the 1,500 Super unit, now fitted with Solex twin-choke carburettors and pistons that gave a 12.5:1 compression ratio for running on alcohol fuels. Bodywork was all-alloy and was built by Weidenhausen, the builder of Glöckler's bodies. They were open two-seaters with the unusual addition of a removable hard top, which was to be used in very high-speed events, though the hard top had a thoroughly claustrophobic effect on drivers and drummed mercilessly, giving the impression of driving in a biscuit tin! Glöckler's cousin, Helm, was to have the privilege of driving 550-01 on its maiden outing, in the Eifelrennen 1,500cc Class at the Nürburgring. The car performed virtually faultlessly and, despite a thorough soaking because the hard top was not fitted for this event, Glöckler was delighted with its handling and his victory.

A couple of weeks later came Le Mans, and Porsche was entering the first two examples of the new model which was seen at Nürburgring. Helm Glöckler partnered Hans Herrmann in 550-01, whilst Richard von Frankenberg drove Chassis 550-02 with Belgian motoring journalist Paul Frere, who was to develop a long driving association with Porsche. With detuned engines to allow the use of pump fuel, the power output was down to 77bhp. However, with hard tops fitted, the cars were timed down the Mulsanne Straight at 124mph (198kph). After a gruelling race, in which the drivers suffered unbearable heat and noise, the von Frankenberg/Frère car set a new 1,500cc class record, finishing fifteenth overall.

Glöckler and Herrmann drove a 550 at the Avus in a July race, without much success, though Herrmann won a 1,500cc class in a sports car race preceding the 1953 German Grand Prix and then took a class win at the Freiburg Hill Climb a week later. But the original 550s had now run their course, giving as much as they could to the development of the new Zuffenhausen racing line. With them, the first pavings of the road to greatness for Porsche had now been laid.

6 From the Quad-Cam 550 to the Single-Seat Porsches

After Helm Glöckler's victory at Nurburgring, followed by his shared drive of 550-01 at Le Mans with Hans Herrmann in partnership with the duo of Richard von Frankenberg and Paul Frère in 550-02 (where the Frankenberg/Frère car did so well), these two cars were refurbished and mildly modified before being shipped to Guatemala. Their new owner, Jaroslav Juhan, a displaced Czech, entered them for the 1953 Carrera Panamericana. He drove 550-01, whilst José Herrarte drove 550-02, which actually went on to a class win ahead of a 356 coupé, Juhan retiring not long after the start of the race.

Much had been learned from the creation and racing of these first two 550s, but now Erwin Komenda and Ernst Furhmann were given the job of developing the car still further. There was still the belief that racing improved the breed – and for Porsche that belief had proved to be fact. For who could argue that the tremendous pace of development at Gmünd and Zuffenhausen was not in a large part down to the sequence of events started by Herbert Kaes back in 1948, when he won that first competitive event in 356-001.

THE NEW 550/1500RS

With a modified ladder frame chassis, the next step in the 550's development was to see a further revision to the rear suspension, putting the torsion bar links into a trailing position once again, though they had to be much longer than before, now 600mm (23in), as the torsion bars were positioned ahead of the engine. The VW-type torsion bar front suspension was retained for the 550 and drum brakes remained as the stopping power at this time. The 2100mm (82in) wheelbase of the production 356 was retained for the 550s, though there really was little else in common between the two types. The Porsche split-ring synchromesh four-speed gearbox was fitted, with three different final drive ratio options.

The real 'magic' of the 1500 Rennsport, though, was its Type 547 four-cam engine. At 1,498cc, the bore was 85mm (3in), whilst the stroke was a diminutive 66mm (2.5in), giving a substantially over-square engine that could yield very considerable improvements in engine speeds whilst giving lower or no more than equal increases in piston speed, compared with its predecessors. The compression ratio of the RS engine was now 9.8:1, whilst it had been 9.5:1 on the prototypes. Twin camshaft-driven distributors provided dual ignition to the engines, whilst two valves per cylinder provided inlet and exhaust gas flows through hemispherical combustion chambers. Fuel supplies came via Weber carburettors now, instead of the earlier Solexes.

The quad-cam engine was so called because each bank of cylinders in the flat-four design had dual overhead camshafts –

Model: Porsche Type 550/1500RS – 1953

Construction	Tubular spaceframe with hand fabricated aluminium alloy bodywork by Weidenhausen, Weinsberg and Wendler
ENGINE	Type 547 (547/1 from sixteenth car built)
Crankcase	Light alloy crankcase with individual cylinders
Cylinder head	Light alloy with inserted valve guides and seats
Cyls/Type	Four, horizontally opposed
Compression	9.5:1
Cooling system	Air, with finned cylinder barrels and belt-driven fan
Bore & Stroke	85mm × 66mm (3.3in × 2.6in)
Capacity	1,498cc (91.4cu in)
Main bearings	Roller main and big end bearings
Valves	Two overhead per cylinder, dual overhead cam actuation
Fuel supply	Dual electric pumps/two Solex 40PJJ carburettors
Power output	110bhp @ 6,200rpm
Ignition system	Dual coil and distributor with twin spark plugs
Lubrication	Dry sump, 8-litre oil tank, gear pump and oil cooling
BRAKES	
Type	Drum front and rear with hydraulic actuation
TRANSMISSION	Four-speed Type 718 – rear wheel drive
Clutch type	Single dry plate
Gear ratios	Various, according to requirements of circuit
Final drive ratio	Various, according to requirements of circuit
SUSPENSION/STEERING	
Front suspension	Independent with double oscillating arms, square-section torsion bars and telescopic shock absorbers
Rear suspension	Independent swing axles, round-section torsion bars and telescopic shock absorbers
Steering type	Spindle with divided unequal length arms
Wheels	Pressed steel 3.25D × 16
Tyres	Front: 5.00 × 16R, Rear: 5.25 × 16 RS Racing
DIMENSIONS	
Wheelbase	2,100mm (81.9in)
Track (front)	1,290mm (50.3in)
Track (rear)	1,250mm (48.8in)
DRY WEIGHT	550kg (1,177lb). From car 16 = 590kg (1,180lb)
MODELS AVAILABLE	Coupé / Spyder
TOP SPEED	136mph (220kph)

From the Quad-Cam 550 to the Single-Seat Porsches

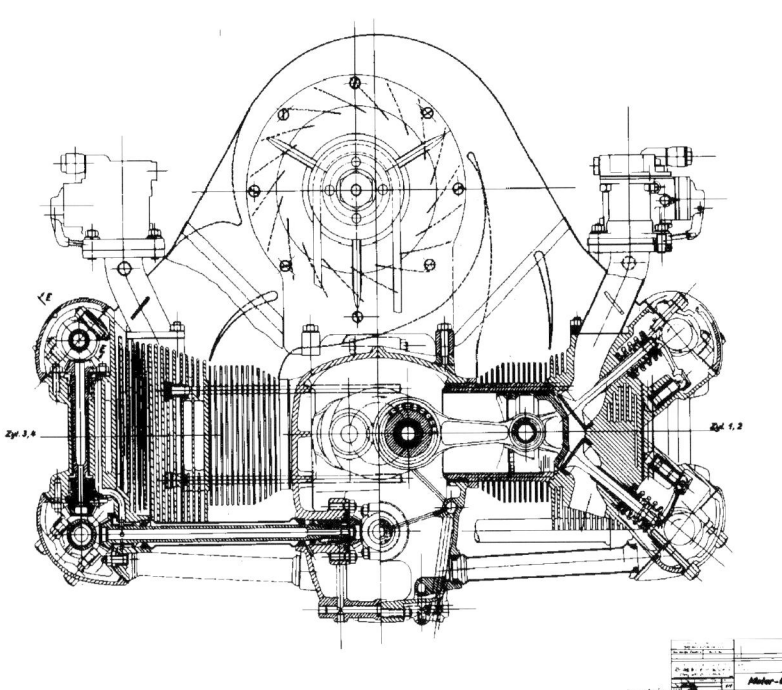

Ernst Fuhrmann's original Type 547 quad-cam engine design for installation into the new 550/1500RS.

with two camshafts per bank, it was four to the engine, thus 'quad-cam'. Most engines of the time used either chain drive or gear drive to rotate the camshafts, but for the Type 547 Ernst Fuhrmann chose to use a drive method more common to aircraft or motorcycle engines. A single rotating shaft to each cylinder bank, driven by bevel gears from the crankshaft, rotated the lower pair of camshafts. Then another, short, shaft ran across each cylinder head, driven from the lower camshaft to operate the upper one. Finger tappets lay between the cam lobe and the valve stem. Timing and valve settings must have been an utter nightmare.

This engine had been designed from a 'clean sheet of paper' and so shared nothing by way of components with any of the pushrod engine types. With the higher compression ratio used on the 547, the power output was capable of being raised to well over 110bhp at engine speeds over 6,500rpm. The torque output was deliberately pitched high, because this was a racing engine by design, though the so-called 'production' engines which were intended for sale to private buyers would be mostly detuned to give something like 85bhp and run on lower compression ratios, down to 8.7:1. The intention was, of course, to give the customers a thoroughly reliable power unit that could bear a little amateur 'tweaking'.

The bodywork on the new 550 was built by Weinsberg to Erwin Komenda's design. Large bulbous rear fins extended to the end of the body from the high rear deck, whilst the cockpit had a full framed windscreen. Chassis Number 550-03 was completed in July 1953 and had its first trial in an event at the Nürburgring on 2 August. The public was not to know it, but this was the debut of the quad-cam engine. They were not to know because the engine cover was never lifted. The Freiburg Hill Climb saw the same chassis out again, with another disappointing result, but once again the engine was not exposed.

Chassis 550-05 was built for exhibition at the Paris Salon in October 1953. This one was built as a road car, with a roadgoing windscreen, windscreen wipers, a folding top, two full seats, slightly modified rear fins and a single cooling grille at the rear. This was the 550/1500RS (Rennsport), in which the quad-cam engine was announced to the public for the first time. It was a car consciously intended for sale to private buyers who would use it for competition, though at this point the engine was to go through a few further modifications before it actually reached production.

More developments took place with the 550, and in January 1954 Chassis Number 550-04 took the public's attention at the Brussels Motor Show. It had an unusual body design, with the rear deck raised up to the level of the top of the windscreen. Small tapering sidescreens were fitted and wind tunnel tests showed that what had effectively become a 'coupé without a top' was aerodynamically almost as 'clean' as a fully enclosed car. The line from the cockpit to the rear end of the car resulted in a somewhat pronounced hump, with the result that the car acquired the nickname of 'The Humpback'. The rear section of the body was made in one piece and was hinged at its lower rear to provide access to the engine, gearbox and rear suspension. It was a feature pioneered by Porsche and soon followed by others, used even to this day.

THE 550 GOES FROM STRENGTH TO STRENGTH

After extensive testing, including Hockenheim in April 1954, a single 550, Number 08, was entered for the Mille Miglia, to be driven by Hans Herrmann and Herbert Linge. Richard von Frankenberg drove a 356 coupé in the same race and both cars put up spirited performances, 550-08 taking Herrmann and Linge to an overall sixth place and a class win in the under 1,500cc Sports category at a very rapid 79.2mph (126kph) race average, whilst the much scarred coupé of von Frankenberg and Sauter won the under 1,600cc GT Class at an amazing 72mph (115kph), followed home by two other 356s.

Next on the international sporting calendar was Le Mans. Fifty-seven cars went to the start, though notably absent were the entries from Austin-Healey, Lancia and Mercedes-Benz. It was a wet and miserable event which was expected to be a battle between Ferrari and Jaguar. Numerous changes had been made to the circuit, with the road between Mulsanne and Arnage having been widened and a piece of the White House farmhouse demolished to improve visibility round the corner. A new grandstand had also been built on the site of the original restaurant and several other improvements were made to the amenities, including enlargement of the public enclosures behind Mulsanne and Arnage.

The duel between Ferrari and Jaguar began from the very start of the race, while further down the field Hans Herrmann and Helmut Polenski set a blistering pace with the 1,500cc Porsche, the car of von Frankenberg and Glöckler having retired earlier with a blown head gasket. By midnight, with the rain having begun again, Herrmann and Polenski were just two minutes behind the Ecurie Francorchamps 'C' Type Jaguar. Halfway through the race, the pair were in ninth place and pressing on, but their pace took its toll and a head gasket blew, bringing another Porsche retirement. The finish was one of the most

From the Quad-Cam 550 to the Single-Seat Porsches

Chassis 550/04 was built with this raised rear deck as an aerodynamic experiment. The shape earned it the nickname 'Humpback'.

exciting ever at Le Mans, with Froilàn Gonzalez's Ferrari crossing the line ahead of Tony Rolt in the leading Jaguar. There were two Porsches in the results too: Claes and Stasse took the 1,500cc Class and finished twelfth overall, while Duntov and Olivier drove the first 1,100cc car home into fourteenth place.

The year 1955 saw a new 550 Spyder, driven by Walter Ringenberg and Richard von Frankenberg, take six new class records at the Monza Autodrome from 200 miles (320km) to six hours, lapping the track at 130mph (208kph) en route. Then came the Sebring 12 Hours Race, in which six Spyders out of seven finished and racing on the US west coast saw Porsches winning race after race. Le Mans brought a 1,500cc class 1–2–3, a 1,500cc win in the Index of Performance and an 1,100cc Class win. Several American competitors, though, were beginning to find that things were getting tougher, as a number of the opposition had installed Type 547 Porsche engines into Cooper chassis as a means of creating quicker cars. Then, in August, Porsche offered a five-speed gearbox to help close the gap between the 'working' four upper gears. September brought a brief revival of Porsche fortunes, with Masten Gregory and Carroll Shelby's 550 taking a class win in the RAC Tourist Trophy Race.

By the end of the year, the original 550's days were over, as a new version, the Type 550A/1500RS was on the scene. Now the chassis was a full spaceframe, instead of the earlier ladder design. Suspension changes involved only the fitting of an anti-roll bar at the front, while at the rear, low pivot swinging arms were used, which were jointed just below the differential in the fashion of Mercedes-Benz design. A larger fuel tank (by nine gallons), wider front brakes which gave an increase of 25 per cent surface contact area and that fifth gear brought the specification up to date.

Model: Porsche Type 550A/1500RS – 1956

Construction	Tubular spaceframe with hand fabricated aluminium alloy bodywork by Wendler
ENGINE	
	Type 547/1 P90-500
Crankcase	Light alloy crankcase with individual cylinders
Cylinder head	Light alloy with inserted valve guides and seats
Cyls/Type	Four, horizontally opposed
Compression	9.8:1
Cooling system	Air, with finned cylinder barrels and belt-driven fan
Bore & Stroke	85mm × 66mm (3.3 × 2.6in)
Capacity	1,498cc (91.4cu in)
Main bearings	Roller main and big end bearings
Valves	Two overhead per cylinder, dual overhead cam actuation
Fuel supply	Dual electric pumps/two Weber 40DCM1 carburettors
Power output	135bhp @ 7,200rpm
Ignition system	Dual coil and distributor with twin spark plugs
Lubrication	Dry sump, 8-litre oil tank, gear pump and oil cooling
BRAKES	
Type	Drum front and rear with hydraulic actuation
TRANSMISSION	Five-speed Type 718 – rear wheel drive
Clutch type	Single dry plate
Gear ratios	Various, according to requirements of circuit
Final drive ratio	Various, according to requirements of circuit
SUSPENSION/STEERING	
Front suspension	Independent with double oscillating arms, square-section torsion bars and telescopic shock absorbers
Rear suspension	Independent swing axles, round-section torsion bars and telescopic shock absorbers
Steering type	ZF steering box with divided unequal length arms
Wheels	Pressed steel 3.25D × 16
Tyres	Front: 5.00 × 16R, Rear: 5.25 × 16 RS Racing
DIMENSIONS	
Wheelbase	2,100mm (81.9in)
Track (front)	1,290mm (50.3in)
Track (rear)	1,250mm (48.8in)
DRY WEIGHT	530kg (1,177lb)
MODELS AVAILABLE	Spyder
TOP SPEED	149mph (240kph)

From the Quad-Cam 550 to the Single-Seat Porsches

Porsche used a base at Teloche, near the Sarthe circuit, for the preparation of cars at each Le Mans race. Here, the team prepares for the 1954 event.

The 1955 Le Mans was Porsche's finest to date, with von Frankenberg and Polenski (Car 37) winning the 1,500cc Class and finishing fourth overall. Here, Frankenberg is pursued by Glöckler in the sixth place car.

From the Quad-Cam 550 to the Single-Seat Porsches

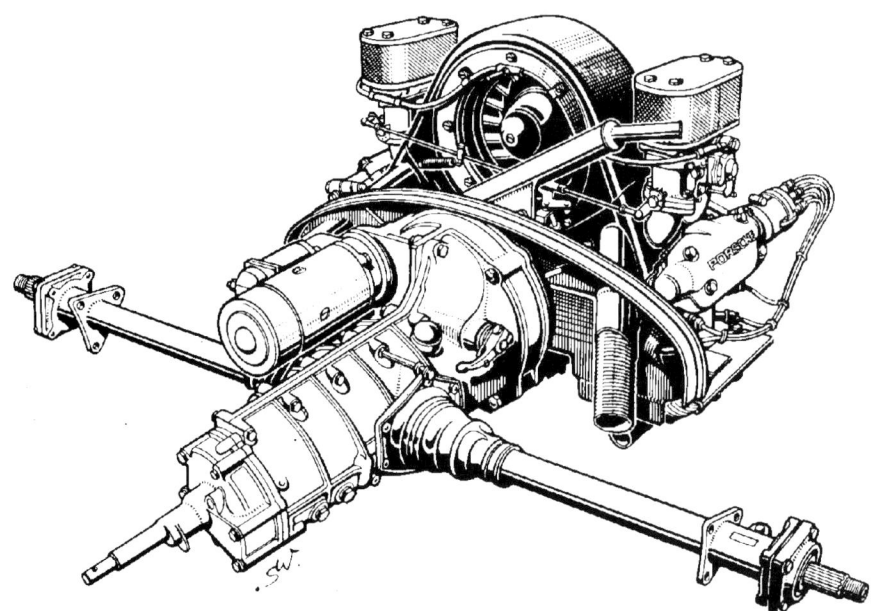

The engine and gearbox assembly of the 550.

Michael May calculated that by fitting a wing above the bodywork, set at a suitable angle, it could create sufficient downforce to so improve the adhesion of the car's tyres that its performance in corners would be vastly improved, as would its potential to win. However, it was disqualified from the 1955 Nürburgring 1,000 Kilometres Race.

Opening the 1956 season, Herrmann and von Trips took sixth place overall, a class win and the Index of Performance at the Sebring 12 Hours. In the Nürburgring 1,000 Kilometres, a poor Mille Miglia was made up for by a superb drive from Wolfgang von Trips and Umberto Maglioli in a 550A, with Hans Herrmann and Richard von Frankenberg in another. The von Trips/Maglioli car came home into fourth place, with the other car fifth, making a very creditable class 1–2. This was also the event in which an aerofoil was seen on a racing car for the first time.

Swiss entrant Michael May had an older 550 to which he had fitted a wing, mounted just above the cockpit and adjustable for varying conditions by the driver to increase the downforce. The effect of the wing was such that he took fourth fastest qualifying time overall, and was then promptly disqualified on the grounds that the wing blocked the view of other drivers. This rather feeble protest resulted in the principle of aerofoil devices being abandoned for over a decade, when they reappeared on Grand Prix cars. The next significant event for Porsche came in June, when Umberto Maglioli persuaded Ferry Porsche to agree to a last minute entry in the Targa Florio for him and Wolfgang von Trips. It really was a shoestring affair in the best of early Porsche tradition, because they took one car, two mechanics and a bag of spares. After the drive of a lifetime, their reward was the first German victory in the Sicilian classic since 1924, when Ferdinand Porsche's 2-litre Mercedes-Benz had won.

Days later came the 1956 Le Mans 24 Hours Race, in which two new 550s were entered. New regulations demanded full height windscreens, so Porsche decided to fit roof panels as well, attaching them at the rear to the hinged engine cover. The two resultant coupés ran another wet Le Mans, one car retiring whilst the other, driven by

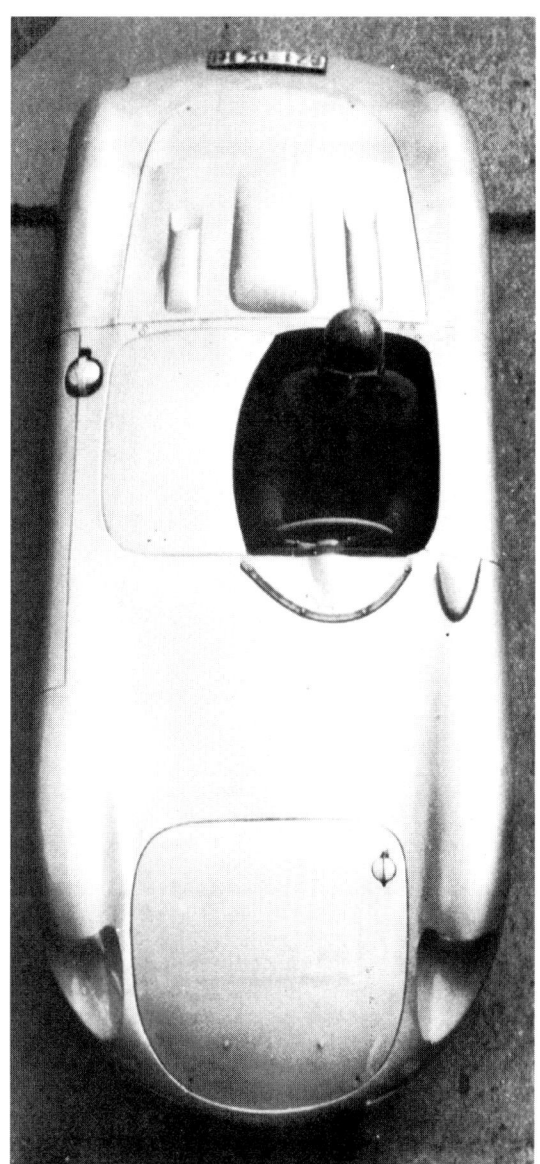

The Type 645 was nicknamed 'Mickey Mouse' for its early handling characteristics, but its narrower track and shorter wheelbase were hoped to give it a competitive edge. All such hopes were shattered when Richard von Frankenberg almost lost his life in a record attempt at the Avusrennenring in Berlin, with the result that the design was promptly abandoned.

Richard von Frankenberg and Wolfgang von Trips, finished fifth overall with yet another class win and second place in the Index of Performance.

At the Rheims 12 Hours Race, Porsches finished 1–2–3, then took the first two places at Solitude. But then came near disaster, when a new-style Spyder, Type 645 and dubbed 'Mickey Mouse' for its dubious handling qualities, went to the Avus track in Berlin. Richard von Frankenberg had named the car, having driven it in all its public appearances, but this time, as he rose on the banking, the car went out of control and veered over the top at speed, throwing out its driver on the way and landing on the outside of the track in flames. Unconscious but unhurt, von Frankenberg never fully recalled the whole incident, while the car itself was allowed to drift into oblivion.

A NEW SPYDER – THE TYPE 718

A new chassis design, specifically aimed at controlling the changes in camber angles during the movement of the torsion bar suspension that had been the experience of the 550s, was labelled Type 718. Because the tube arrangement in this new frame presented a letter 'K' in profile, the car quickly became known as the RSK. The torsion bars were relocated, the bodyline was much lower and several detail changes appeared. The front end had a much cleaner line, with faired-in headlamps, while the rear end had cooling grilles to draw air from the car's aerodynamic backwash. At the Nürburgring 1,000 Kilometres, the first prototype was unstable, so small vertical fins were fitted at the rear. At Le Mans, it was found to be no faster than a 550, so the company spent the rest of the year developing and improving it, entering the odd hill climb to register a presence.

As the 1957 season opened, the 718 had two new engines available: the 547/4 was called the 1600 (actually 1,587cc from 87.5mm (3.4in) bore and 66mm (2.5in) stroke) and the 547/5 was labelled the 1700 (1,679cc from 90mm (3.5in) bore and 66mm (2.5in) stroke). New high-lift cams were fitted and American-made valve springs closed the valves. The policy of short-run development by entering the cars in 2-litre

The 718RSK as it rolled out of the racing shop for the first time and before it acquired its tail fins.

From the Quad-Cam 550 to the Single-Seat Porsches

Model: Porsche Type 718/1500RSK/1600RSK – 1957/8

Construction	Tubular spaceframe with hand fabricated aluminium alloy bodywork
ENGINE	Type 547/3 (1500), Type 547/4 (1600)
Crankcase	Light alloy crankcase with individual cylinders
Cylinder head	Light alloy with inserted valve guides and seats
Cyls/Type	Four, horizontally opposed
Compression	9.8:1
Cooling system	Air, with finned cylinder barrels and belt-driven fan
Bore & Stroke	85mm × 66mm/87.5mm × 66mm (3.3 × 2.6/3.4 × 2.6in)
Capacity	1,498cc/1,587.5cc (91.4/96.8cu in)
Main bearings	Roller main and big end bearings
Valves	Two overhead per cylinder, dual overhead cam actuation
Fuel supply	Dual electric pumps/two Weber 40DCM1 or 46IDM carburettors
Power output	148bhp @ 8,000rpm/160bhp @ 7,800rpm
Ignition system	Dual coil and distributor with twin spark plugs
Lubrication	Dry sump, 8-litre oil tank, gear pump and oil cooling
BRAKES	
Type	11-inch drum front and rear with hydraulic actuation
TRANSMISSION	Five-speed Type 718 – rear wheel drive
Clutch type	Single dry plate
Gear ratios	Various, according to requirements of circuit
Final drive ratio	Various, according to requirements of circuit
SUSPENSION/STEERING	
Front suspension	Independent with double oscillating arms, square-section torsion bars and telescopic shock absorbers
Rear suspension	Independent swing axles, round-section torsion bars and telescopic shock absorbers
Steering type	ZF centre-point steering box with divided equal length arms
Wheels	Pressed steel 3.25D × 16
Tyres	Front: 5.00 × 16R, Rear: 5.25 × 16 RS Racing
DIMENSIONS	
Wheelbase	2,100mm (81.9in)
Track (front)	1,290mm (50.3in)
Track (rear)	1,250mm (48.8in)
DRY WEIGHT	530kg (1,177lb)
MODELS AVAILABLE	Spyder (one 1,500 modified to central seating for F2)
TOP SPEED	149mph (240kph)

Model: Porsche Type 718 RS60 – 1959

Construction	Tubular spaceframe with hand fabricated aluminium alloy bodywork
ENGINE	Type 547/3 (1500), Type 547/4 (1600)
Crankcase	Light alloy crankcase with individual cylinders
Cylinder head	Light alloy with inserted valve guides and seats
Cyls/Type	Four, horizontally opposed
Compression	9.8:1
Cooling system	Air, with finned cylinder barrels and belt-driven fan
Bore & Stroke	85mm × 66mm/87.5mm × 66mm/88mm × 66mm (3.3 × 2.6/3.4 × 2.6/3.43 × 2.6in)
Capacity	1,498cc/1,587.5cc/1,605cc (91.4/96.8/97.9cu in)
Main bearings	Roller main and big end bearings
Valves	Two overhead per cylinder, dual overhead cam actuation
Fuel supply	Dual electric pumps/two Weber 46IDM carburettors
Power output	150bhp @ 7,800rpm/160bhp @ 7,800rpm/170bhp @ 7,800rpm
Ignition system	Dual coil and distributor with twin spark plugs
Lubrication	Dry sump, 8-litre oil tank, gear pump and oil cooling
BRAKES	
Type	11-inch drum front and rear with hydraulic actuation
TRANSMISSION	Five-speed Type 718 – rear wheel drive
Clutch type	Single dry plate
Gear ratios	Various, according to requirements of circuit
Final drive ratio	Various, according to requirements of circuit
SUSPENSION/STEERING	
Front suspension	Independent with double oscillating arms, square-section torsion bars and Koni telescopic shock absorbers
Rear suspension	Independent swing axles, superimposed triangles and telescopic shock absorbers
Steering type	ZF centre-point steering box with divided equal length arms
Wheels	4.5J × 15 front, 5J × 15 rear
Tyres	Front: 5.00 × 15R, Rear: 5.25 × 15 RS Racing
DIMENSIONS	
Wheelbase	2,200mm (85.8in)
Track (front)	1,290mm (50.3in)
Track (rear)	1,250mm (48.8in)
DRY WEIGHT	550kg (1,222lb)
MODELS AVAILABLE	Spyder
TOP SPEED	155mph (250kph)

From the Quad-Cam 550 to the Single-Seat Porsches

This picture shows the 718 centre-seat car used in the early stages of Porsche's entry into Formula Two. Note the tail fins.

class hill climbs continued through the year. One interlude in the 1957 sporting calendar was the Mille Miglia, the twenty-fourth and last as a result of a terrible accident in which Alfonso de Portago and Eddie Nelson crashed close to the finish, killing themselves and ten spectators. The Porsche contingent ran a spectacular race, with Umberto Maglioli finishing fifth overall and running away with the 1,500cc Sports category, followed by two other Porsches to make it a class 1–2–3. Herbert Linge crossed the line to take the 1,600cc Class and was followed by another pair of Porsches to make it a 1–2–3 there, too.

Bodywork on the 718 came from Wendler of Reutingen and, by the beginning of 1958, it was thought that the cars were now ready to be raced seriously, so an entry was made for the Targa Florio. Edgar Barth and Jean

Here, Jean Behra shows the pace of the centre-seat RSK in the 1958 Rouen F2 race, as he won the event with ease.

Behra took the car to Sicily and, as the result of a lot of development work and a brilliant drive, they finished second overall and won their class. The world was later to discover that Porsche had finally abandoned torsion bar rear suspension in favour of coil springs and telescopic dampers with Watts linkage. The performance justified the decision.

The rest of 1958 saw the RSK perform well. In the 1958 Le Mans race, Jean Behra and Hans Herrmann won the 1,600cc Class, finishing third overall, while Edgar Barth and Paul Frere came in behind their teammates to finish fourth and take the 1,500cc Class. A 550A followed Barth and Frere to give Porsche their best overall result at Le Mans yet. Now it was time for the next stage in the development of the 718. Formula Two single-seat racing had enjoyed a revival of interest and Porsche was persuaded to build a car with the seat in the middle using the Barth/Frere Le Mans car. This was fielded at the French Grand Prix Formula Two event at Rheims, driven by Jean Behra, who romped home ahead of the Cooper, Ferrari and Lotus opposition. Edgar Barth came second at Nürburgring and Masten Gregory won his class at the Avus Formula Two event later in the year.

The sports-racing Porsche continued to be officially described as Type 718 until 1961, when the 718-RS-61 became the last of the line. Developed from the RS-60, this last model was reckoned to be capable of 150mph (240kph), but it did not give quite the same good account of itself as the RS-60 had, the earlier model winning such major races as the Targa Florio. Porsche now had major names in the world of racing drivers to rely on, such as Jo Bonnier, Dan Gurney, Graham Hill and Stirling Moss, and in North America launched such names as Bob Holbert and Roger Penske into sports car racing. But the RS-61 should not be dismissed, as it led to the development of a magnificent line of cars, which we will discuss later.

THE FORMULA TWO SINGLE SEATER

Since the first single seater was created out of the 718, its construction was never likely to take as long as if the design had started

The RS60, with its deeper windscreen and slightly longer wheelbase. This is the example which is in the Porsche Museum.

From the Quad-Cam 550 to the Single-Seat Porsches

Masten Gregory and Bob Holbert seen here steamrollering their way to an overall fifth place and Class win aboard an RS61 in the 1961 Le Mans 24 Hours.

from a 'clean sheet of paper'. Even so, it was somewhat surprising to find that construction took only weeks from the decision to build it. The wheelbase of the new single seater was 2,200mm (86in), whilst the front and rear tracks were 1,300mm (50in) and 1,260mm (49in) respectively. The engine was a type 547/3, which gave 155bhp and the gearbox was a new six-speed unit which was aimed at keeping the engine speed as

This example of the RS61 had a roof and was run in the prototype class at the 1961 Le Mans.

constant as possible throughout the gears, as the power output was on the high end at 7,800rpm with not much happening below 5,000rpm.

Surprisingly, the brakes on this new single seater were drum rather than disc, partly because the engineering team felt that the results of recent tests of Lockheed's disc brakes had not been convincing, so they preferred to stick to what they knew, increasing the surface contact area of the shoes. The ribbed brake drums and carriers were made of cast elektron and the hand-beaten alloy body weighed in at a mere 65lb (30kg) – not much by comparison with modern fibreglass products, perhaps, but pretty lightweight for its material and time.

Now that they had a real single seater, the Competitions department were keen to race it and the next available event was the Monaco Grand Prix. However, having conceded to the creation of this new machine, Ferry Porsche was still apprehensive about allowing it into the public view, and when the car was taken to the Nürburgring shortly after dawn on 4 May 1959, where it was to be test-driven by Wolfgang von Trips, Dr Porsche stipulated that it must achieve a lap of 9 minutes 30 seconds, or no race at Monaco.

Typically, it rained and the car failed to achieve anything like the time required. So they waited a day, and it was dry the following morning. The team now had three laps in which to achieve their goal. The first lap yielded 9:47 – not promising. Then von Trips came home with a 9:39 and finally, after standing on everything, he turned in a 9:29.8, just beating the challenge. With a bit of chassis tweaking, von Trips had said that he was sure he could have come home with a 9:25; then, with typical modesty, he added that he thought Stirling Moss could take ten seconds even off that time!

Hopes were high as Team Porsche went to Monte Carlo, especially as von Trips was one of only three drivers to squeeze a Formula Two car into a race of just sixteen cars. Clearly, as a Formula One Grand Prix, the full Grand Prix cars came first, but qualifying times were the final measure on a grid that was restricted because of the tight nature of the street circuit. But Porsche's race was to last less than a lap and a half, as von Trips slid into a wall at St Devote, taking Bruce Halford's Lotus 16 and Cliff Allison's Ferrari 246 out of the race with him. Ferry Porsche was clearly distressed with the realization of his worst fears and the Monaco Grand Prix was an event to be forgotten as quickly as possible, though it was not the end of single-seat racing for Zuffenhausen.

On 5 July, there was a French Formula Two Grand Prix at Rheims, with two works Porsches on the grid – the first being the old centre-seat 718RSK, which had run so well the year before, driven by Wolfgang von Trips, and the second was a new 718F2 for Swedish driver Jo Bonnier. The other car with Porsche power was the single-seater Behra Porsche, to be driven by Hans Herrmann. Perhaps predictably, Stirling Moss was the race winner after what has been described as a 'battle royal', but Hans Herrmann surprised everyone by taking second place. He was followed home by Bonnier, who put up a sparkling drive.

The factory cars did little else now for the rest of the season, as time was spent on further development of the Formula Two Porsche. The official works view of the French result was one of mild disappointment, as it was felt that improved streamlining might have given Jo Bonnier a better result. So new bodylines were experimented with and extensive testing was carried out at Hockenheim. Stirling Moss was one of those who tried out the car there, and he

Model: Porsche Type 718 RS61 – 1960

Construction	Tubular spaceframe with hand fabricated aluminium alloy bodywork
ENGINE	Type 547/3 (1500), Type 547/4 (1600), Type 587/3 (2000)
Crankcase	Light alloy crankcase with individual cylinders
Cylinder head	Light alloy with inserted valve guides and seats
Cyls/Type	Four, horizontally opposed
Compression	9.8:1
Cooling system	Air, with finned cylinder barrels & belt-driven fan
Bore & Stroke	85mm × 66mm/87.5mm × 66mm/92mm × 74mm (3.3 × 2.6/3.4 × 2.6/3.6 × 2.9in)
Capacity	1,498cc/1,587.5cc/1,966cc (91.4/96.8/119.9cu in)
Main bearings	Roller bearings on Types 547, plain bearings on Type 587
Valves	Two overhead per cylinder, dual overhead cam actuation
Fuel supply	Dual electric pumps/two Weber 46IDM 1 carburettors
Power output	150bhp @ 7,800rpm/160bhp @ 7,800rpm/185bhp @ 7,200rpm
Ignition system	Dual coil and distributor with twin spark plugs
Lubrication	Dry sump, 8-litre oil tank, gear pump and oil cooling
BRAKES	
Type	11-inch drum front and rear with hydraulic actuation
TRANSMISSION	Five-speed Type 718 – rear wheel drive
Clutch type	Single dry plate
Gear ratios	Various, according to requirements of circuit
Final drive ratio	4.428:1 or 5.160:1
SUSPENSION/STEERING	
Front suspension	Independent with double oscillating arms, square-section torsion bars and Koni dual-action telescopic shock absorbers
Rear suspension	Independent swing axles, round section torsion bars and Koni dual-action telescopic shock absorbers
Steering type	ZF centre-point steering box with divided equal length arms
Wheels	4.5J × 15 front, 5J × 15 rear
Tyres	Front: 5.50 × 15R, Rear: 5.90 × 15 RS Racing
DIMENSIONS	
Wheelbase	2,200mm (85.8in)
Track (front)	1,290mm (50.3in)
Track (rear)	1,250mm (48.8in)
DRY WEIGHT	550kg (1,222lb), 590kg (1,311lb) with 587 engine
MODELS AVAILABLE	Spyder
TOP SPEED	160mph (255kph)

From the Quad-Cam 550 to the Single-Seat Porsches

Jo Bonnier aboard his 718F2 single seater before the start of the 1959 Rheims Formula Two Grand Prix.

was sufficiently impressed for RRC 'Rob' Walker, his team sponsor, to borrow one for the forthcoming 1960 season.

Larger carburettors were fitted to the Walker/Moss car, with 46mm (1.8in) throat Webers being finally selected, and a five-speed gearbox was created by closing off the first of the original six gears in the 718F2. In March 1960, Moss took the car to Syracuse and set a blistering pace, leading by 29 seconds at the halfway stage of the race, when disaster struck. He had set a new lap record shortly before the engine dropped a valve, putting him out of the race. Porsche protested to ATE, the makers of the valves who, it turned out, had supplied a batch of valves to production car standard, not racing specification.

Undeterred, Moss took the Porsche car to Belgium to race, with Jo Bonnier and Olivier Gendebien in a pair of works cars. Moss had the lead, but misfortune befell him again, as he lost a gear and spun, giving his victory to Jack Brabham's Cooper. Moss managed second, followed into third place by Gendebien. At the Aintree 200, Moss led Bonnier and Graham Hill into a Porsche 1–2–3 after the Coopers had dropped out. At Solitude, the four Porsches were second, third, fourth and fifth; in Britain third and fourth, then on home territory, at the Nürburgring, five out of the first six cars home were Porsches. One of them was Wolfgang von Trips, who now drove for Ferrari, but as they did not race in Germany, he was allowed to drive there for Porsche. A solitary third in Denmark was followed by a 1–2–3 procession in Austria, then first and second in the Cape and South African events. And that was 1960.

FORMULA TWO GROWS UP

The reason so much interest had been shown in Formula Two since 1957 was because of the decision by the FIA (Federation Internationale Automobile) to reduce the engine

Model: Porsche Type 718 F2/ 1500 Single Seater – 1958/9

Construction	Tubular spaceframe with hand fabricated aluminium alloy bodywork
ENGINE	Type 547/3 (1500)
Crankcase	Light alloy crankcase with individual cylinders
Cylinder head	Light alloy with inserted valve guides and seats
Cyls/Type	Four, horizontally opposed
Compression	9.8:1
Cooling system	Air, with finned cylinder barrels and belt-driven fan
Bore & Stroke	85mm × 66mm (3.3 × 2.6in)
Capacity	1,498cc (91.4cu in)
Main bearings	Roller main and big end bearings
Valves	Two overhead per cylinder, dual overhead cam actuation
Fuel supply	Dual electric pumps/two Weber 46IDM 1 carburettors
Power output	150bhp @ 7,800rpm
Ignition system	Dual coil and distributor with twin spark plugs
Lubrication	Dry sump, 8-litre oil tank, gear pump and oil cooling
BRAKES	
Type	11-inch drum front and rear with hydraulic actuation
TRANSMISSION	Six-speed Type 718 – rear wheel drive
Clutch type	Single dry plate
Gear ratios	Various, according to requirements of circuit
Final drive ratio	Various, according to requirements of circuit
SUSPENSION/STEERING	
Front suspension	Independent with double oscillating arms, square-section torsion bars and telescopic shock absorbers
Rear suspension	Independent swing axles, round-section torsion bars and telescopic shock absorbers
Steering type	ZF centre-point steering box with divided equal length arms
Wheels	3.25 × 15 front, 4.5 × 15 rear
Tyres	Front: 5.00 × 15R, Rear: 6.00 × 15 RS Racing
DIMENSIONS	
Wheelbase	2,200mm (85.8in)
Track (front)	1,300mm (50.7in)
Track (rear)	1,260mm (49.1in)
DRY WEIGHT	470kg (1044lb)
MODELS AVAILABLE	Formula Two single seater
TOP SPEED	155mph (250kph)

From the Quad-Cam 550 to the Single-Seat Porsches

Stirling Moss, in the Rob Walker Porsche 718F2 leads Edgar Barth's similar car during the 1960 Formula Two German Grand Prix, run on the South Circuit of Nürburgring.

size of Grand Prix Formula One cars to 1,500cc. Many manufacturers were not happy about the change, but it gave companies like Porsche the opportunity to firmly establish themselves as serious international players. Lotus was another company which might have found it very difficult to progress in Grand Prix racing without the benefit of the reduction in engine size. In fact, as it turned out, Formula One became more exciting as a result of the change.

Porsche began the new Grand Prix season using the previous year's Formula Two cars, with Dan Gurney and Jo Bonnier as the principal team drivers. Stirling Moss was now driving a Lotus 18 for Rob Walker, although Hans Herrmann was still with Porsche and drove in some Grand Prix events. Their first Championship event under the new formula was the 1961 Monaco Grand Prix. Wolfgang von Trips was driving for Ferrari, but Gurney, Bonnier and Herrmann were there, in ninth, tenth and twelfth positions on the grid.

Everybody expected Monaco to yield a Ferrari win, but they had not reckoned on the guile of Stirling Moss, who snatched the victory from Ritchie Ginther. Third place went to Phil Hill and fourth to Wolfgang von Trips. The Porsche of Dan Gurney was fifth, Hans Herrmann made ninth and Jo Bonnier was well down the field in twelfth place. Not the best of results for Porsche, but not a disgrace either. A week later, at Zandvoort, three Porsches went out to do battle again, this time driven by Gurney, Bonnier and Carel de Beaufort. The result was disappointing with Gurney tenth, Bonnier eleventh and de Beaufort fourteenth.

The French Grand Prix in June was something else. For Porsche, Dan Gurney made fourth row of the grid, with Jo Bonnier in the row behind and Carel de Beaufort well back. Gurney was determined that this race would be different for his team. Ferrari's Wolfgang von Trips lost his engine on Lap 18, Ritchie Ginther lost his oil pressure and went out of the race on Lap 41, whilst Phil

From the Quad-Cam 550 to the Single-Seat Porsches

Dan Gurney charges out of Station Hairpin at Monaco to finish fifth in the 1961 Monaco Grand Prix.

Hill, who had been in the lead, spun and stalled his engine, losing two laps in the process of restarting. This let Giancarlo Baghetti through and he didn't put a foot wrong, going on to win ahead of Dan Gurney in second. Jo Bonnier came seventh, but de Beaufort went out with an engine failure on Lap 23.

The British Grand Prix was next on the calendar and, after winning a place on the front row of the grid, Jo Bonnier was expected to do better than he actually did. At the end of the first lap he was in fifth place, where he remained to the finish, with Gurney a couple of places behind and de Beaufort down at the tail end. The German Grand Prix had a similar start, with Bonnier once more on the front row of the grid, but the older Porsches seemed unable to keep up the pace and certainly Bonnier's race was run on Lap 5. Gurney managed another seventh place, whilst Hans Herrmann and Carel de Beaufort finished thirteenth and fourteenth.

In Italy, the Porsches did not start well up on the grid, and the race itself took a tragic turn when von Trips was killed as his car went over the Parabolica after a collision with Jim Clark. Driving like a demon, Dan Gurney finished second and de Beaufort was seventh. Gurney saw another second at his home Grand Prix at Watkins Glen, but fellow countryman Phil Hill was World Champion for Ferrari. The Championship challenge was over now, but Jo Bonnier and Edgar Barth went to South Africa to see if they could improve their fortunes there. They did moderately well, but did not come home with any wins under their belts.

The 1962 season was just more of the same for Porsche. The Type 787/1 chassis had succeeded the 718 and the long-awaited purpose-designed Formula One car, the F1-804-4, was built, but failed to make it to the track. Engineer Michael May had developed the Four to a level at which it was felt it could now win (it produced more

Model: Porsche Type F1-804/4 Single Seater – 1961

Construction	Tubular spaceframe with hand fabricated aluminium alloy single seat bodywork
ENGINE	Type 547/6 (1500)
Crankcase	Light alloy crankcase with individual cylinders
Cylinder head	Light alloy with inserted valve guides and seats
Cyls/Type	Four, horizontally opposed
Compression	10.31
Cooling system	Air, with finned cylinder barrels and belt-driven fan
Bore & Stroke	85mm × 66mm (3.3 × 2.6in)
Capacity	1,498cc (91.4cu in)
Main bearings	Roller main and big end bearings
Valves	Two overhead per cylinder, dual overhead cam actuation
Fuel supply	Dual electric pumps/two Weber 40DCOE carbs or fuel injection
Power output	187bhp @ 8,000rpm
Ignition system	Dual coil and distributor with twin spark plugs
Lubrication	Dry sump, 8-litre oil tank, gear pump and oil cooling
BRAKES	
Type	Disc brakes all round
TRANSMISSION	Six-speed Type 718 – rear wheel drive
Clutch type	Single dry plate
Gear ratios	Various, according to requirements of circuit
Final drive ratio	Various, according to requirements of circuit
SUSPENSION/STEERING	
Front suspension	'A' arms with longitudinal torsion bars and telescopic shock absorbers
Rear suspension	'A' arms with longitudinal torsion bars and telescopic shock absorbers
Steering type	ZF centre-point steering box with divided equal length arms
Wheels	4.5 × 15 front, 5.0 × 15 rear
Tyres	Front: 5.00 × 15R, Rear: 6.00 × 15 RS Racing
DIMENSIONS	
Wheelbase	2,300mm (89.7in)
Track (front)	1,300mm (50.7in)
Track (rear)	1,330mm (51.9in)
DRY WEIGHT	450kg (1,000lb)
MODELS AVAILABLE	Formula One single seater
TOP SPEED	167 mph (270kph)

Not exactly where it all began, but the Cisitalia Grand Prix car certainly helped pay for the development of the 356, which is why the picture is here. Whilst Porsche was receiving design royalties from Volkswagen, the Cisitalia was an extremely useful design exercise to the company, even though it never raced.

Two very interesting examples of early Cabriolets: the front one is a 1952, with the 'bent' windscreen, whilst the one in the background is an earlier model with the split two-piece windscreen.

The America Roadster was the first attempt to produce a purely sporty low-cost Porsche for the US market. This one is in the Porsche Museum at Stuttgart.

The 356A Coupé brought the 356 from a rather quaint-looking little car to being a serious grand touring coupé. The car in the background is a 1954 Speedster.

The America was followed by the Speedster, which was an immense success. This one, though bumperless, is a very pretty example. The yellow colour sets it off very well.

The Porsche Type 597 'Jagdwagen' was an attempt to attract military sales. This one is a 1958 definitive example, from which the cross-country 'Hunter' was developed.

The Type 787 single-seater went from Formula Two to Formula One and did well in the hands of Dan Gurney, but not well enough to merit Porsche staying in single-seat motor racing.

Whilst Porsche didn't enjoy brilliant success with the Formula Two or Formula One cars, the 718RSK/60 brought great success in the area where Porsche was best known – sports car racing.

Compare the grey 356B Cabriolet on the left with the blue 356SC on the right and the only difference you'll see at a glance is the road wheels, as both are T-6 bodied.

The 356C Coupé was the final variant of the 356 and was a refined and elegant car, as these two shots show.

Heads! Front ends of the 356B T-6, the 356C T-6 and the 356SC T-6. The 356C, with its front lid open, shows how little space there was for even the smallest bag.

Tails! The principal difference from the rear of these cars is the badging. The 356B carries the '90' motif, whilst the 356C Coupé carries the 'C' and the blue Cabrio is identified as a top-of-the-range 'SC'.

The improvements over the years to the interior of the 356 are epitomized here in the 'C' Coupé with its rear fold-down jump seats. Not too comfortable for a long journey, though.

Two nice detail shots of the 356SC Cabriolet, showing the very tidy engine compartment and the steering wheel and dash.

The 914-4 was quite a pretty car, but seen by many as 'not quite a Porsche'. Even so, it gave a good account of itself on the road and track.

On the track, the 914-4 was very popular for a while. Many, like this one, acquired 911-type wheels, which were available on the 914-6. The script on the side, though, tells you clearly what this one is.

Detail design on the 914 was good, with the 'hoop' shrouding a rollover bar. Door handles were tidy, too. Yellow was a popular colour for this model.

The F1-804-4 was to be the final flat-four Formula One car from Porsche. Developed by Michael May, it won no races, but provided the platform from which Porsche did finally win a Grand Prix, albeit with an eight-cylinder engine.

power than the succeeding eight) and had installed it with a horizontally mounted fan, but was then told that the eight-cylinder engine was so far advanced as to make it unnecessary to develop the Four any further. The new car was actually ready to race, but the recently appointed works director of Porsche, Hans Tomala, cancelled the race entry for the Pau Grand Prix. May was furious. It turned out that his services were also dispensed with, so he left Stuttgart and went to work for Ferrari. Porsche's remaining Grand Prix hopes would now rest on the flat-eight F1-804-8. Dan Gurney won the French Grand Prix at Rouen in 1962, the only Porsche Grand Prix win in that car. Hardly surprisingly, Porsche finally abandoned single-seat racing to concentrate more of its attention on the manufacture of cars for sale and to pursue its interests in securing the World Sports Car Championship.

7 The Product Grows – To the 356A and Beyond

In the mid-1950s, the key to Porsche's commercial success was undoubtedly the 356, although, of course, there were other contributors to the company's coffers, not least royalties from Volkswagen designs, as the 'Beetle' continued to grow in popularity. Porsche's participation in motor sport had always been aimed at raising the profile of the company's name and the reputation of its products, which is why, in those days, Porsche never spent huge sums of money on advertising, nor on lavish stands at the many international motor shows where it exhibited. The company also tended to encourage private entrants to compete in sporting events, because while success brought credit to the vehicle's manufacturer, lack of success brought it no blame.

Making cars for sale, however, was the prime objective, even competitive cars in controlled numbers. To this end, the 356 had to be upgraded on a continuous basis in order to keep, and improve, its market share. The America Roadster had made its mark, but it was not going to make a lot of money for Porsche, so another model had to supplant it. That model, the Speedster, would arguably become the most famous open Porsche model ever produced, and was the brainchild of America's principal Porsche distributor, Max Hoffman. Strange, perhaps, that a car produced down to a price, and a very sharp price at that, should prove to be such a milestone in Porsche history.

MOVING TOWARDS A NEW LINE

15 March 1954 was a milestone date at Zuffenhausen, for that was the day on which the five-thousandth Porsche left the assembly hall. Ferry Porsche was its driver, and he was justifiably publicly acknowledged as the motivating force behind the company he and his father had founded. Interestingly, it was around this time that Heinz Nordhoff, Chairman of Volkswagen, despatched his sales director to Zuffenhausen with an offer he was sure Dr Porsche would be unable to refuse.

The post Nordhoff had in mind was that of Development Director at Volkswagen's Brunswick research centre. The principal condition was that the Porsche company be wound up and Ferry Porsche devote his whole time to Volkswagen. Hardly surprisingly, Nordhoff was rebutted. He had failed to reckon with the fierce sense of pride and independence bred into the Porsche family and heightened not least by their experiences at the hands of their inquisitors in the late 1940s.

Before Nordhoff's offer was made – and before the five-thousandth car left the works – a number of product developments had come about to ensure that the continuing growth in sales was maintained. After the changes brought about by the introduction of the 1953 models, the range had settled down for a while, but in November, for the

The Product Grows – To the 356A and Beyond

The five-thousandth Porsche, a 356 coupé, which rolled out of Zuffenhausen on 15 March 1954.

1954 season, a new variant of the 1,300 engine was announced. This was the 1300S, Type 589, engine, aimed to provide a strong contender for the 1,300cc Class of racing in Europe and to offer a sportier version of the 1,300 as a road car.

The new engine had a bore of 74.5mm (2.9in) and used the Hirth multi-piece roller-bearing crankshaft of 74mm (2.85in) throw, giving a displacement of 1,290cc. The compression ratio, at 8.2:1, matched that of the 1500S unit. With a 'warm' camshaft and Solex 32PBJ carburettors, the almost perfectly square engine proved capable of coming up with 60bhp at 5,500rpm. This made the new 1,300 engine the fastest running pushrod engine so far produced at Zuffenhausen. This specification was bound to be a success.

In the United States, Porsches were beginning to be seen as expensive cars, perhaps a little too expensive to retain their sales momentum. So Max Hoffman came to the rescue once again, with the suggestion that the factory create a lower priced Porsche for wider sales potential. By eliminating the fold-down rear seat, the adjustable passenger seatback, the sun visor, the wheel trims and the radio, the price was pulled down to $3,445. The new 'economy' model Porsche was to be called the 'America' in that continent (the 'Normal' elsewhere) and, standing at almost $800 below the price of $4,284 for the 1,500S Coupé, was thought to be a potentially bright seller. The factory obliged Mr Hoffman and immediately Porsche sales rose, even against the much lower priced competition from the British motor industry.

A cabriolet version of the 'America' was also offered, at a price premium of $250. This brought the owner a car with wind-up windows, a luxury few other sports cars offered (the Alfa Romeo Spyder was one) and a fully padded soft top, unlike the

Model: Porsche Type 356 1100/1300 (A&S)/1500 (&S) – 1954

Construction	Pressed steel fabricated and welded box-section chassis with unitary steel coupé or cabriolet bodywork
ENGINE	Types 369 (1100)/ 506 (1300)/589 (1300S)/546 (1500)/528 (1500S)
Crankcase	Light alloy crankcase with individual cylinders
Cylinder head	Light alloy with inserted valve guides and seats
Cyls/Type	Four, horizontally opposed
Compression	1100 = 7.0:1, 1300 = 6.5:1, 1500 = 7.0:1
Cooling system	Air, with finned cylinder barrels and belt-driven fan
Bore & Stroke	1100 = 73.5 × 64mm (2.9 × 2.5in), 1300A = 80 × 64mm (3.1 × 2.5in), 1300S = 74.5 × 74mm (2.9 × 2.88in), 1500 = 80 × 74mm (3.1 × 2.88in)
Capacity	1086cc/1,286cc (66.2/78.4cu in), (1300A)/1,290cc (78.7cu in), (1300S)/1,488cc (90.8cu in)
Main bearings	Four main journals (roller big ends/composite crank in 1500)
Valves	Two overhead per cylinder, pushrod actuation
Fuel supply	Mechanical pump/two Solex 32PBI or 40PBIC (1500S)
Power output	40bhp/44bhp @ 4,200 /60bhp @ 5,500/55bhp @ 4,400/70bhp @ 5,000rpm
Ignition system	Coil and distributor with auto advance/retard
Lubrication	Wet sump, gear pump and oil cooling
BRAKES	
Type	Drum front and rear with hydraulic actuation
TRANSMISSION	Four-speed gearbox mounted ahead of the engine – rear wheel drive
Clutch type	Single dry plate
Gear ratios	1 = 13.91:1, 2 = 7.70:1, 3 = 4.94:1, 4 = 3.5 7:1. R = 15.575:1
Final drive ratio	4.375:1
SUSPENSION/STEERING	
Front suspension	Transverse torsion bars/trailing parallel links/telescopic shocks
Rear suspension	Transverse torsion bars/trailing parallel links/telescopic shocks
Steering type	VW type worm and peg with unequal arms
Wheels	Pressed steel 3.25D × 16
Tyres	5.00 × 16 cross-ply sports

DIMENSIONS	**Cabriolet**	**Coupé:**	**Speedster**
Overall length	3,950mm	3,950mm	3,950mm (151.1in)
Overall width	1,660mm	1,660mm	1,660mm (64.7in)
Overall height	1,300mm	1,300mm (50.7in)	1,250mm (48.7in)
Wheelbase	2,100mm	2,100mm	2,100mm (81.9in)
Track (front)	1,290mm	1,290mm	1,290mm (50.3in)
Track (rear)	1,250mm	1,250mm	1,250mm (48.8in)

MODELS AVAILABLE	Cabriolet/Coupé/Speedster
TOP SPEED	1100/87mph (140kph), 1300A/90mph (145kph), 1300S/95mph(152kph), 1500/100mph (160kph)

The Product Grows – To the 356A and Beyond

The 1,300cc Type 589 engine, with the Hirth roller-bearing crankshaft, was the fastest running Zuffenhausen power unit to date.

unlined tops offered on many other cars. And the Porsche Cabrio was reckoned to be just as competitive as the coupé. This was particularly well demonstrated by Art Bunker and Richard Thompson when they went out and won just about everything in sight to secure the SCCA Class F Production Sports Car racing championship in 1954.

Innovations which came into production during 1954 included the introduction of small grilles inboard of the sidelights. These were intended to provide an aperture for the horns to sound through and an airflow slot for brake cooling. Windscreen washers had been around for a little while now, but Porsche was one of the earliest manufacturers to fit them as standard equipment. It was another addition worthy of note, especially from a safety point of view. Several ideas for the improvement of the suspension were tried out during 1954, in particular the front anti-roll bar, which was introduced into the 356 specification in November, just in time for the 1955 model range.

A MOST NOTABLE PORSCHE – THE SPEEDSTER

It was in 1954 that the most significant new Porsche model ever – in the United States – was announced to a waiting

The Product Grows – To the 356A and Beyond

public. This was the Speedster roadster. Its inspiration was Max Hoffman who, when supplies of the America Roadster dried up, went to Ferry Porsche and made it plain that he foresaw a downturn in Porsche sales if something was not done to beat the competition from Alfa Romeo's Spyder and Triumph's TR2, and the rumour of a new sports car from MG (that was to be the MGA). Hoffman's challenge to Zuffenhausen was to produce a car that could sell for $3,000 or less. A tall order!

In recognition of the fact that Max Hoffman knew his market well, the Porsche team went to work to produce the car he wanted at the price he wanted. Typical of Porsche, there were to be no short cuts as far as the chassis was concerned. The production cabriolet chassis was taken as the basis for this new car and the drawings for that model's body were examined in the minutest detail to take out any element of excess weight in the design before the coachbuilders, Reutter's, were consulted. Areas which were immediately available for pruning were body trims, the interior and the glassware. The windscreen was reduced in height and wind-up side windows were abandoned in favour of slot-in sidescreens.

Erwin Komenda and Reutter now took the standard cabriolet body as their starting point and went about lightening it. They simplified the structure from Porsche's suggestions, stripped out all but the basics of the interior, revised the dashboard and created a car which looked very much like an inverted bathtub. The process of redesign began with the addition of three panels into the rear deck to extend it forward. Then, the doors were shortened to adapt to the revamped rear end. Even the soft top came in for the weight-watching treatment, now being smaller than that of the cabriolet, and with the lining stripped off. One side-effect of the new design was that when the hood was raised the occupants found themselves in almost total darkness, as well as with a serious stoop, as the roof was so much lower than its more orthodox sibling's.

This spartan little car was offered for sale in North America at $2,995, meeting Max

A Porsche for under $3,000? Impossible! But it wasn't, for the Speedster, introduced in 1954, really did sell for under $3,000 – and in some numbers

The Product Grows – To the 356A and Beyond

The hard top for the Speedster did little to improve the visibility out of the car, but did improve the aerodynamics a little.

Hoffman's target – just. Being light in weight, relatively low in price and displaying Porsche handling, it was an instant hit with sports car enthusiasts on the east and west coasts, many of whom spent almost every weekend at local club racing events at such places as Watkins Glen, Monterey and Torrey Pines. Johnny von Neumann took a Speedster to a very early success by winning the SCCA's 1,500cc Production Sports Car race at Torrey Pines. It was among the first of many.

The basic price Speedster was fitted with the standard 1,500 engine, producing 55bhp. For an extra $500, you could have the 70bhp 1500S power unit. With closer ratio gears coupled to the 'S' engine, the car was capable of an amazing ten-second 0–60mph (0–96kph) time. It is worth noting that many a car made in the last decade of the twentieth century would be hard pressed to achieve that sort of acceleration. And if you wanted a 'cleaner' airflow over your car, it wasn't long before you could get a factory option fibreglass hard top to clip on in place of the hood frame and soft top – it was a bit lighter, too, but, whilst it gave slightly better all-round vision, it did little to improve the stoop suffered by the driver and passenger. But wasn't the fun of driving a Speedster worth it? A lot of people thought so.

Announced late in 1954, it is probably surprising that as many as a couple of hundred cars were built in that year, serial numbered 80001 to 80200, especially considering the fact that the Speedster was always intended to be a limited volume model. The first few cars had no extra badging, but then the scripted badge 'Speedster' was added above the alloy trim strip on the front wings. The next year,

The Product Grows – To the 356A and Beyond

1955, brought fewer cars, in two batches totalling 134 units, the 34 in the first batch and the other 100 following. In 1956, 1,156 left the factory, and just a few more a year later. Production then fell to 552 and in the final year of the Speedster, 1959, there were only thirty-two cars built. But more of that later, for we have yet to see the development of the rest of the range.

CONTINUING TOWARDS THE 'A' SERIES

The most important change to come at the end of 1954 was an unheralded series of modifications to the whole range of Porsche engines. In particular, a new crankcase came into production, now a three-piece aluminium alloy assembly instead of the previous two-piece unit and larger than the original VW casing. Capacity for an extra litre of oil was one instant benefit, another being that the front main bearing, along with the distributor drive and fuel pump drive, as well as the oil pump, were carried in the front casting. Larger bearing webs inside the crankcase made for a wholly stronger assembly and the exterior shape was modified for improved cooling, whilst larger cylinder openings were provided which would allow for larger bore cylinders to be fitted at some time in the future.

Still with a four-speed gearbox, the new line-up of Porsches for 1955 had engines of 1,300cc and 1,500cc available, though the old 1,100 was dropped. All the engines carried the designation '/2' after the engine type, to show that they were of the new design. In 1955, Porsches offered for sale in the United States were labelled 'Continental', but that upset the Ford Motor Company whose Lincoln model of the same name claimed priority, at least in that continent (there was a similar touching of nerves before World War II in Britain, when Riley contemplated calling its Touring Saloon the

The 1955 'Continental' cabriolet was relabelled 'European', as rumblings came from the Lincoln Division of Ford over the use of the name.

The Product Grows – To the 356A and Beyond

For the 1956 model year, Porsche introduced the 356A, seen here in cabriolet form, which was quickly identifiable by the deeper luggage compartment handle adorned with the Porsche shield.

'Continental' but was warned off by Rolls-Royce, who had used the model name since before World War I). Not surprisingly, Porsche decided not to put the issue to the legal test and withdrew the name, relabelling the range 'European', though they soon abandoned any general policy of naming, reserving the principle of naming for specific models.

At the 1955 Frankfurt Motor Show, the first distinct step from the original Type 356 was taken in model designation. There were sufficient changes to the specification to justify the car now being called the 356A. Starting with the changes that were to be seen immediately, the trim strip that appeared on the Speedster was now seen on the bodywork of the 'A'. The lid to the front luggage compartment now had a deeper handle which bore the Porsche crest, featuring, like a certain other make of car, a prancing horse in its centre.

Perhaps the most significant visual change heralded by the 356A was the windscreen. Gone was the legacy of the original split windscreen, the bent screen of the post-1952 models; the windscreen of the new model was a gentle horizontal curve and inside the car. In addition, the dashboard now had a padded top panel, with a large centrally positioned rev counter, the speedometer being on the left of it and the supplementary instruments, oil temperature and fuel gauge, on the right in a single circular dial. Self-cancelling flashing direction indicators were a new feature, along with a headlamp flasher, provision for a radio in the centre of the dash, and a passenger grab handle and lockable glove box on the right of the dash panel (on left-hand drive models).

Other new features of the 356A were to do with driving the car, rather than the way it looked. The ride was softened a little, with larger shock absorbers fitted and a more substantial front anti-roll bar. The road wheels were now wider than before, in fact their 4.5 inch (114mm) width caused concern among some of the tyre manufacturers, because they thought it too wide for the 5.60×15 tyres selected for the car. Porsche's reckoning was that the wider rims helped to put more of the tread on to the surface, which may be why the tyre makers were worried, as this would put more stress on the tyre walls. A steering damper was

The Product Grows – To the 356A and Beyond

Model: Porsche Type 356A 1300cc /1600cc – 1955

Construction	Pressed steel fabricated and welded box-section chassis with unitary steel coupé or cabriolet bodywork
ENGINE	Type 506/2 (1300)/589-2 (1300S)/616/1 (1600)/616/2 (1600S)
Crankcase	Light alloy crankcase with individual cylinders
Cylinder head	Light alloy with inserted valve guides and seats
Cyls/Type	Four, horizontally opposed
Compression	T506/2 = 6.5:1, T589/2 = 8.2:1, T616/1 = 7.0:1, T616/2 = 8.5:1
Cooling system	Air, with finned cylinder barrels & belt-driven fan
Bore & Stroke	1,300 = 74.5mm × 74mm, 1,600 = 82.5mm × 74mm
Capacity	1,300 = 1290cc, 1,600 = 1582cc
Main bearings	Four main journals/roller bearing big ends on composite crank
Valves	Two overhead per cylinder, pushrod actuation
Fuel supply	Mechanical pump/two Solex 32PBJ or 40PBIC/Zenith 32NDIX carbs
Power output	1300 = 60bhp/5,500 , 1300S = 44bhp/4,200, 1600 = 70bhp/5,000, 1600S = 75bhp/5,000
Ignition system	Coil and distributor with auto advance/retard
Lubrication	Wet sump, gear pump and oil cooling (magnetic filter)
BRAKES	
Type	Drum front and rear with hydraulic actuation
TRANSMISSION	Porsche Type 644 (716 from 1958) four-speed synchro plus reverse
Clutch type	Single dry plate
Gear ratios	3.182:1/1.765:1/1:1/0.815:1, R3.56:1 or 3rd/4th @ 1.227:1/0.885:1
Final drive ratio	4.428:1 – 4.857:1 optional
SUSPENSION/STEERING	
Front suspension	Transverse torsion bars/trailing parallel links/telescopic shocks
Rear suspension	Transverse torsion bars/trailing parallel links/telescopic shocks
Steering type	ZF Worm & stud, with divided unequal length arms
Wheels	Pressed steel 3.25D × 16
Tyres	5.00 × 16 cross-ply

DIMENSIONS	**Cabriolet:**	**Coupé:**	**Convertible:**	**Speedster:**
Overall length	3,950mm	3,950mm	3,950mm	3,950mm (151.1in)
Overall width	1,670mm	1,670mm	1,670mm	1,670mm (65.1in)
Overall height	1,310mm	1,310mm (51.1in)	1,270mm (49.5in)	1,220mm (47.6in)
Wheelbase	2,100mm	2,100mm	2,100mm	2,100mm (81.9in)
Track (front)	1,306mm	1,306mm	1,306mm	1,306mm (50.1in)
Track (rear)	1,272mm	1,272mm	1,272mm	1,272mm (49.6in)

MODELS AVAILABLE	Cabriolet/coupé/convertible/Speedster
TOP SPEED	90mph (145kph)/100mph (160kph)

The Product Grows – To the 356A and Beyond

The 356A coupé was the epitome of the comfortable sports car.

added to the revised and strengthened geometry of the steering gear.

Now that the new engine designs were proven, with the bigger three-piece crankcase, it was time to take advantage of those larger cylinder barrel holes by offering a bigger displacement power unit. The new version was 1,582cc, commonly to be known as the 1600, Type 616/1 for the Normal and 616/2 for the Super. The lower powered version had a compression ratio of 7.5:1 and gave 60bhp at 4,500rpm, whilst the 1600S produced 75bhp from a compression ratio of 8.5:1 and an engine speed of 5,000rpm. The smaller 1300S and the 1600S retained the roller bearing crankshaft, whilst the new cast alloy inlet manifolds carried Solex 40PIBC carburettors. The gearbox had new mountings and the clutch release bearing was modified to make for smoother gear changes.

The 356A was an instant hit. Like its cousin of growing distance, the Volkswagen 'Beetle', this new version of the 356 retained the basic line, but now it had features which were common among motor cars of its age, like the curved windscreen and lighting equipment. It had better performance and now had a heater which worked. With the improved suspension, the handling was slightly better, but, more importantly, for those who wanted a comfortable small sporting car, this was it, relatively speaking. For in those days, comfort and sporting cars were not synonymous. Sports cars were generally noted for good roadholding, a harsh ride and poor weather protection. The Porsche 356A certainly had the roadholding, but it had a pretty smooth ride, a roof and quite a few creature comforts.

1 December 1955 was another significant day for Ferry Porsche and his company, for this was the twenty-fifth anniversary of the formal establishment of the Porsche Design Bureau. Also in 1955, Porsche finally recovered possession of the original Zuffenhausen buildings and land. The United States Army had, at long last, decided it could function quite adequately without the Porsche site. Immediately possession was restored, most of the administrative staff of the company moved into the old buildings. These included

107

The Product Grows – To the 356A and Beyond

The US market version of the 356 incorporated over-riders on the bumpers to cope with 'nudges' from a wide range of domestic vehicles.

in particular the finance, sales, purchasing and technical affairs departments.

In the meantime, small changes continued to be made to the 356 through 1956 into 1957. For example, cars exported to the United States acquired bumper overriders to cope with the much higher bumper heights of cars manufactured in the US. By 1957, the cam gear on the 'Normal' engines was manufactured of aluminium, carburettors were warmed from the heat exchangers and then the gearbox was replaced with the new Type 644, which used a single casting as the main casing. This was stronger than the older three-piece unit and had the advantage of infinitely variable gear combinations, as well as being easier to repair than the Type 519.

The most momentous change to occur in 1957, first revealed at the Frankfurt Motor

Rear end changes; the T-0 and T-2 tail light arrangements.

The Product Grows – To the 356A and Beyond

Show, was the arrival of a new body for the 356. This was the T-2 body, on which the dual round tail lights and direction indicators were replaced with a teardrop-shaped single lens rear light positioned horizontally. Then the rear registration plate light, the bezel of which also had the reverse light built in, was mounted below the plate, instead of above it. Other aspects of the T-2 were: relocated interior light and repositioned ashtray; improved seat backrests and reshaped seat cushions. The 1,300 engine was also dropped, along with the Hirth multi-piece roller-bearing crankshaft. A new diaphragm pressure plate replaced the spring plate in the clutch and Zenith carburettors with replaceable venturi were now used on the engines. Finally, the 'Normal' engine acquired iron cylinder barrels, partly to reduce production cost, and partly to cut down noise from the engine. Whilst there would clearly be a weight penalty from using iron cylinder barrels, it wouldn't make much difference to performance.

OTHER AVENUES OF PROFIT FOR PORSCHE

Whilst development and production of the Porsche 356 continued apace, there were other revenue-earning activities at Zuffenhausen. The company continued to earn royalties from Volkswagen for Porsche designs, but, more significantly, one older product was still being manufactured, whilst a new one was about to be embarked upon. The old product was the agricultural tractor designed by Porsche back in the 1940s, whilst the new one was the creation of a 4×4 military light car, much along the lines of the wartime Volkswagen 'Kübelwagen'.

The Porsche-Schlepper Type 111 agricultural tractor was designed under Ferdinand Porsche's supervision. It had been in production by a company called Allgaier since 1947 and they had built some 25,000 units in that time. However, Ferry Porsche and Albert Prinzing, the man who had done so much to spearhead the growth of Porsche in the early days at Stuttgart, both felt that there was now a strong case to expand the tractor business to maximize its potential. With the support of the Mannesmann group, a new factory was built at Friedrichshafen and Prinzing left Zuffenhausen to take up the post of general manager of the new plant, which went by the name of Porsche Diesel Motorenbau GMBH. This facility was to continue manufacturing agricultural tractors into the 1960s, with much royalty money going to Zuffenhausen to bolster its coffers.

Engines were also part of the Allgaier product line. Static generator engines made up a significant part of the original firm's

This is the most widely known Porsche agricultural tractor, the Type 111, which found its way to British shores via Grays of Fetterangus.

The Product Grows – To the 356A and Beyond

Gyrodyne produced this military helicopter as an experiment for the US Marine Corps.

sales. When the Friedrichshafen plant was built, the sale of engines for pump, generator and static power uses increased apace, as did, of course, sales of complete tractors. But the growing demands on the Porsche car business made it more difficult to keep pace with developments in the agricultural tractor industry, at a time when it was undergoing a period of major change. There were many large companies whose main business was tractors and they were going through drastic restructuring, spending sums far greater than Porsche Diesel Motorenbau GMBH could even dream of affording. It was therefore predictable that the Porsche tractor interest would fade.

Engines had an interest for Ferry Porsche in other areas, too. The air-cooled flat-four engine had been selected by the Gyrodyne Corporation for its lightweight observation helicopter, built for evaluation by the US Marine Corps. The Porsche aviation engines were designated Type 678, with various sub-numbers for the different versions and power ratings. By 1959, in the US market there were three variants of the 678 engine, priced at between $968 and $1,379. On the other hand, there was the Type 729 marine engine, which was produced in higher numbers than the aero units. Fifty-six Type 729 engines were built in 1954, rising to 1,250 in 1959, with over sixty per cent exported.

THE MILITARY 4×4 PROJECT

Even as Porsche was moving towards a reorganization of its involvement in the tractor business, the design office was looking outwards for design and manufacturing work that could underpin the business of car production. 'Underpinning' car production basically meant adding a product that could be produced in volume against a single sales order, thereby also strengthening the buying power and supply lines from outside contractors. The result of that quest was a decision to fund, as a private venture, the design and build of a military vehicle for the newly reorganizing armed forces of the Federal Republic of Germany.

The Product Grows – To the 356A and Beyond

The Type 678 engine was a successful venture into the world of aviation for Porsche.

Ferry Porsche cast his mind back to the days when his father had created the 'Kübelwagen' for the military, and had applied what he had learnt through this process to the vehicle he was then involved with, which went on to volume production as a totally reliable and durable vehicle – the Volkswagen. Times were different now, but the concept of using a military design to develop and 'prove' a car was not so different. The car in question was the Porsche 356, and the military vehicle was to be the Porsche Design Type 597 'Jagdwagen'. Design work began in 1953 and the first

The Type 597 'Jagdwagen' appeared in military prototype form in 1955.

111

Model: Porsche Type 597 Jagdwagen – 1957/8

Construction	Fabricated steel platform chassis with unitary steel military utility bodywork
ENGINE	Porsche Type 546 or Type 616/1
Crankcase	Light alloy crankcase with individual cylinders
Cylinder head	Light alloy with inserted valve guides and seats
Cyls/Type	Four, horizontally opposed
Compression	6.5:1
Cooling system	Air, with finned cylinder barrels and belt-driven fan
Bore & Stroke	1500 = 80 × 74mm (3.1 × 2.9in), 1600 = 82.5mm × 74mm (3.2 × 2.9in)
Capacity	1,488cc (90.8cu in) and 1,582cc (96.5cu in)
Main bearings	Four main journals
Valves	Two overhead per cylinder, pushrod actuation
Fuel supply	Mechanical pump/1 Solex 32PBI
Power output	50bhp @ 4,500rpm/55bhp @ 4,500rpm
Ignition system	Coil and distributor with auto advance/retard
Lubrication	Wet sump, gear pump, magentic filter and oil cooling
BRAKES	
Type	Drum front and rear with hydraulic actuation
TRANSMISSION	Four-speed gearbox/two or four-wheel drive, double reduction rear hubs
Clutch type	Single dry plate
Gear ratios	1 = 15.678:1, 2 = 11.05:1, 3 = 6.955:1, 4 = 5.2:1. R = 29.25:1
Final drive ratio	6.5:1 with low range gears at 1.8:1 reduction on above ratios
SUSPENSION/STEERING	
Front suspension	Transverse torsion bars/trailing parallel links/telescopic shocks
Rear suspension	Transverse torsion bars/trailing parallel links/telescopic shocks
Steering type	VW type worm and peg with unequal arms
Wheels	Pressed steel 5.00F × 16
Tyres	6.00 × 16 cross-ply
DIMENSIONS	
Overall length	3,600mm (140.4in)
Overall width	1,560mm (60.8in)
Overall height	1,580mm (61.6in) with top raised
Wheelbase	2,100mm (81.9in)
Track (front)	1,290mm (50.3in)
Track (rear)	1,250mm (48.8in)
MODELS AVAILABLE	Utility four-seater
TOP SPEED	62mph (99kph)

The Product Grows – To the 356A and Beyond

By 1958, the Type 597 had acquired corrugated panels, in the idiom of the wartime 'Kübelwagen', as a means of increasing structural strength. In this form, it was also offered as the civilian 'Hunter'.

example rolled out of the factory just two years later.

The Jagdwagen was essentially a shorter, chunkier development of an accumulation of ideas from the wartime VW Kübelwagen Types 86 and 87. It was a 4×4, but borrowed much of its transmission from the Grand Prix Cisitalia of 1947–48. Larger section tyres on wider rims, thanks in large part to the developments in tyre technology over a dozen years or so, meant that the Porsche had better traction than its predecessor. It also had a substantially better gearbox and more powerful engine.

The unitary construction of the new Porsche was stronger and lighter than the old Kübelwagen. The now well proven torsion bar suspension of the sporting Porsche was employed on this military vehicle. After all, if it could withstand the rigours of the Carrera Panamericana, there was not much the new *Wehrmacht* could throw at it that would cause it to break. Two body designs were tried, one with corrugated 'ribs' formed into the panelwork to strengthen it and resist the usual military knocks to which such a vehicle would inevitably be prone. The other variation used plain panels, to provide an alternative testbed. Both versions used a flat two-piece windscreen, with wipers to both halves and this could be folded forward to a flat position as required.

On the utility side, the vehicle was constructed with a trio of recesses in the front end. The outermost, just inboard of the quite substantial front bumper, carried the spare wheel, which was held in place by a simple three-point strap. Behind this was a slot for a NATO-type jerrican, which was felt to be safer positioned and easier to locate than when hung off a bracket on the back, as on the old US Army Jeep. Next to the jerrican was the fuel tank. No attempt was made to cover it; it was mounted on rubber-lined straps and was designed to be easily removable so that, in case of a leak or damage, it could be quickly replaced in the field.

Whilst the Jagdwagen was never going to handle like a Porsche Speedster, it had a solid feel to it and one thing that could be reasonably guaranteed was its reliability. It had a limited optional four-wheel drive, selected from the driver's seat, which whilst not capable of propelling the vehicle through water, would allow it to float without any

This was the Convertible 'D', the body built by Drauze (hence the 'D') as a successor to the Speedster.

ill effect. However, a political decision gave the production of the *Wehrmacht's* new generation 'Jeep' to a competitor. Ferry Porsche was so angry that he declared he would never again sanction the development of a military vehicle without a positive order on somebody's desk. He did no more than have the Jagdwagen modified as necessary to turn it into a civilian cross-country 4×4, to be named the 'Hunter'. Sadly for Porsche, the concept of the recreational 4×4 was about thirty years too soon, and so only seventy-one examples were sold before the model was discontinued in 1958.

THE FINAL PHASE OF THE 356A

By the end of 1957 3,283 coupés, 542 cabriolets and 1,416 Speedsters had been built in an excellent year for production and car sales, quite apart from earnings on other activities. But the 1958 model year brought change, particularly to the Speedster. For some time, Ferry Porsche had been unhappy that the spartan nature of the original Speedster was not in keeping with the range of other Porsche models, and so the Convertible Model D was introduced to replace the earlier model. The 'D' stood for Drauz, the coachbuilder who supplied the bodies for the new model, which had a higher windscreen, better interior trim and more convenient top. The result was a somewhat heavier car which cost $3,695, an extra $700.

Technical Programme 3 would have been expected to replace T-2 in normal circumstances, but because it took a different direction to Technical Programme 2, it was abandoned, so there was no T-3. The new models in the T-4 range were to feature shorter gearshift throws, the return to a hinged front quarter light, an anti-glare tilting interior mirror and an improved heater control slide. These T-4 features found their way into the 356A, ultimately gestating into the next generation of Porsche as the 356B, but now as the T-5.

8　The Mighty Carrera 356

Whilst the 356 was the mainstay of Porsche's product line, and thus its principal source of income, the Porsche organization was already a multifaceted jewel. There were design commissions from other companies; there was continuing design work for Volkswagen AG; there were aero engines and marine engines; there was the private venture military general purpose 4×4 Jagdwagen/Hunter; and there were racing cars.

The continuing link with Volkswagen was not surprising, as Ferdinand Porsche had been primarily responsible for the creation of the VW Beetle. The connection of product commonality was fading year on year, as the Porsche model line-up became more and more individual by design, and whilst all this development was taking place at the production end, the Zuffenhausen design team was working to bring race technology closer to production technology, in line with the Porsche philosophy that racing improved the breed.

The Carrera Panamericana was not only Porsche's most gruelling test in its early days of competition, it was looked upon by those at Zuffenhausen as the true proving ground of the 356, especially regarding the US market, since the event was 'in their backyard'. So, when Porsche decided to produce a road car powered by the quad-cam Type 547 engine, the original version was to be named the 356A 1500GS Carrera in recognition of the make's success there and to denote a car that was fast and resilient.

START OF A NEW LINE – THE 1500 CARRERA

It has to be said that the idea of putting the most powerful engine available into a road-registerable sports car was not new to Porsche. Before World War II, Ferdinand Porsche had dreamt up the idea of designing a road car around the mighty Auto-Union V-16 Grand Prix power unit. The result of that design idea was the Porsche Design Type 52. It was quite a large sports car, though only a two-seater. The tamed engine was intended to provide a car to compete with anything that Bugatti, with the streamlined 'Tank' Type 57, or Alfa Romeo, with the magnificent 8C2900, could throw at the German challenge. Of course, it all came to nothing, and the Type 52 never left the drawing board, as more pressing matters were to occupy Europe over the next few years.

The idea of the Type 52 was not lost, however, for Ferry Porsche decided to re-examine the concept in the 1950s. The difference was that *his* design did leave the drawing board to become a truly exciting sports car, the Carrera 1500GS. After a couple of years of running the Type 547 quad-cam engine in the 550RS, it found its way into the rear end of a 356, albeit by a

The Mighty Carrera 356

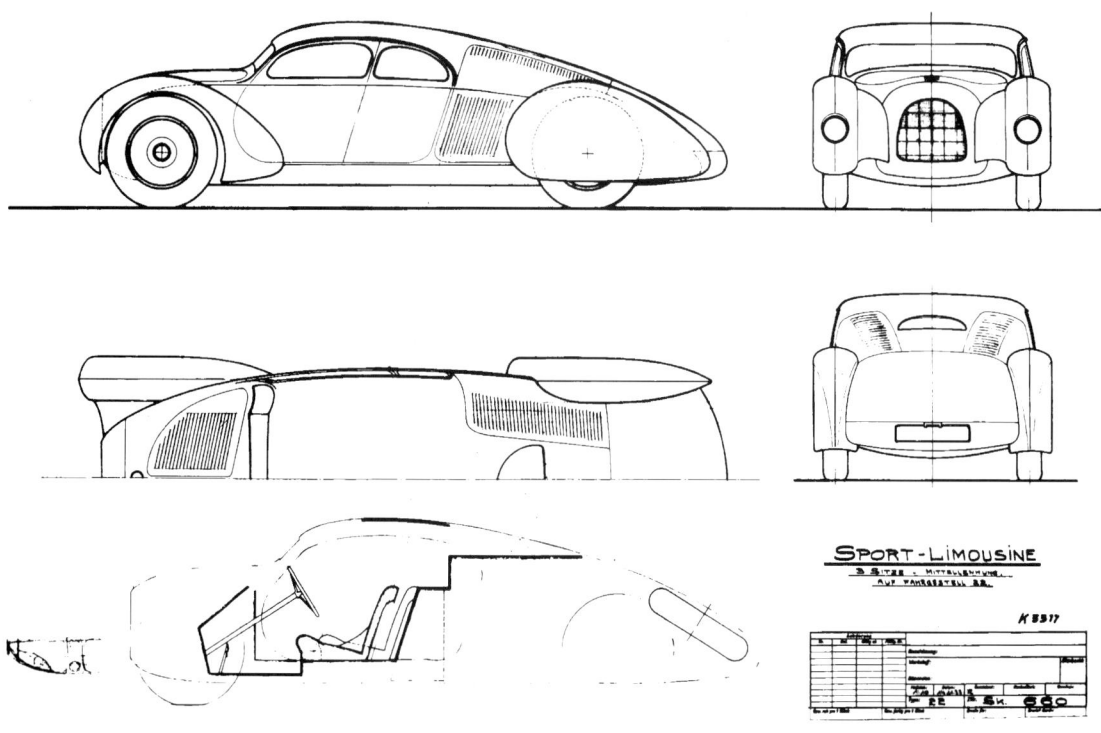

Forerunner of the Carrera? This was the Porsche Design Type 52, a roadgoing adaptation of the V-16 Auto-Union Grand Prix car. It has been suggested that this was where the thinking began for the implant of a raceworthy engine into an ultra-high performance enclosed sports car.

very tight squeeze – so tight in fact that it has often been said that the easiest way to adjust valve clearances and tune the engine was to remove it from the car!

Porsche had produced the Speedster in 1953 as a startling new, but low-cost, sporting car for the Americas, but the Carrera was to stand at the other extreme: it would be a very expensive vehicle, though its performance would be beyond question. The Frankfurt Motor Show was the debut for the Carrera, where it enjoyed a rapturous reception. The German *Auto Motor und Sport* magazine described the engine, the 547/1, in almost reverent tones. The article told us that the crankcase, cylinders and cylinder heads were all made of light aluminium alloys, with running surfaces that were hard chrome plated.

The writer of the review, H U Wieselmann, was neither a newcomer to Porsche nor a novice in the world of sporting cars, but even he seemed in awe of a piston speed of 7.7 metres per second (just about dead on 25 feet per second) at 100kph (62.5mph) in fourth gear. We are told that the valves

The Mighty Carrera 356

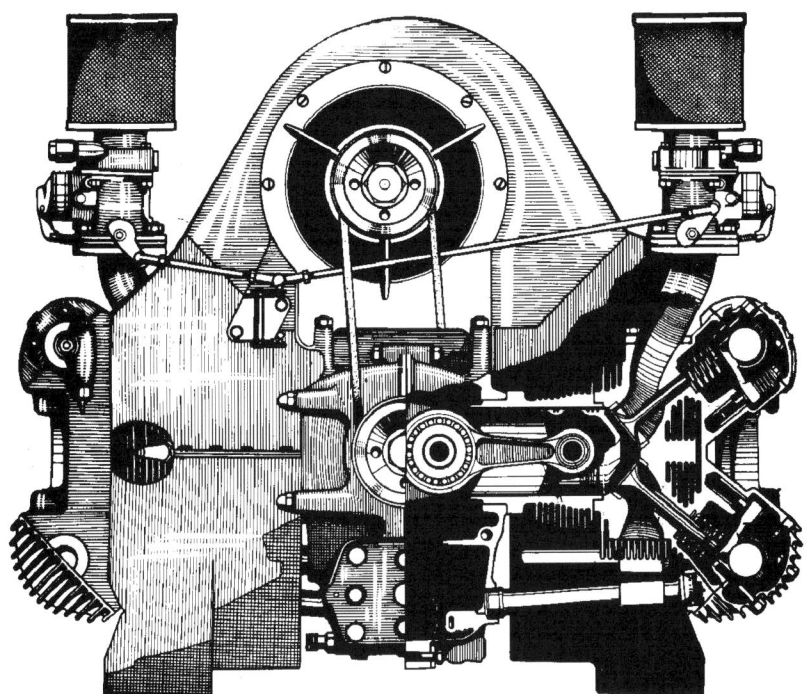

The engine of the Carrera was the Type 547/1, which looked little different from the power unit of the 550RS cars, except that it had quite large air filters to the carburettors.

were set at a 78-degree angle to each other in the combustion chamber and that sparks were provided by dual ignition, with two plugs per cylinder. Wieselmann explains the camshaft drives, which were much more akin to aircraft principles than those of cars, had a shaft driven by the crankshaft at the front of each cylinder bank operating the camshafts via skew gears. There were then, and are still, mixed views as to the wisdom of using shafts and skew gears in preference to roller chains or gear drives for camshaft rotation. Setting all the clearances on a skew gear driven shaft is more difficult, but the result was clearly thought by Porsche to be worth it, in the belief that it produced less power loss.

With much tighter tolerances than the original 547 engine of the 550 Spyder, and a compression ratio of only 9.0:1, the Carrera was expected to have a lower level of engine noise than the racing car. But its performance was expected to be startling – and startling it certainly was! With an extra twenty-five or so horsepower over the most powerful pushrod Porsche engine available at that time, this car, despite its higher price, was set to make an impact on the North American market that would certainly dent the Alfa Romeo Giulietta's market, if not that of the competitive British sports cars on offer. Despite its price, though, the Porsche would certainly persuade a number of British car owners seeking to trade upmarket to take another look at it.

On the road, Wieselmann extracted almost 200kph (124mph) out of the Carrera test car at his disposal, the first road test car released by the factory. Running on shorter third and fourth gear ratios than the pushrod models, as well as on larger

Model: Porsche Type 356A Carrera 1500GS – 1955

Construction	Pressed steel fabricated and welded box-section chassis with unitary steel coupé or cabriolet bodywork
ENGINE	Type 547/1 P90-500
Crankcase	Light alloy crankcase with individual cylinders
Cylinder head	Light alloy with inserted valve guides and seats
Cyls/Type	Four, horizontally opposed
Compression	9:1
Cooling system	Air, with finned cylinder barrels and belt-driven fan
Bore & Stroke	85mm × 66mm (3.3 × 2.6in)
Capacity	1,498cc (91.4cu in)
Main bearings	Roller main and big end bearings
Valves	Two overhead per cylinder, dual overhead cam actuation
Fuel supply	Dual electric pumps/two Solex 40PJJ carburettors
Power output	100bhp @ 6,500rpm
Ignition system	Dual coil and distributor with twin spark plugs
Lubrication	Wet sump, gear pump, magnetic filter and oil cooling
BRAKES	
Type	Drum front and rear (2LS front) with hydraulic actuation
TRANSMISSION	Type 716/5 – Four-speed synchromesh plus reverse
Clutch type	Single dry plate
Gear ratios	Std = 3.09:1/1.765:1/1.23:1/0.885:1 – Reverse = 3.55:1
Final drive ratio	4.428:1 or 5.16:1
SUSPENSION/STEERING	
Front suspension	Independent with double oscillating arms, square-section torsion bars and telescopic shock absorbers
Rear suspension	Independent swing axles, round-section torsion bars and telescopic shock absorbers
Steering type	ZF worm/stud steering box with divided unequal length arms
Wheels	Pressed steel 4J × 15
Tyres	5.90 × 15 Sport tread
DIMENSIONS	
Wheelbase	2,100mm (81.9in)
Track (front)	1,306mm (50.9in)
Track (rear)	1,272mm (49.6in)
DRY WEIGHT	930kg (1,860lb)
MODELS AVAILABLE	Coupé/cabriolet
TOP SPEED	124mph (200kph)

The Mighty Carrera 356

The 356A Carrera's identity was not immediately obvious until you spotted the 'Carrera' script badge just ahead of the doors.

diameter tyres (5.90 × 15s), the Carrera ran up to sixty in just under eleven seconds and, as the bias-belted crossply tyres 'grew' as the road speed increased, so the car seemed to reach its maximum more quickly. Yet despite all this on-tap performance, the car was observed as being docile in traffic ('as willing as a VW' was the expression used) and very easy to start, thanks in no small part to its twin electric fuel pumps. This was a very relevant point, as quite often sports cars with engines at a high state of tune had the reputation of being very difficult, if not positively awkward, to start.

Another reviewer who praised just about every aspect of the Carrera was Hans Tanner, a man more generally reckoned to be a Ferrari enthusiast (he wrote the first definitive history of Ferrari); his view, therefore, would be considered by many to be all the more valuable. Tanner also thought the Carrera to be remarkably docile, yet capable of true race-winning performance, as many Carrera owners were to prove. Hans Tanner's test car was a Carrera Speedster, out of which he teased the catalogued 200kph without too much trouble, whereas the car driven by Wieselmann had been a coupé.

As you approached a 356 Carrera, there were few obvious differences between it and the other Porsche models. The sharp-eyed would note the 'Carrera' script on the side of the car and might spot the larger tyres, though that was less likely. Walk round to the back of the car and the twin exhaust pipes were an immediate giveaway. The other giveaway came as the curious climbed inside the car and noticed the speedometer went up to 160mph, whilst the rev counter showed 8,000rpm. Clearly, this was no ordinary Porsche, if any Porsche could ever be described as ordinary!

THE CARRERA LINE-UP

The 356 Carrera 1500 was offered in coupé form, as well as cabriolet and Speedster. Because the American market was split

The Mighty Carrera 356

Looking at the tail end of this 1958 Carrera (the view most other motorists had of this car), the horizontal louvres in the engine cover are the immediate giveaway of the car's identity. Inset: inside the '58 Carrera GT, everything is functional – note the strap for lowering the window instead of the more customary winder (a quick acting weight-saving device).

over what it wanted from the Carrera, Porsche decided that two variants had to be offered to satisfy all needs. There was a large body of enthusiasts who did not care about the car coming without a heater as standard. They were the ones who wanted to take the car out to their local race circuits and turn in the fastest laps. On the other hand, there was the body of enthusiasts who had no concern for competition, but wanted an all-weather sports touring car that was reliable, fast and fun to drive.

So what did Porsche do? In 1957, they simply went to work to create two models out of one. For the sporting enthusiast, there was the GT, with light bumpers, wider 60mm (2.3in) front brakes and a 20-gallon (90-litre) fuel tank. The GT also had leather straps to lower the plexiglass windows, instead of winding mechanism and glass, whilst the seats were the same bucket type that had been originally fitted to the Speedster. Then they used light alloy instead of steel for the lids, doors and road wheels, although the wheels had steel centres for extra strength.

On the other hand, the Carrera De Luxe, as the non-racers' model was called, had the full interior kit. This included the full seats fitted to other Porsche models, wind-up windows and a petrol–electric heater – yes, a heater, fitted as standard (although not operable without the ignition switched on, so effectively a heater for use only when on the move). All this added up to a weight difference between the two models of around 45kg (100lb).

A number of people in the competition fraternity on the west coast of America were not too happy about having to wait

The Mighty Carrera 356

To oblige the Speedster fraternity, Porsche produced a Carrera version of that model, too.

so long for what they saw as a usable car. But Porsche were anxious, as ever, to 'get it right', so when they did offer the GT, it came in Speedster form as well as coupé. Of course, the Speedster was the one the racers wanted, as it was the lightest of all, weighing in at just 810kg (1,786lb). Surprisingly, perhaps, the Speedster was also available in De Luxe form (though it seems unlikely that many people wanted that version, as 'Speedster' and 'De Luxe' just didn't seem to go together!).

In another world, of course, the De Luxe fraternity wanted to be able to pose with something a little more comfortable than a spartan Speedster GT. Not for them the less-than-luxurious bucket seats, or pull-up windows that could get scratched. And no heater for those cool autumn evenings was just intolerable! So, the factory obliged that group with a choice of Speedster (for the motorist who liked other people to think he was a super-sport), or the cabriolet for the driver who wanted to be able to put the top down in the best of summer days or even a hard top for the owner who wanted something a little more distinctive. So there it was: Porsche had provided a wide range of Carreras to choose from, and the customers duly made their choices, bringing problems to the factory in their wake.

The roller-bearing Type 547 engine was a fine power unit and generally ran well when being watched over by expert mechanics and when running at fairly high engine speeds. The 547 definitely did not like being laboured, demonstrating itself to be very unhappy when run at low speed or idled for a long time, as in heavy traffic situations. In particular, the bearings did not like slow running, as this did not lubricate them properly, and so quite a few broken roller bearings found their way into the warranty claim statistics for no reason other than that they were being used in ways the designers had not intended.

Out on the track, the engine ran with few problems and the experience of the 550 had already shown that, as long as it was topped up with oil and properly adjusted, it would run for long distances without stopping. Everyday road conditions were another thing: the 547 would overheat. and oil plugs in traffic, if not properly tuned on a regular

Model: Porsche Type 356A Carrera 1500GS De Luxe – 1956/7

Construction	Pressed steel fabricated and welded box-section chassis with unitary steel coupé or cabriolet bodywork
ENGINE	Type 547/1 (P90-500)
Crankcase	Light alloy crankcase with individual cylinders
Cylinder head	Light alloy with inserted valve guides and seats
Cyls/Type	Four, horizontally opposed
Compression	9:1
Cooling system	Air, with finned cylinder barrels and belt-driven fan
Bore & Stroke	85mm × 66mm (3.3 × 2.6in)
Capacity	1,498cc (91.4cu in)
Main bearings	Roller main and big end bearings
Valves	Two overhead per cylinder, dual overhead cam actuation
Fuel supply	Dual electric pumps/two Solex 40PJJ-4 carburettors
Power output	100bhp @ 6,500rpm
Ignition system	Dual coil and distributor with twin spark plugs
Lubrication	Dry sump, 8-litre oil tank, gear pump and oil cooling
BRAKES	
Type	Drum front and rear (2LS front) with hydraulic actuation
TRANSMISSION	Type 714/1 – four-speed synchromesh plus reverse
Clutch type	Single dry plate
Gear ratios	Std = 3.09:1/1.765:1/1.23:1/0.885:1 – Reverse = 3.55:1
Final drive ratio	4.428:1 standard
SUSPENSION/STEERING	
Front suspension	Independent with double oscillating arms, square-section torsion bars and telescopic shock absorbers
Rear suspension	Independent swing axles, round-section torsion bars and telescopic shock absorbers
Steering type	ZF worm/stud steering box with divided unequal length arms
Wheels	Pressed steel 4J × 15
Tyres	5.90 × 15 Sport tread
DIMENSIONS	
Wheelbase	2,100mm (81.9in)
Track (front)	1,306mm (50.9in)
Track (rear)	1,272mm (49.6in)
DRY WEIGHT	Coupé/cabriolet: 930kg (1,860lb), Speedster: 885kg (1,770lb)
MODELS AVAILABLE	Coupé/cabriolet/Speedster
TOP SPEED	124mph (200kph)/Speedster 130mph (210kph)

basis, would simply fail. This was not Porsche's fault, though of course it got the blame. It was not necessarily even the owners' fault that the quad-cam engine was less satisfactory than a pushrod for certain uses. A finely tuned machine needed extra care over a more commonplace device, and certain drivers probably would have been better off spending their money on a pushrod-engined Porsche.

Proving the point of what a Carrera could do, Rolf Goetze took his specially prepared 1,529cc Carrera Speedster to Monza Autodrome in March 1957, intent on taking a record or two. His target was the 24 Hour Two-Litre Class Record. He failed to make the 24 hours, but he did set a new 1,000-Mile and 2,000-Kilometre record and turned in a fastest lap of 128mph (205kph) on the way. Then, Claude Storez won the Marathon de la Route outright in a Porsche, ahead of some pretty heavy metal.

With the FIA's uprating of the old International Class F 1,500cc limit to 1,600cc, Porsche was faced with the need to modify the quad-cam engine. Klaus Rucker took advantage of this situation to eliminate the roller bearings and introduce the Type 692/1 engine, with plain main and big end bearings. This made for a less temperamental power unit in the eyes of many, and certainly made for a more potent car in the hands of the 'fast boys'. The engine rapidly developed into the 692/2 and by mid-1958, heat tubes had been introduced to warm the carburettors, whilst a ZF limited slip differential was offered as an optional extra.

Now, this limited slip diff contained a set of elliptically shaped bearings which rode between two plates that had radiating ridges on them. It worked, but those bearings were as vulnerable to neglect as the roller-bearing engine. By now, also, the lower-ratio final drive of 4.86:1 was dropped in favour of the 4.428 gears, with the very low 5.17:1 still offered for those who wanted faster acceleration. The hill climbers and sprinters were the people who would want rubber-rending acceleration at the expense of top speed, so a 95mph (152kph) top speed was no embarrassment to them.

One of the most momentous achievements of the 1600 Carrera was its Class win in the 1957 Mille Miglia. In fact, Porsches took the first three places in the 1,600cc Class of that race, with Alfa Romeo cleaning up in the 1,300cc Class. Umberto Maglioli, in a 550A, had taken first place in the 1,500cc

Rolfe Goetze in action on his record run at Monza in his modified 1,529cc Carrera Speedster.

Model: Porsche Type 356A Carrera 1500GS GT – 1957

Construction	Pressed steel fabricated and welded box-section chassis with unitary steel coupé or cabriolet bodywork – alloy doors and hoods
ENGINE	Type 547/1
Crankcase	Light alloy crankcase with individual cylinders
Cylinder head	Light alloy with inserted valve guides and seats
Cyls/Type	Four, horizontally opposed
Compression	9:1
Cooling system	Air, with finned cylinder barrels and belt-driven fan
Bore & Stroke	85mm × 66mm (3.3 × 2.6in)
Capacity	1,498cc (91.4cu in)
Main bearings	Roller main and big end bearings
Valves	Two overhead per cylinder, dual overhead cam actuation
Fuel supply	Dual electric pumps/two Solex 40PJJ-4 carburettors
Power output	110bhp @ 6,400rpm
Ignition system	Dual coil and distributor with twin spark plugs
Lubrication	Wet sump with gear pump, magnetic filter and oil cooling
BRAKES	
Type	Drum front and rear (2LS front) with hydraulic actuation
TRANSMISSION	Type 714/1 – four-speed synchromesh plus reverse
Clutch type	Single dry plate
Gear ratios	Std = 3.09:1/1.765:1/1.23:1/0.885:1 – Reverse = 3.55:1
Final drive ratio	4.428:1 standard, 4.875:1 optional
SUSPENSION/STEERING	
Front suspension	Independent with double oscillating arms, square-section torsion bars and telescopic shock absorbers
Rear suspension	Independent swing axles, round-section torsion bars and telescopic shock absorbers
Steering type	ZF worm/stud steering box with divided unequal length arms
Wheels	Pressed steel 4J × 15
Tyres	5.90 × 15 Sport tread
DIMENSIONS	
Wheelbase	2,100mm (81.9in)
Track (front)	1,306mm (50.9in)
Track (rear)	1,272mm (49.6in)
DRY WEIGHT	Coupé/cabriolet: 930kg (1,860lb), Speedster: 885kg (1,770lb)
MODELS AVAILABLE	Coupé/cabriolet/hard top/Speedster
TOP SPEED	124mph (200kph)/Speedster 130mph (210kph)

Model: Porsche Type 356A Carrera 1600GS De Luxe – 1958

Construction	Pressed steel fabricated and welded box-section chassis with unitary steel coupé or cabriolet bodywork
ENGINE	Type 692/2 (P93-001/P93-139)
Crankcase	Light alloy crankcase with individual cylinders
Cylinder head	Light alloy with inserted valve guides and seats
Cyls/Type	Four, horizontally opposed
Compression	9.5:1
Cooling system	Air, with finned cylinder barrels and belt-driven fan
Bore & Stroke	87.5mm × 66mm (3.4 × 2.6in)
Capacity	1,587.5cc (96.8cu in)
Main bearings	Plain bearings throughout
Valves	Two overhead per cylinder, dual overhead cam actuation
Fuel supply	Dual electric pumps/two Solex 40PJJ-4 carburettors
Power output	105bhp @ 6,500rpm
Ignition system	Dual coil and distributor with twin spark plugs
Lubrication	Dry sump, 8-litre oil tank, gear pump and twin front oil coolers
BRAKES	
Type	Drum front and rear (2LS front) with hydraulic actuation
TRANSMISSION	Type 714/1 – four-speed synchromesh plus reverse
Clutch type	Single dry plate
Gear ratios	Std = 3.09:1/1.765:1/1.23:1/0.885:1 – Reverse = 3.55:1
Final drive ratio	4.428:1 standard, 4.857 optional
SUSPENSION/STEERING	
Front suspension	Independent with double oscillating arms, square-section torsion bars and telescopic shock absorbers
Rear suspension	Independent swing axles, round-section torsion bars and telescopic shock absorbers
Steering type	ZF worm/stud steering box with divided unequal length arms
Wheels	Pressed steel 4J × 15
Tyres	5.90 × 15 Sport tread
DIMENSIONS	
Wheelbase	2,100mm (81.9in)
Track (front)	1,306mm (50.9in)
Track (rear)	1,272mm (49.6in)
DRY WEIGHT	Coupé/cabriolet: 940kg (1,880lb)
MODELS AVAILABLE	Coupé/cabriolet
TOP SPEED	124mph (200kph)

The Mighty Carrera 356

The Strahle/Linge Carrera 1600 finished fourteenth overall in the last Mille Miglia.

Sports/Racing Class and managed a staggering fifth overall, displacing many larger cars on the way and following three Ferraris and a Maserati, with less than forty-five minutes between him and the overall winner, Piero Taruffi.

That race was the twenty-fourth and final Mille Miglia. Despite its tragic end, for Porsche it was a great success. Not only did Maglioli romp away with the 1,500 Sports Class, but a Carrera 1600, driven by Strahle and Linge, led a whole procession of Porsches in the 1,600cc GT Class to a 1–2–3 in the official listings, while the Strahle/Linge car finished fourteenth overall, a pretty remarkable achievement, especially considering there was a whole train of Porsches bringing up the rear.

TO THE SECOND GENERATION

When the catalogue for the 1960 model year was released from Zuffenhausen, there were no Carreras included in it. It looked as though this was the end of the road for the Carrera line. Many enthusiasts concluded that they would have to settle for the 1600 Super 90 as their competitive mount which, whilst capable of being tuned to turn in a pretty crisp performance, was no true match for the Carrera. However, Porsche had decided that a Carrera had to be part of the 356 'B' Series programme, but it was just a little late in bringing it to the market.

Accepting that less than one hundred De Luxe Carreras had found customers, when the factory released the new 693/3 engined model, it was decided that it would be available only in GT form. The /3 series engine had a higher compression ratio, 9.8:1, and now came home with 115bhp at 6,500rpm. The extra horsepower did not have much effect on the car's top speed, but it did improve intermediate performance. So, by the time this T-5 bodied version was made available, if you wanted a Carrera, then you bought a Carrera GT. But your Carrera GT did not come in Speedster form, for the

The Mighty Carrera 356

Following other models in the T-5 series 356 range was the 356B Carrera, now only a GT model, the De Luxe variant having been dropped.

The 356 2000GS Carrera 2 was powered by the new Type 587 2-litre engine.

Model: Porsche Type 356B 1600GS Carrera GT – 1960

Construction	Pressed steel fabricated and welded box-section chassis with unitary steel coupé bodywork
ENGINE	Type 692/3 (P95-001/P95-112)
Crankcase	Light alloy crankcase with individual cylinders
Cylinder head	Light alloy with inserted valve guides and seats
Cyls/Type	Four, horizontally opposed
Compression	9.8:1
Cooling system	Air, with finned cylinder barrels & belt-driven fan
Bore & Stroke	87.5mm × 66mm (3.4 × 2.6in)
Capacity	1,587.5cc (96.8cu in)
Main bearings	Plain bearings throughout
Valves	Two overhead per cylinder, dual overhead cam actuation
Fuel supply	Dual electric pumps/two Solex 40PJJ-4 carburettors
Power output	115bhp @ 6,500rpm
Ignition system	Dual coil and distributor with twin spark plugs
Lubrication	Wet sump, gear pump and magnetic filter
BRAKES	
Type	Drum front and rear (2LS front) with hydraulic actuation
TRANSMISSION	Type 714/1-3-4 four-speed synchromesh plus reverse
Clutch type	Single dry plate
Gear ratios	Std = 3.09:1/1.765:1/1.23:1/0.885:1 – Reverse = 3.55:1
Final drive ratio	4.428:1 standard, 5.16 optional
SUSPENSION/STEERING	
Front suspension	Independent with double oscillating arms, square-section torsion bars and telescopic shock absorbers
Rear suspension	Independent swing axles, round-section torsion bars and telescopic shock absorbers
Steering type	ZF worm/stud steering box with divided unequal length arms
Wheels	Pressed steel 4.5J × 15
Tyres	5.90 × 15 Sport tread or 165 × 15 radial
DIMENSIONS	
Wheelbase	2,100mm (81.9in)
Track (front)	1,306mm (50.9in)
Track (rear)	1,272mm (49.6in)
DRY WEIGHT	Coupé: 845kg (1,877lb)
MODELS AVAILABLE	Coupé
TOP SPEED	124mph (200kph)

Model: Porsche Type 356B/C 2000GS Carrera 2 – 1961

Construction	Pressed steel fabricated and welded box-section chassis with unitary steel coupé bodywork
ENGINE	Type 587/1 (P97-001)
Crankcase	Light alloy crankcase with individual cylinders
Cylinder head	Light alloy with inserted valve guides and seats
Cyls/Type	Four, horizontally opposed
Compression	9.5:1
Cooling system	Air, with finned cylinder barrels and belt-driven fan
Bore & Stroke	92mm × 74mm (3.6 × 2.9in)
Capacity	1,966cc (119.9cu in)
Main bearings	Roller bearings throughout
Valves	Two overhead per cylinder, dual overhead cam actuation
Fuel supply	Dual electric pumps/two Solex 40PJJ-4 carburettors
Power output	130bhp @ 6,200rpm
Ignition system	Dual coil and distributor with twin spark plugs
Lubrication	Wet sump, gear pump and magnetic filter
BRAKES	
Type	Porsche-Teves disc brakes Type 695 with ring disc
TRANSMISSION	B = Type 714/2A (Europe) 714/8A (US), C = 741/9A 4-synchro + rev
Clutch type	Single dry plate
Gear ratios	Std = 3.09:1/1.765:1/1.227:1/0.885:1 – Reverse = 5.6:1
Final drive ratio	4.428:1 standard
SUSPENSION/STEERING	
Front suspension	Independent with double oscillating arms, square-section torsion bars and telescopic shock absorbers
Rear suspension	Independent swing axles, round-section torsion bars and telescopic shock absorbers
Steering type	ZF worm/stud steering box with divided unequal length arms
Wheels	Pressed steel 4.5J × 15
Tyres	165 × 15 radial
DIMENSIONS	
Wheelbase	2,100mm (81.9in)
Track (front)	1,306mm (50.9in)
Track (rear)	1,272mm (49.6in)
DRY WEIGHT	Coupé: 1,010kg (2,244lb)
MODELS AVAILABLE	Coupé
TOP SPEED	124mph (200kph)

Model: Porsche Type 356C 2000GS Carrera 2 GT – 1963

Construction	Pressed steel fabricated and welded box-section chassis with unitary steel coupé or cabriolet bodywork
ENGINE	Type 587/2 (P98-001)
Crankcase	Light alloy crankcase with Ferral sliding surfaces to cylinders
Cylinder head	Light alloy with inserted valve guides and seats
Cyls/Type	Four, horizontally opposed
Compression	9.5:1
Cooling system	Air, with finned cylinder barrels and belt-driven fan
Bore & Stroke	92mm × 74mm (3.6 × 2.9in)
Capacity	1,966cc (119.9cu in)
Main bearings	Plain bearings throughout
Valves	Two overhead per cylinder, dual overhead cam actuation
Fuel supply	Bendix electric pump/two Weber 46 IDM-2 carburettors
Power output	130bhp @ 6,200rpm
Ignition system	Dual coil and distributor with twin spark plugs
Lubrication	Wet sump, gear pump and magnetic filter
BRAKES	
Type	Porsche-Teves disc brakes Type 695 with ring disc
TRANSMISSION	Type 741/9A 4-speed synchromesh plus reverse
Clutch type	Single dry plate
Gear ratios	Std = 3.09:1/1.765:1/1.227:1/0.885:1 – Reverse = 5.6:1
Final drive ratio	4.428:1 standard
SUSPENSION/STEERING	
Front suspension	Independent with double oscillating arms, square-section torsion bars and telescopic shock absorbers
Rear suspension	Independent swing axles, round-section torsion bars and telescopic shock absorbers
Steering type	ZF worm/stud steering box with divided unequal length arms
Wheels	Pressed steel 4.5J × 15
Tyres	165 × 15 radial
DIMENSIONS	
Wheelbase	2,100mm (81.9in)
Track (front)	1,306mm (50.9in)
Track (rear)	1,272mm (49.6in)
DRY WEIGHT	Coupé: 1,020kg (2,266lb)
MODELS AVAILABLE	Coupé
TOP SPEED	124mph (200kph)

The Mighty Carrera 356

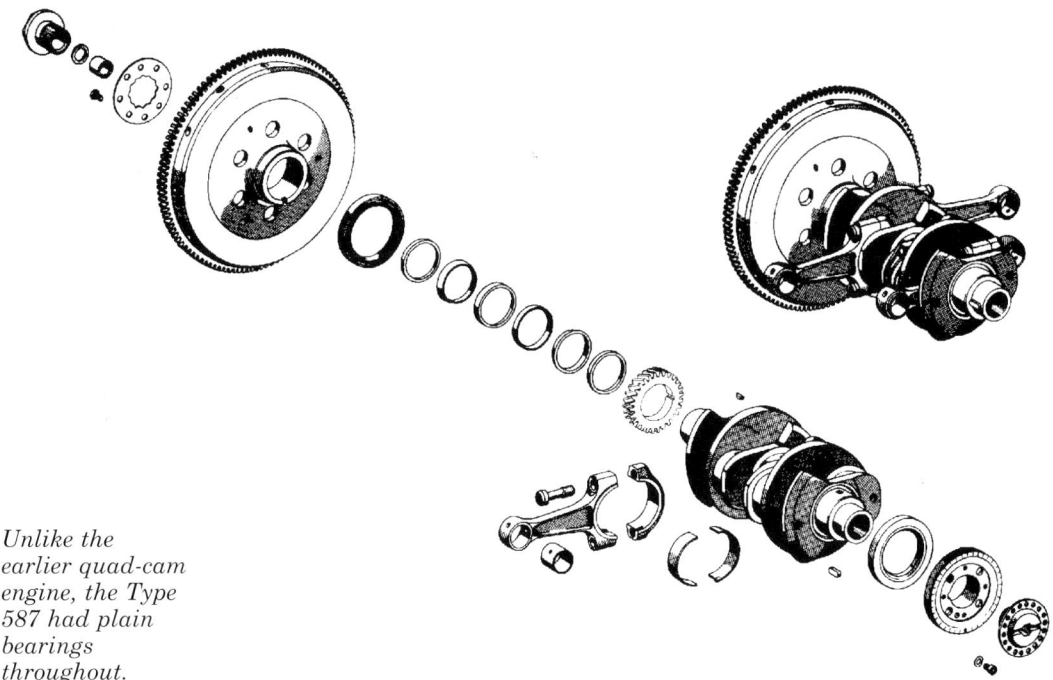

Unlike the earlier quad-cam engine, the Type 587 had plain bearings throughout.

Speedster's days had come to an end. In fact, of the thirty-two Speedster GTs produced in 1959, the last seven were fitted with 1600 Super 90 pushrod engines. Four of those pushrod GT Speedsters went to the Block dealership in Oakland, California, and were fitted with amazingly low final drives of 6.3:1 for hill climbing. This gave them stunning acceleration, but a frightening potential for blowing up engines!

The development of the pushrod models in the 'B' and 'C' Series of the 356 is covered elsewhere, but the 356 roadgoing Carrera story continues here. After the 692/3-engined 1600 Carrera GT had made its mark on the world of road and sporting cars, the next in line was to be the 2-litre version. The 356 2000GS Carrera 2 was to be the most powerful 'street' Carrera produced so far, with something approaching fifty per cent greater power output than any of the pushrod-engined models. But in the process of creating this new model, the 692 engine had reached its zenith, so was replaced by a new 1,966cc unit, the Type 587, an engine already tried and tested in the 718RSK racer.

The 587 engine was an Ernst Fuhrmann design which saw its debut in the 718RSK chassis, where it was 'de-bugged' prior to being let loose on the streets. However, this new engine was 50mm (2in) wider than the 692 as a result of the longer stroke, so it was going to be a bit of a problem squeezing it into a T-5 Series 356. Flatter, rectangular camboxes made a small difference, but not enough to make the new engine any more accessible than its predecessors when fitted into a 356, although somehow Porsche managed to make it slightly easier to reach the spark plugs in this new power unit. Other features of the 587 in the Carrera included large rectangular air filters, one per bank, and the now standard quad-cam feature of twin ignition, the distributors being positioned in a vee just

The Mighty Carrera 356

Last of the four-cylinder Carreras was the 356C variant.

inside the engine cover. The 587 engine, unlike the original 547 type, had plain bearings throughout.

Public sales of the Carrera 2 were higher than those for any previous Carrera variant, with some 437 examples finding homes about the world. The model spanned both T-5 and T-6 body units, therefore being offered as both 356B 2000GS Carrera 2 and 356C 2000GS Carrera 2. The original 356B versions were fitted with drum brakes, but by April 1962 Porsche's own design of annular disc brakes was being fitted. These were reckoned to be a highly successful brake installation, although Porsche warned its customers to warm up the brakes before putting them to hard use. As the final version of the 356, the 'C' Series, with the T-6 body, came into production, so the annular discs were dropped, most probably for reasons of manufacturing cost, and were replaced with Dunlop-ATE disc brakes, these being reckoned the best disc brake available at that time.

The Carrera 2 had the distinction of being the first 'street' Porsche to be able to turn in a sub-10 second 0 to 60mph (96kph) acceleration, at a time when you would expect to buy a much larger and more potent machine to achieve that. Such acceleration was to be expected of an Aston Martin, a Ferrari or a Maserati, but not of a car with an engine of less than half their power output (and probably half their size), so this was a milestone in Porsche history. Also, this final version of the Carrera was offered only in De Luxe form, it being felt that there was enough power available now to drag along a few luxuries, like the new Eberspacher interior heater and well-padded seats, wind-up windows and perhaps even a radio. In all respects, this was a worthy 'last of the line' and predecessor to an even more worthy successor – the magnificent 911.

THE CARRERA OUT THERE

There was a whole string of successes in Porsche 356s over the years, starting with that tremendous run in the 1957 Mille Miglia. Within the same year, the Strahle/Denk Carrera took a Class win in the 1,600cc Class at the Nürburgring 1,000 Kilometres Race, then Storez, Bonnier and Barth won their class, whilst Richard von Frankenberg took the 1,600cc Class at the 12 Heures du Rheims in France. Huschke von Hanstein won the Special GT Class in the Swiss Hill Climb Grand Prix and then, of course, there was the Storez/Buchet outright win of the Liège–Rome–Liège Rally in a Carrera.

Storez and Buchet raised the curtain on international successes for the Porsche Carrera in 1958, with a Class win in the Rallye Lyon–Charbonnieres. Then Porsche's international success list embraced the United States of America, with a 1,600cc Class win from von Hanstein and Linge in a Carrera at the Sebring 12 Hours Race in Florida. This was a tough event that all European car makers needed to win if they were to sell their sports car products in that country, but it fell to few to win outright. Porsche's performance, however, was seen as pretty good, all in all, especially as they were not throwing huge sums of money into competition.

In 1958, hill climbs seemed to take more of the laurels after Sebring, although Strahle and Walter brought home a 1,600cc Class win from the Nürburgring 1,000 Kilometres and shortly afterwards from the Targa Florio, a race fast becoming known as the toughest sports car race in Europe. Next came the Mont Ventoux Hill Climb and the Trento-Bondone Hill Climb Class victories from von Hanstein, followed by more of the same at the Schauinsland Hill Climb, the The Swiss Hillclimb Championship and the Gaisbergrennen in Austria. In the Coppa Intereuropa at Monza, von Hanstein rounded off that season in Europe with a 2-litre Class win, trying out a 2-litre version of the quad-cam long before it was to be offered to the public for sale.

Opening up the 1959 Season in the United States, von Hanstein went back to Sebring to partner Carel de Beaufort for another run at the 12 Hours Race. Once again, they won the 1,600cc Class after a gruelling drive. But in North America, of course, it was not just about visitors coming in and winning events under factory patronage. Americans wanted to win in their own backyard, and to facilitate this Porsche put in a team of their own specialists to roam the United States and support local effort by making sure that things were being done properly.

Much, of course, was down to the local dealerships, because without setting up a very expensive operation, which was neither Porsche's policy nor was it affordable, there was no way that local competitors could ever achieve their aspirations, even at club racing level. Porsche's contribution to this was to position two support personnel, Hermann Briem in the west and Herbert Tramm in New York, to give help to racers and dealers alike. While the tremendous efforts made by Max Hoffman had a profound effect from the beginning, others, like Johnny von Neumann and Vasek Polak in California, also gave dealer support.

Vasek Polak's situation was really quite interesting. He had been an outstanding motorcycle racer in his native Czechoslovakia, had managed to escape from the communist regime and found his way to New York. Being an engine tuner of some skill, he persuaded Max Hoffman to give him a job as a mechanic. It did not take him long to earn enough to buy a Speedster, which he then began to race, developing a reputation as an 'ace' tuner in the process. California's sunshine was soon too much to resist, so he climbed into his Speedster one day and drove off to the west coast, where he became well known for his prowess in extracting the most from a quad-cam Porsche engine. By December 1959, Polak had earned enough, in cash and respect, to be able to set himself up as the first-ever all-Porsche dealer in the United States, locating himself at Manhattan Beach in California.

People like Vasek Polak, Max Hoffman and Johnny von Neumann were a very large part of the success of Porsche in North

The Mighty Carrera 356

The 1964 Monte Carlo Rally saw a Class win for Porsche with another Carrera.

America, but it has to be said that none of them were above calling for the help and advice of Hermann Briem and Herbert Tramm when they faced problems or felt they could use the confirmation of another opinion when trying out something new. Briem and Tramm also, of course, came into contact with anybody and everybody who raced a Porsche, from club racers who were running on a shoestring budget, to professionals who were funded by corporate entrants, and even to film stars, like the great Steve McQueen, who drove a black Speedster indecently quickly.

Success upon success followed the Carrera wherever it went to race or rally. There was great satisfaction in America when a local pair, Sheppard and Dungan, won their Class at the Sebring 12 Hours of 1960, whilst von Hanstein and Bohnen won the 2-litre Class of the Buenos Aires 1,000 Kilometres, and the Boutin/Motte Carrera secured an outright win of the Rallye Lyon–Charbonnieres in France. There were also Class wins that year at Le Mans, at the Nürburgring 1,000 Kilometres and a two-in-a-row Class win for von Hanstein, with different partners, at the 1,000 Kilometres de Paris, one in 1960, the other a year later.

Class wins also came to Porsches in the 1961 French Grand Prix Sports Car Race at Rouen, the 1962 Monte Carlo and Tulip Rallies, the 1963 Tulip Rally, the 500 Kilometre Race at Spa Francorchamps, the Nürburgring 1,000 Kilometres and several other major events in the 1963 sporting calendar. A Class win in the 1964 Monte Carlo Rally was followed by several more rally successes in that and the following year. Even after the 356 was officially discontinued, it was still winning front-line events, taking a 1,600cc Class win in the 1966 Targa Florio and the Nürburgring 1,000. The Carrera was an outstanding car of its time and did much to consolidate the name and reputation of Porsche on the road, in rallies and on the track.

9 Towards a New Age – The Carrera GTL, the 356B, 2000 GS-GT and the 904GTS

We continue with a racing flavour into this Chapter, as the Carrera develops into something much more specialized, via the Carrera GTL, which first took form in metal in 1960. It was to become quite a landmark in Porsche history, as the whole design was entrusted to Carlo Abarth without any form of engineering drawings prior to its creation, other than stylist's sketches. It was also a combination of several different companies' input and went on to establish another niche in Porsche sporting history.

The 365B 2000 GS-GT was a logical progression from the Carrera GTL and the 718RSK. Created in 1963, this car became known as the 'Dreikantschaber', or 'Triangular Scraper', a nickname earned by its unusual shape. This car was to go on to earn more laurels for Porsche, but the true *pièce de résistance* of Carrera Fours had to be the Type 904GTS Carrera, which brought an entirely new shape and much new technology to Porsche and to motor racing, in the process of paving the way for Porsche's greatest competition successes.

INTRODUCING THE TYPE 356B CARRERA GTL

In chronological terms, the Carrera GTL should have appeared in the previous Chapter, but in development terms, its rightful place is here, as part of the development programme that ultimately gave us the 904.

The GTL story begins with a meeting in Frankfurt, between Ferry Porsche, Walter Schmidt and Klaus von Rucker – all from Porsche – and a naturalized Italian now named Carlo Abarth. The family name 'Abarth' was Austrian, whilst 'Carlo' was clearly an Italianization of the Germanic name 'Carl'. Like Rudolf Hruska, Abarth was born in Austria and decided after World War II that he would be more comfortable living in Italy. He knew the country and liked the place, so settled in Turin. He had already established a reputation as a high performance engine tuner, as a performance parts manufacturer and occasional car builder. He had built the diminutive Fiat Abarth Grand Touring coupés which did so well, for one example, in the 1957 Mille Miglia.

It was because of Abarth's contact with Italian coachbuilders and because of his involvement in the Cisitalia project back in 1947, that he was invited to talk to the Porsche Group in this Frankfurt meeting. The directors of Porsche had come to realize that the Carrera was a heavy beast by now, even in GT form, and so they were looking for a way of reducing weight to provide a

Rudolf Hruska

You might ask why this name appears in a Porsche book, when Hruska's greatest claim to fame, indeed his epitaph, was Alfa Romeo's renowned Alfasud. Well, there is justification, because firstly Hruska worked with Porsche Design and secondly because he was instrumental in bringing together Piero Dusio and Ferry Porsche when Dusio was looking for someone to design him a Grand Prix car and when Porsche was looking for a means of raising the cash to pay for his father's and brother-in-law's release from jail via a million-franc bail bond for each. The result was highly productive, in that Dusio got his car (though it never reached a start line) and Porsche won back his relatives.

Rudolf Hruska was also an Austrian, born in Vienna in 1915. He graduated from the Vienna Engineering Institute in 1935 and went to work for Magirus in Ulm. They were famous for their enormously reliable air-cooled diesel engines and fire appliances. An old friend from his student days was Karl Rabe, which is how he came to join Porsche Design in 1938. He was soon involved in the Volkswagen design project and also in the creation of the factory where it was to be built at Wolfsburg. He remained there as a production engineer until 1942.

Then, as the war intensified, Hruska found himself assigned to the *Tiger* battle tank project and later to other military tracked vehicles, which brought him full circle when a half-tracked version of the VW 'Kübelwagen' was dreamed up. A lucky break came next, as he was placed in charge of organizing production supplies for Porsche's Type 111 Volkstraktor, a small agricultural tractor which was intended to be cheap and improve German agricultural efficiency. Hruska's quest for components took him to Italy, where he stayed until 1945 under the patronage of OM.

As the war ended, Rudolf Hruska went to Gmünd, where he completed his work on the tractor project. Then he returned to Italy, where he worked on the Cisitalia project after meeting Piero Dusio. Hruska knew Carlo Abarth, who was a friend of Dusio and of Tazio Nuvolari (who, of course, knew Ferdinand Porsche from the Auto-Union days). Hruska persuaded Dusio to go to Porsche Design for his new Grand Prix car and then took part in the development programme. After that, he went to work with Finmeccanica in Italy as consultant engineer for the Alfa Romeo 1900 Series production.

When the Carrera GTL was in the planning stage with Carlo Abarth, Hruska became involved with Porsche again. This time he acted as an intermediary between Porsche and the designer, Franco Scaglione, as well as with Bertone and Zagato, the latter firm being chosen as the manufacturer of the body shells for Abarth to install on to the chassis from Zuffenhausen. Rudolf Hruska stayed with Alfa Romeo and went on to create the Alfasud, Alfa Romeo's flat-four engined car, as well as the factory at Pomigliano d'Arco, where it was built.

This view of the 356B Carrera GTL shows a very clean and attractive line, though it gives no hint of the problems of water-tightness and other difficulties encountered in bringing the cars to build.

lighter potential racer, primarily for private entrants who didn't want to see Alfa Romeo, or Lotus, or perhaps even MG, take away all they'd built up by winning the races they felt they should be winning.

It was originally agreed that Abarth would create two-seat coupé bodies for Porsche on the 356B platform. It was observed that the bodies should be "as light as possible", but aiming to comply with the FIA's homologation regulations for GT cars. There were to be twenty cars built, with a first body going for approval by Porsche before the other nineteen were to be completed. Abarth quoted a price of one million Lire per body, which was to include the amortization of the wooden bucks, so that if more bodies were ordered after the initial twenty, these would cost the lower figure of 800,000 Lire each. It was then arranged that Porsche would send a single chassis to Turin on 1 October, preceded by a chassis drawing.

Now it seems that those at Porsche were not entirely confident that Abarth could produce all these bodies in his own workshops, so Franz Xaver Reimspriess was despatched from Zuffenhausen to Italy to meet with Carlo Abarth to follow up the arrival of the initial chassis, but also to meet with others in Italy to explore possible alternatives if all didn't go well with Abarth. He met Piero Dusio Jr, son of the founder of Cisitalia, he went to Bertone and then met up with Rudolf Hruska, who was a close friend of Nuccio Bertone, where he discussed the development of the GTL (Gran Turismo Leicht).

Hruska would have liked the production contract to go to Bertone, but another friendly acquaintance of his came on to the scene in the course of discussions. This was Franco Scaglione, who had been very much involved, with Hruska, in the development of the line of Alfa Romeo's Giulietta Sprint Coupé. Ultimately, it was to be Scaglione who would draw out the shape of the Porsche's new GT car. All this was brought together by Reimspriess, who must have been an incredibly skilled diplomat to pull it all off, and he finished up with Carlo Abarth managing the Italian end of the project with quite a free hand, with Scaglione doing the styling design and with Zagato, not Bertone, constructing the bodies.

Model: Porsche Type 356B GTL Carrera Abarth – 1960

Construction	Pressed steel fabricated and welded box-section chassis. Aluminium alloy bodywork designed by Scaglione and constructed by Zagato
ENGINE	Type 692/3A (P96-001)
Crankcase	Light alloy crankcase with individual cylinders
Cylinder head	Light alloy with inserted valve guides and seats
Cyls/Type	Four, horizontally opposed
Compression	9.8:1
Cooling system	Air, with finned cylinder barrels and belt-driven fan
Bore & stroke	87.5mm × 66mm (3.44 × 2.6in)
Capacity	1,587cc (96.84cu in)
Main bearings	Plain bearings throughout
Valves	Two overhead per cylinder, dual overhead cam actuation
Fuel supply	Dual electric pumps/2 Solex 40PJJ-4 or Weber 40 DCM-2 carburetters
Power output	115bhp @ 6,500 rpm
Ignition system	Dual coil and distributor with twin spark plugs
Lubrication	Dry sump, 8 litre oil tank, gear pump and magnetic filter
BRAKES	
Type	Drum front and rear (2LS front); later discs all round
TRANSMISSION	Type 714/5-6-7-8 4-speed synchromesh plus reverse
Clutch type	Single dry plate
Gear ratios	Std = 3.09:1 / 1.765:1 / 1.23:1 / 0.885:1 Reverse = 3.55:1
Final drive ratio	4.428:1 standard, 5.16 optional
SUSPENSION/STEERING	
Front suspension	Independent with double oscillating arms, square-section torsion bars and telescopic shock absorbers
Rear suspension	Independent swing axles, round-section torsion bars and telescopic shock absorbers
Steering type	ZF worm/stud steering box with divided unequal length arms
Wheels	Pressed steel 4.5J × 15
Tyres	5.90 × 15 Sport/Racing
DIMENSIONS	
Wheelbase	2,100mm (81.9in)
Track (front)	1,306mm (50.9in)
Track (rear)	1,272mm (49.6in)
DRY WEIGHT	Coupé: 780kg (1,733lb)
MODELS AVAILABLE	Coupé
TOP SPEED	136mph (220kph)

Towards a New Age

Originally, the rear panel had only twelve louvres, the six each side at the bottom, plus the hinged air scoop just below the rear window for cooling, but the rest soon appeared after early track testing.

Abarth would complete the final assembly of the GTL bodies and mount them on to the Porsche chassis, carrying out road testing prior to delivery back to Zuffenhausen. The first car built emerged in early 1960 and carried few of the louvres for which the Carrera GTL became so well known later. A single, adjustable, air scoop sat just below the rear window and a set of six louvres was positioned each side of the rear licence plate position. It was a very clean and attractive vehicle and weighed in at around fifty kilograms below the weight of the 356 Carrera 1600 GT, which in turn had taken fifty kilos off the De Luxe weight.

It was now time for Franz Xaver Reimspriess to go back to Abarth and examine the first car, as well as to establish a delivery programme for the remaining nineteen cars. It was not the most enjoyable of visits, for a number of things were found to need change before full production could proceed, though most of the changes made were to do with things 'under the skin' so the manufacture of panelwork could continue relatively unhindered. However, the oil cooler needed to be shrouded; the shape of the fuel tank had to be modified to leave more room for the occupants; and the oil tank mounting had to be changed to allow better cooling and ease of access. That was in February 1960 and Porsche wanted a car 'shaken down' and fit to enter the Targa Florio in May.

News of the build programme came as less than good news to Reimspriess, too, for whilst the first two cars were promised for February, the modifications called for would clearly delay them. The next delivery would be of one car in March, five in April, six in May and six in June. The first prototype left Turin alone in February and when it reached Stuttgart, did not meet with instant acclaim, except for the shape. It had leaked rainwater, the driver's seat was almost impossible to get into for anyone over one-and-a-half metres tall and the finish was not up to the standard expected, so there were discussions – heated discussions. Even so, by the end of March, every GTL to be built was sold.

The second car did come up to scratch and all the modifications called for had been incorporated. The finish was infinitely

Towards a New Age

Linge and Walter drove this Carrera GTL to an eleventh Porsche Class win at Le Mans in 1960.

better than the first and, in the words of one commentator, it was good enough to perform at the Targa Florio 'straight out of the box'. In fact, Herbert Linge and Paul Strahle took the car to an easy class win in Sicily, then on to another at the Nurburgring 1,000 Kilometres, fitted with experimental disc brakes, then Linge co-drove the car to another Class win, and eleventh overall, at Le Mans in June. The Porsche Carrera 1600GTL had arrived.

Eventually, all the GTLs were delivered, but in use they began to give problems. It must be remembered that Porsche sold most of these cars to racing customers, who expected certain things of Porsche in return for their DM25,000 apiece. The lightweight structure brought its own problems, like hinged panels needing to be reinforced to minimize the risk of tearing metal. The biggest problem seemed to be the windscreen, which was mounted on a very narrow rubber moulding, which meant it passed stress through the bodywork, with the inevitable breaking of metal – and Porsche's warranty bank! To make things worse, the Italian glassware was not type approved in Germany. Then there was the decision to replace the window winding mechanisms with a leather strap and pegs, as had been done with the earlier GT Carrera. Other little problems had to be dealt with, too, before the GTL could be described as acceptable.

Out on the road or track, the GTL proved to be not quite what had been promised or expected. For example, it weighed in at only 20–30 kilograms below the GT and so its 0–60 time was down, turning in 8.8 seconds where something substantially better had been expected. Even so, it could reach 110mph in only 26.5 seconds, compared with 38.9 in a Carrera 2, so the new car had its redeeming features. It was, like many Porsches, a rather slow starter, but once wound up, could hold its own against its opposition. When the 2-litre Type 587 engine appeared, the GTL was now a competitive motor car and proved it by taking another class win in the 1961 Targa Florio. Greatest disappointment of that race, though, was the fact that Stirling Moss, driving a Camoradi Porsche, was comfortably in the lead when, just a stone's throw from the finish, his car broke down and he lost the race to Wolfgang von Trips's Ferrari. Not far behind Moss, however, Jo Bonnier and Dan Gurney had piloted their 718 RS60 into second place overall.

THE 356B 2000GS-GT ARRIVES

That two race cars outwardly so similar in appearance could be so different in fact is perhaps not too surprising when one considers that the two cars in question were Porsches. The two models were the 718 RS-61 and the 356B 2000GS-GT, the former being built on a tubular spaceframe chassis whilst the latter was, quite simply, a 356 chassis, though it was a little more than 'quite simply a 356 chassis'. Both used flat-four quad-cam engines and both used the Porsche synchromesh gearbox. Both were sports racers, and while the 718 had its engine ahead of the gearbox and rear wheels, whilst the 2000GS-GT had the traditional 356 engine/gearbox layout.

Only two 356B 2000GS-GTs were built and their primary purpose was to keep the Porsche banner flying on the race tracks until their successor was ready to take their place. That said, consideration was given to the possibility of manufacturing a small batch for sale to customers who wanted to race in the GT Prototype category. The idea was dropped for two reasons, firstly that the Carrera GTL had already cost Porsche a substantial sum in warranty claims, and secondly that there was a much more exciting project on the way from which Porsche did not want to be distracted.

The whole basis for constructing these two cars – the rarest Carreras of all – was that Porsche wanted to take advantage of a loophole in the regulations for GT cars which required only that the chassis and the engine must have been produced in numbers greater than 100 to qualify for entry. There was no restriction on bodywork styling, so it was decided at Zuffenhausen that the body style of the RS61 'with a lid' would be used, if slightly modified. The principal modification was the engine cover, which was not, on this model, a fully raising tail end, but just a panel, which meant that the whole roof could be integral with the body.

When first seen, many people thought (and some hoped) that this was the new Carrera, the car to replace the GTL. Little did they know that the body on this car leaked every bit as much as the Abarth car had and their body warranty claims might have been just as high as they had been on the GTL in its early days. That said, the GTL was still around, of course, and was still winning races and hill-climbs. But the *Dreikantschaber* (literally translated to mean 'triangular scraper', but colloquially as the 'wedge') was to have its day and prove that it could travel even faster than its Italian-bodied predecessor.

The principle was to take two 356B chassis and build on to them bodies in the style of the 718-RS61 Coupés that had been built for the 1961 Le Mans 24-Hours Race. Because the whole rear end of the body was not hinged up on the 2000GS-GT, in the fashion of the RS61, it was possible to make the roof in one piece, as an integral part of the body, and so put glass in the rear quarter, which had previously been quite a blind spot. This feature was, of course, the immediate identifier of the 2000GS-GT from the RS61. The engine of the 2000GS-GT was the two-litre Type

Model: Porsche Type 356B 2000 GS-GT (Dreikantschaber) – 1963

Construction	Tubular spaceframe with hand fabricated aluminium alloy bodywork by Weidenhausen and Weinsberg
ENGINE	Type 587/3 (2000)
Crankcase	Light alloy crankcase with individual cylinders
Cylinder head	Light alloy with inserted valve guides and seats
Cyls/Type	Four, horizontally opposed
Compression	9.8:1
Cooling system	Air, with finned cylinder barrels and belt-driven fan
Bore & stroke	92mm × 74mm (3.6 × 2.4in)
Capacity	1,966cc (119.9cu in)
Main bearings	Roller bearings on Hirth composite crankshaft
Valves	Two overhead per cylinder, dual overhead cam actuation
Fuel supply	Dual electric pumps/2 Weber 46IDM 2 carburetters
Power output	160bhp @ 6,600 rpm
Ignition system	Dual coil and distributor with twin spark plugs
Lubrication	Dry sump, 8 litre oil tank, gear pump and oil cooling
BRAKES	
Type	Porche/Teves discs front and rear
TRANSMISSION	5-speed synchro Type 718 – rear wheel drive
Clutch type	Single dry plate
Gear ratios	Various, according to requirements of circuit
Final drive ratio	4.428:1 standard
SUSPENSION/STEERING	
Front suspension	Independent with double oscillating arms, square-section torsion bars and Koni dual action telescopic shock absorbers
Rear suspension	Independent swing axles, round section torsion bars and Koni dual action telescopic shock absorbers
Steering type	ZF centre-point steering box with divided equal length arms
Wheels	4.5J × 15 front. 5J × 15 rear
Tyres	Front: 5.50 × 15R. Rear 5.90 × 15 RS Racing
DIMENSIONS	
Wheelbase	2,100mm (81.9in)
Track (front)	1,306mm (50.9in)
Track (rear)	1,272mm (49.5in)
DRY WEIGHT	820kg (1,822lb)
MODELS AVAILABLE	Racing Coupé
TOP SPEED	146mph (235kph)

Only two 356B 2000GS-GTs were built, designed along the lines of the 718 RS61 coupé and aimed at bridging the gap between the Carrera GTL Abarth and the Carrera 904GTS.

587/3. The cars were very fast and spent their whole lives in competition, the first major outing being Sebring in 1963, where the two cars finished ninth and tenth overall.

Porsche won the 1963 Targa Florio with an eight cylinder engined RS61, driven by Jo Bonnier and Carlo Abate. Behind them, sandwiching a Ferrari between first and third place cars, came Herbert Linge and Edgar Barth with the first of the 2000GS-GTs, then another Ferrari in a sandwich between it and the second GS-GT driven by Strahle and Pucci. Winning the GT Class in the Targa Florio justified the whole exercise and the cars went on to the Nürburgring for the next round in the Sports Car season.

In the paddock at the 1963 Targa Florio (obviously before the race, because it's clean and unmarked) is the Edgar Barth/Herbert Linge 2000GS-GT which was placed third in the race, the Bonnier/Abate eight-cylinder car coming home first.

Once again, the works entered two eight-cylinder cars, one to be driven by Edgar Barth and Herbert Linge, whilst the other was piloted by Phil Hill and Jo Bonnier, whilst a solo 2000GS-GT was driven by H J Walter and B Pon. The Hill/Bonnier car was doing well, running in the lead and expected to win at one stage, but as has often been said in motor racing before: 'The race isn't won until it's won', for Hill was half a lap ahead of his nearest rival, Willy Mairesse in a Ferrari, when disaster struck. Mike Parkes had stuffed his Ferrari into a wall at the Aremberg Hairpin and the debris lay on the track. Hill came upon this, got crossed up on the slippery surface and overturned his car.

With both eight-cylinder Porsches now out, Edgar Barth and Herbert Linge took over the Walther/Pon car, which was lying in sixth place, and went back into the race. By sheer dogged driving, they hauled the Carrera 2000GSGT through the traffic into fourth place. It was a hard gruelling race, in weather which varied between fair and foul, but Porsche spirits rose as they realized another Class win.

Le Mans was next, where once more the Carrera Fours were sent to back up the two eight-cylinder machines. Neither Carrera finished that event, one going out after over-revving its engine, the other dropping a valve. It was sad, because these two cars had been timed down Mulsanne at 143mph and 149mph respectively, making them the fastest Carreras to date and dispelling the story of the Abarth Carreras being the fastest ever. After this, the GS-GT was 'running out of steam'. The 904 prototype was on the track in 1964 and the 2000GS-GT didn't do particularly well either at Sebring or Daytona that year, though they had picked up a few hill climb points in 1963. These, then, were the last true 356 derivatives, passing into history to make way for what some describe as the most exciting Porsche ever built – the 904.

LAST OF THE CARRERA FOURS: THE 904GTS

The only feature of this new car which connected it to the 356 line of Porsches was the engine. Even before the Carrera 2000GS-GT was built, this car was on the drawing board of Ferdinand Alexander 'Butzi' Porsche. In February 1963, a wooden body buck was sent to Heinkel Flugzeugbau for the construction of a glass-reinforced plastic body shell – yes, fibreglass! The chassis was really quite simple – two longitudinal fabricated box section members with an integral subframe at the rear to support engine, transmission and suspension and three other cross-members.

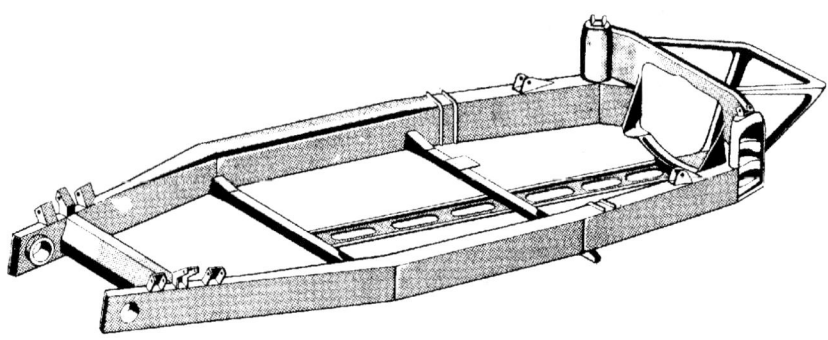

The chassis of the 904 GTS, from the maker's parts manual.

Towards a New Age

The reasoning behind the decision to create the 904 was that Carlo Abarth had made it clear that he would like to move up a from the 1,000cc Class and build a 2-litre car for competition in the FIA's Grand Touring Championship during the 1963 Season. He enlisted the skills of Hans Herrmann as his lead driver and entered into an agreement with Simca for the use of their 2-litre four-cylinder engine.

Worse than that, Alfa Romeo had decided it was time to uprate and update its Sprint Zagato, which had done so well in the

An interesting view in the Heinkel workshops, of the GTS glass-fibre body being mounted on to a chassis.

The Alfa Romeo SZ ('Sprint Zagato') was to be succeeded by . . .

. . . the Alfa Romeo TZ ('Tubolare Zagato' – tubular chassis Zagato), which was the most serious threat faced by Porsche.

Towards a New Age

1,300cc Class. So they were developing the Giulia TZ (*Tubolare Zagato – Tubolare* meaning simply 'tubular' for the spaceframe chassis) at the same time as Porsche were working on the 904. The TZ was probably the greatest threat, because Alfa Romeo, like Porsche, keenly supported private entrants and so there was almost always a large contingent of Alfas in any major race and, as Porsche had walked away on many occasions with the 1,600cc Class, so Alfa Romeo almost always followed suit in the 1,300cc Class.

Apart from these two contenders for supremacy over Porsche, there was then Lotus in Great Britain, who had by now developed the Elan. The roadgoing Elan, also using fibreglass for its bodywork (Lotus had used the material since 1957 when they introduced the Elite), had an awesome standing start 0–60mph (96kph) time of less than eight seconds in production form. In full race trim, using Cosworth-developed Ford power, it could be expected to be a formidable contestant, for Lotus knew how to race and were expected to do outstandingly well on the 1963 Grand Prix scene.

History tells us that they did, with Jim Clark winning the Grand Prix World Championship.

Apart from facing up to what the competition was doing, the Porsche management team was still licking its wounds from its venture into Grand Prix racing which, whilst it secured one win in its first season, cost an enormous sum in comparison to the publicity value of sports car racing, so the time was right to create a new winner. So, whilst 'Butzi' Porsche was beavering away designing the most elegant Porsche racer ever built, the engineering team was working at producing a chassis that was substantial enough to support the new glass-fibre body and provide the road-holding essential to success in such places as the Targa Florio and the Nürburgring circuits.

Ladder-type frames are not renowned for being rigid, but this one was designed with the body in mind, so that the combined strength and rigidity of chassis and body would be greater than that of a 356 Coupé body. The body sections were so designed that, when they were glued or bolted (or in

The finished 904GTS.

Towards a New Age

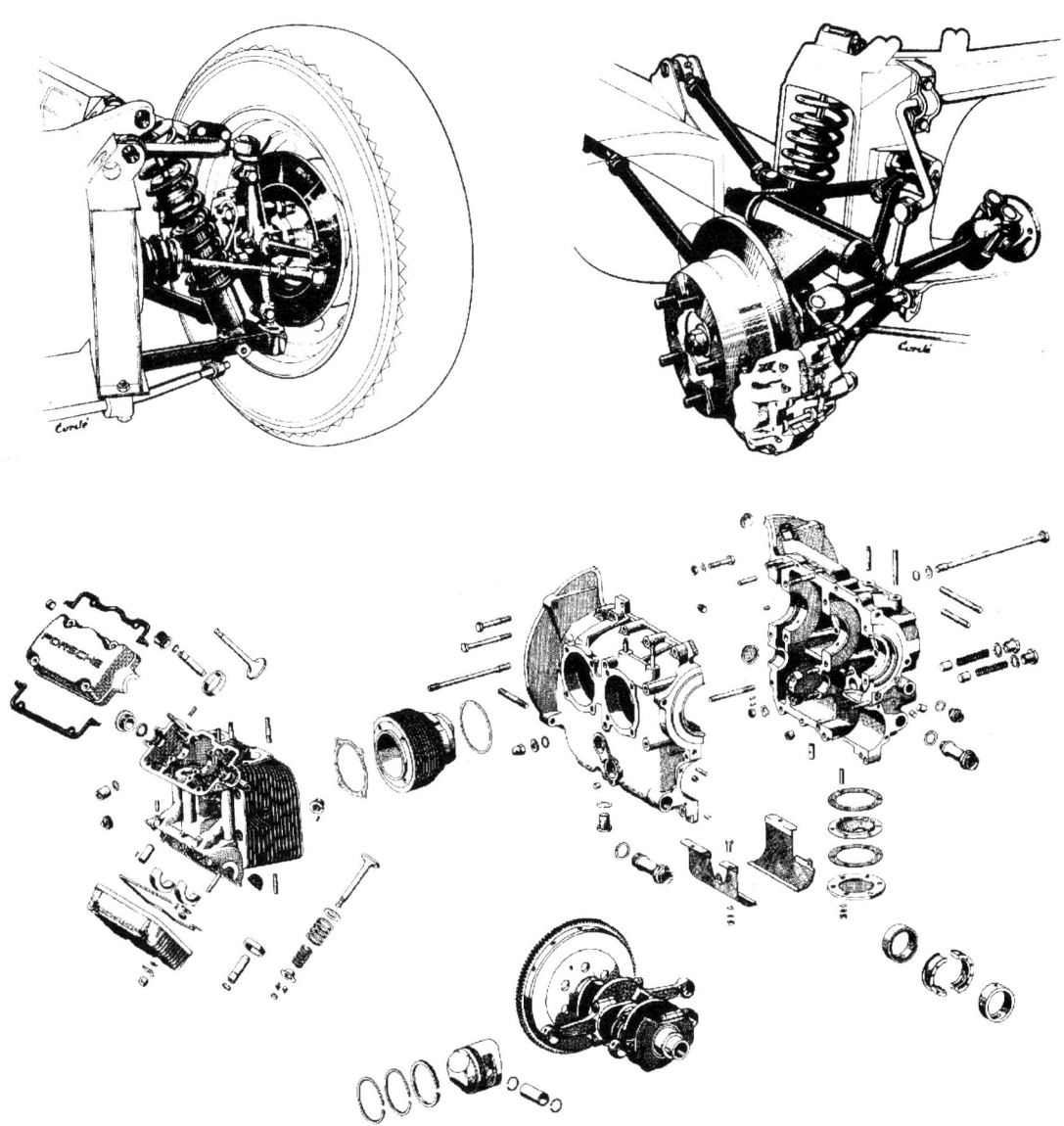

An exploded view of the 547/3 engine which powered the Carrera GTS and the suspension (front and rear) which provided the ride

some parts, both), they created a structural box that was torsionally rigid and yet very light. The structure was different from Lotus's designs, in that the Lotus chassis was a steel box section backbone which, even when attached to its body, was not going to be as rigid as the Porsche. This design was covered by German Patent Number 1275372.

Hans Mezger was assigned the task of developing the 587/3 quad-cam engine so as to extract more than its standard 155bhp.

Indeed, the power target for the Carrera GTS engine was set at 180bhp, which was not as far-fetched as it might have seemed, when one considers that 187bhp was extracted from a 1,500cc engine in the Type 804-4 Formula One car a couple of years before. They actually obtained 180bhp from the test engine at 7,200rpm. The reason for the decision to improve the 587 engine, instead of continuing to develop the new six-cylinder 2-litre was that the six was not as far advanced as planned, so a standby engine for the 904GTS was the eight-cylinder Type 771 2-litre already used and which gave 210bhp.

TESTING AND RACING THE 904GTS CARRERA

Three prototypes were built and on 29 August 1963, the first went to Weissach, Porsche's proving ground about 25km (16 miles) from Stuttgart. The first tests were run on Dunlop 5.50 × 15 racing tyres. Then road tests were conducted on normal road radial tyres, before the car was taken to the Nürburgring for testing under more arduous running conditions. Early problems were mostly associated with body cracking and bonding breaks, though on one car, the tyres rubbed on the bodywork, on another the trans-axle was giving problems and gearshifting was proving difficult, whilst on all the prototypes, brake cooling proved a problem.

As a result of the testing programme, various modifications were made, many unseen and connected with the bolting and bonding of the body to the chassis, others more obvious, like the brake cooling air scoops added just behind the doors. Continued testing ran into October and the pressure increased, as the first customer cars had been promised by February, and not least because the Sebring 12 Hours Race was scheduled for March. A final test session was embarked on in November at Nürburgring, in which the car turned in a lap time of 9 minutes and 30 seconds. That was it. The car was now considered sufficiently de-bugged to commence production. The price had been fixed at DM29,700 (about US $7,425) and the official name of 'Carrera GTS' was accorded it for the car's press debut at Solitude.

Edgar Barth and Herbert Linge were the demonstration drivers at the press debut, which proved to be the success that had been hoped for. The press wrote in glowing terms of this elegant, fast and not expensive sports racing car (the price was roughly half that of a roadgoing Ferrari of the time). A few days after this general press presentation, Bernard Cahier, a noted French journalist, was given a private review session by Huschke von Hanstein. The two took the car back to the Solitude circuit and tested the car's potential raceworthiness in typical early winter conditions of cold and slush. Cahier then drove the 904 back over country roads to Zuffenhausen and was impressed. He found the car responsive and sure-footed, even in the wet, though he did not like the draughts and leaks of the prototype.

Production of the 904 began in late November 1963, with the first few cars delivered to Zuffenhausen as bonded assemblies of fibreglass and steel. That brought problems, as Porsche found the task of finishing them in that semi-assembled state quite difficult. As a result, Heinkel Flugzeugbau was asked to take the job further, installing electric wiring and interior trim, finish painting and glazing the body units before delivery. Then Porsche added the suspensions, engine/transmission units and internal/external detail to bring the cars to a drivable state. They had to

Pon and van Zalinge drove this 904GTS to third place overall, and a twelfth Class win, at the 1964 Le Mans 24 Hours.

speed things up, as February was fast approaching, homologation had to be certified before that time and, to add a little extra pressure, the space in which the 904s were being built had been allocated for early production of the new 911 model.

Now came the real test. The first international race for the 904GTS was the Sebring 12 Hours, where clutch problems beset the prospects of a result. On to Sicily for the Targa Florio and full vindication of the four-cylinder car. The Porsche eight-cylinder 2-litres failed, leaving Zuffenhausen's reputation in the hands of the newcomer. 904s finished first, second and third, trouncing Ford on the way, although Ferrari had kept its cars at home that day. Customer and works cars alike were entered for the Nürburgring 1,000 Kilometres, where the first Porsche home was Ben Pon's 904, finishing third overall. At Le Mans, Porsches did even better, relatively, with five cars entered and five cars finishing – in seventh, eighth, tenth, eleventh and twelfth places (up to this point, only the British Riley company had done better, with six cars entered and six finishing with a fistful of prizes and a near-win on the way, but Porsche would see that record off in time). At Rheims, all eight cars entered finished, the first among them fifth overall. The only dull spot in Porsche's 1964 year was the RAC Tourist Trophy Race at Goodwood, where 904s fell second and third to a Lotus Elan. But the World 2-litre GT Championship for 1964 went to Porsche.

The year 1965 saw the rise of multi-cylinder engines, Ferrari in particular coming in with the V-6 engined 166SP. Fortunately for Porsche, Ferrari was not pursuing the GT category, but it still threatened the German firm's supremacy. In response, Porsche introduced a modification to the 587/3 engine's specification. It started with an increase in the inlet valve size to 50mm (2in) and modified valve timing to 90/94/100/72, giving a valve overlap increase of 23 degrees at 162, raising the power output to 185bhp at 7,200rpm. Just to confound those who saw the 904 as a pure racer, the factory entered one in the 1965 Monte Carlo Rally and, to everyone's surprise, it finished second overall. This was followed by a fifth place in the Targa Florio and first in the Index of Performance at Le Mans, placed fifth overall at the end.

The 904 was, and is, a legend. Ferdinand Porsche III was rightly given credit for producing what, in the eyes of many, was one of the most elegant Porsches ever – and

Model: Porsche Type 904 Carrera GTS – 1963

Construction	Fabricated box-section outrigger typechassis frame with GRP body panels bonded and bolted to the frame (bonding by Heinkel)
ENGINE	Type 587/3 (2000) located ahead of the transmission
Crankcase	Light alloy crankcase with individual cylinders
Cylinder head	Light alloy with inserted valve guides and seats
Cyls/Type	Four, horizontally opposed
Compression	9.8:1
Cooling system	Air, with finned cylinder barrels and belt-driven fan
Bore & stroke	92mm × 74mm (3.6 × 2.4in)
Capacity	1,966cc (119.9cu in)
Main bearings	Plain bearings to main and big-end journals
Valves	Two overhead per cylinder, dual overhead cam actuation
Fuel supply	Dual electric pumps/2 Weber 46IDM 2 carburetters
Power output	155bhp @ 6,900 rpm
Ignition system	Dual coil and distributor with twin spark plugs
Lubrication	Dry sump, 8 litre oil tank, gear pump and oil cooling
BRAKES	
Type	ATE/Dunlop discs front and rear
TRANSMISSION	5-speed synchro Type 904/0 – rear wheel drive
Clutch type	Single dry plate
Gear ratios	Various, according to requirements of circuit
Final drive ratio	4.428:1 standard
SUSPENSION/STEERING	
Front suspension	Independent with unequal length "A" arms and coil springs double outside telescopic shock absorbers
Rear suspension	Independent with unequal length "A" arms and struts with coil springs outside telescopic shock absorbers
Steering type	ZF rack and pinion
Wheels	4.5J × 15 front. 5J × 15 rear
Tyres	Front: 5.50 × 15R. Rear 6.50 × 15 RS Racing
DIMENSIONS	
Wheelbase	2,300mm (90.6in)
Track (front)	1,316mm (51.81in)
Track (rear)	1,312mm (51.65in)
DRY WEIGHT	650kg (1,444lb)
MODELS AVAILABLE	Racing Coupé
TOP SPEED	163mph (263kph)

Towards a New Age

The 1965 Monte Carlo Rally saw Porsche secure a surprise second place overall in this 904.

a successful racer at that. There was, and is, a downside, in that under hard use, bodywork and chassis could try to part company – rust got at the chassis and restoration experts have not found the 904 an easy task. But no-one can take away the tremendous, almost instant success of this magnificent 2-litre. Time and the development of multi-cylinder engines eclipsed this last four-cylinder racing Porsche, though it would continue in use with eight- and six-cylinder engines until the 906 came on the scene to introduce the new era of Porsche racing.

10 From T-5 to T-6 and 356B to 356C

The casual observer could easily wonder whether the frenetic pace of Porsche's racing programme left any time for the development of its production cars. Of course, that was not the case, as Porsche used sports car racing, and its brief sojourn into single-seat racing via Formula Two and Formula One, to improve and develop its production car range – back again to the Ferdinand Porsche adage of many years before that racing improves the breed.

In this Chapter, we see the development of the Porsche product, from the 356B to the 356C, the last of the original series of four-cylinder Porsche production cars. The next car in four-cylinder Porsches was to be the 'new kid on the block' in the form of the 912, but that comes later. The development of the 356 into this last variant is a fascinating story, not dissimilar in many ways from that of the Volkswagen, in that the basic outline remained identifiable for many years. In the world of sports cars, it is certainly unusual for a car to retain its basic shape and form for so long – and be successful as well.

The development of the 356 over fifteen years is the story of deep research, of investigation into customer reactions and expectations and of creative application of race technology to road cars. In this final phase, the T-5 body evolved logically into the next phase, the T-6, which itself then evolved from 356B to 356C, becoming the springboard for an even more successful Porsche, arguably the most successful sports car ever built.

CONTINUING THE 356 LINE WITH THE T-5

It was in the summer of 1958 that the first of the many meetings which led to the creation of the T-5 took place. As the meetings progressed, such far-fetched ideas as air suspension were talked of, though not-so-far-fetched ideas as Watts linkage and fuel injection were also considered. Blocking synchromesh has often been thought to have been a feature of the new bodied model, which was to be designated the 356B, though in fact it came with the last of the 356As.

In the course of establishing what features should be incorporated into the 356A's successor, the management team examined very closely a schedule of complaints from Porsche customers who were transferring their allegiance to other makes. All the features known to have caused problems were listed and set out in priority. Then a list of the makes to which dissatisfied customers had transferred was examined, and the specification characteristics of those cars were also listed. At the end of this process, Porsche had a clear idea of what it had to do. Now, consideration had to be given to how those factors could be brought into the Porsche 356B.

From T-5 to T-6 and 356B to 356C

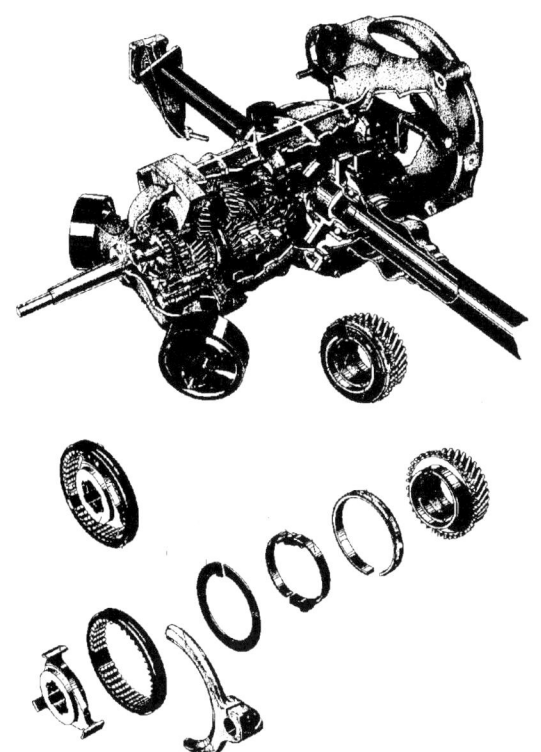

The blocking synchromesh which replaced the split-ring synchro in earlier Porsche models.

In November 1958, the specification for the proposed 356B was approved by Dr Ferry Porsche, then the design and engineering teams went to work to create the new car, which was announced to the public on 11 June 1959. The Porsche 356B was born. Mechanical features of the new model included the continuing use of the 616/1 engine (the 'Normal' or 'Dame' engine still being available, producing 60bhp) with a new 'Super 90', using the 616/7 engine of 90bhp. Behind the engine options came the Type 741 gearbox, with a shortened gearshift lever, and Alfin brake drums were fitted to provide improved brake cooling (the principle of these was that an aluminium alloy finned drum was shrunk on to a steel ring which was the friction surface contact) and lower unsprung weight.

Other features of the new 356B included a wider body, with a higher, rounded front end which raised the headlamps, giving it a slightly more chunky appearance. This was further added to by a small increase in the overall height and the new bumpers. The bumpers on this new car were more

The 356B coupé, with its raised bumpers and higher front-end line, was not approved of in all enthusiast quarters, but certainly made for a cleaner general appearance.

substantial than on previous models and were positioned higher than before. This was very much an appeasement of American customers, many of whom had discovered too late that the bumpers on their 356 sat at a level below that of most American cars. In a country where it is not uncommon to touch bumpers when parking, the Porsche bumper usually came off worse and could even find itself tangled with the offending vehicle and badly damaged in the process.

To combat the bumper problem still further, large chrome overriders were also fitted, to make sure that almost any vehicle, except perhaps the odd pick-up or 4 × 4, would touch them instead of either becoming entangled with the bumper or doing damage to the bodywork. Another feature which raised the bumpers was the increased tyre size, to 5.90 × 15 cross-plies or 165 × 15 radials. Other bodywork changes included enlarged horn grilles, a new, longer hood handle on the front which bore the Porsche prancing horse badge, new licence place lights mounted on the rear bumper, and a pair of separate rear reflectors (mounted above the bumpers in the United States, but below them in Europe).

New comfort features included the return of opening quarter lights in front of the door windows, the provision of warm air ducting to the rear window (a welcome addition to the 356, because many owners of earlier models had bitterly criticized the fact that, unless they drove with the side windows open, they could not see through the back when they came to reverse). A new black three-spoke steering wheel was accompanied by a steering column combination stalk-type switch which operated the direction indicators, high and low headlight beam and headlamp flasher. Would-be rear seat passengers were much better provided for now, with two 'jump-seats' with seat squabs positioned 60mm lower and with individual hinged fold-down backrests.

Out on the road, the basic ('Dame'-engined) 1,600 turned in a respectable top speed of 90mph (144kph), a decent speed for a relatively low state of tune in what could

This head-on view shows the bumpers and over-riders to excellent effect

Model: Porsche Type 356B 1600/1600S/1600S-90 – 1959/60

Construction	Pressed steel fabricated and welded box-section chassis with unitary steel coupé or cabriolet bodywork
ENGINE	Type 616/1(1600), 616/2 & 616/12 (1600S), 616/7 (1600 S-90)
Crankcase	Light alloy with grey iron cylinders (1600/S) or light alloy (1600 S-90) cylinders
Cylinder head	Light alloy with inserted valve guides and seats
Cyls/Type	Four, horizontally opposed
Compression	1600 = 7.5:1, 1600S = 8.5:1, 1600S-90 = 9.0:1
Cooling system	Air, with finned cylinder barrels and belt-driven fan
Bore & Stroke	82.5mm × 74mm (3.2 × 2.9in)
Capacity	1,582cc (96.5cu in)
Main bearings	Plain bearings throughout
Valves	Two overhead per cylinder, pushrod actuation
Fuel supply	Mechanical pump/two Zenith 32NDIX (1600/S) or two Solex 40PJJ-4 (1600S-90)
Power output	1600 = 60 bhp /4,500, 1600S = 75bhp/5,000, 1600 S-90 = 90bhp/5,500 rpm
Ignition system	Coil and distributor with auto advance/retard
Lubrication	Wet sump, gear pump and oil cooling (magnetic filter)
BRAKES	
Type	Drum front and rear with hydraulic actuation
TRANSMISSION	Porsche Type 741/1 (74½ in 1600S-90 to '61, then 741A) four speed synchro & reverse
Clutch type	Single dry plate
Gear ratios	1 = 13.682:1, 2 = 7.815:1, 3 = 5.003:1, 4 = 3.609:1 – R = 15.764:1
Final drive ratio	4.428:1 standard
SUSPENSION/STEERING	
Front suspension	Transverse torsion bars/trailing parallel links/telescopic shocks
Rear suspension	Transverse torsion bars/two trailing arms/telescopic shocks
Steering type	ZF Worm and stud, with divided tie rods and hydraulic damper
Wheels	Pressed steel 4.5J × 15
Tyres	5.60 × 15 Sport (1,600/1,600S), 165 × 15 (1,600S-90)

DIMENSIONS	Cabriolet:	Coupé:	Hard top:	Roadster:
Overall length	3,960mm	3,960mm	3,960mm (154.4in)	3,950mm (154.1in)
Overall width	1,670mm	1,670mm	1,670mm	1,670mm (65.1in)
Overall height	1,320mm	1,320mm (51.5in)	1,295mm (50.5in)	1,283mm (50.0in)
Wheelbase	2,100mm	2,100mm	2,100mm	2,100mm (81.9in)
Track (front)	1,306mm	1,306mm	1,306mm	1,306mm (50.9in)
Track (rear)	1,272mm	1,272mm	1,272mm	1,272mm (49.6in)

MODELS AVAILABLE	Cabriolet/coupé/hard top/Roadster
TOP SPEED	90mph (145kph)/100mph (160kph)/115mph (185kph)

best be described as a 'touring' car. The other two models in the range, the 1600S and the 1600 Super-90, were both capable of three-figure top speeds, the 'S' producing 100mph (160kph), whilst the Super-90 came in at 115mph (184kph), with the 616/7 engine. To enable the driver to handle the extra power of the Super-90, Koni Sport shock absorbers were fitted to control the vertical movement of the larger tyres. To provide still more control, a transverse spring was mounted underneath the gearbox and attached at each end to the axle tubes pivoting at the gearbox.

This auxiliary spring was intended to push the inner wheel in cornering down against the road with the same force as it pressed against the loaded wheel, so applying equal force and improving rear end grip and traction. In consequence of this spring being fitted, it was decided also to reduce the diameter of the rear torsion bars from 24.1mm to 23mm (0.94in to 0.89in), creating a slight increase in roll, but nothing unacceptable. In general then, the handling of the 356B was somewhat improved from the 356A, whilst better braking induced the would-be competitive driver to push the car a little harder in the knowledge that it could take it. Certainly, the 1600 Super-90 was bought by many people with the specific aim of competition in mind, as the performance envelope of the Super-90 was not all that far behind the Carrera and one major consideration for amateurs was that it cost less and took a lot less time to maintain. What was more, the Super-90 was more tractable for street use than the Carrera.

Back in 1952, Porsche had embarked upon a study into the feasibility of manufacturing a four-seat version of the 356 under the Type Number 530. Two prototypes were built at that time, although the car did not go into production, as the management team at Zuffenhausen thought it would not be economic, and in any case the 356 was at full production. However, the concept of four-seater Porsches did not end there.

Wendler of Reutlingen, who had built 550RS bodies for Porsche during the early quad-cam racing days, took it upon themselves to develop and offer for sale a four-seat version of the 356. It was a two-door vehicle with an extended wheelbase and restyled rear end. A trunk-like structure appeared at the back of the car, slightly resembling a cabriolet tail, but with Mercedes-Benz vertically positioned tail lights to give it a more upright appearance. The front end of the Wendler Sedan looked very much like the original 356B, so as one approached a passer-by, the observer had a bit of a surprise as the rest of the car went by.

Beutler of Thun, who had made such an attractive cabriolet body on the Gmünd 356, created this four-seat Sedan on the 356B T-5 chassis.

Model: Porsche Type 356B 1600/1600S Sedan – 1961/2

Construction	Pressed steel fabricated and welded box-section chassis with aluminium alloy four-seater coackwork by Beutler
ENGINE	Type 616/1(1600), 616/2 (1600S)
Crankcase	Light alloy with grey iron cylinders
Cylinder head	Light alloy with inserted valve guides and seats
Cyls/Type	Four, horizontally opposed
Compression	1600 = 7.5:1, 1600S = 8.5:1
Cooling system	Air, with finned cylinder barrels and belt-driven fan
Bore & Stroke	82.5mm × 74mm (3.2 × 2.9in)
Capacity	1,582cc (96.5cu in)
Main bearings	Plain bearings throughout
Valves	Two overhead per cylinder, pushrod actuation
Fuel supply	Mechanical pump/two Zenith 32NDIX
Power output	1600 = 60bhp @ 4,500, 1600S = 75bhp @ 5,000
Ignition system	Coil and distributor with auto advance/retard
Lubrication	Wet sump, gear pump and oil cooling (magnetic filter)
BRAKES	
Type	Drum front and rear with hydraulic actuation
TRANSMISSION	Porsche Type 741/1 four-speed plus reverse
Clutch type	Single dry plate
Gear ratios	1 = 13.682:1, 2 = 7.815:1, 3 = 5.003:1, 4 = 3.609:1 – R = 15.764:1
Final drive ratio	4.428:1 standard
SUSPENSION/STEERING	
Front suspension	Transverse torsion bars/trailing parallel links/telescopic shocks
Rear suspension	Transverse torsion bars/two trailing arms/telescopic shocks
Steering type	ZF Worm & stud, with divided tie rods & hydraulic damper
Wheels	Pressed steel 5.0J × 15
Tyres	5.90 × 15 Sport
DIMENSIONS	**Sedan:**
Overall length	4,530mm (176.7in) (1600) or 4,500mm (175.5in) (1600S)
Overall width	1,680mm (65.5in)
Overall height	1,350mm (52.7in)
Wheelbase	2,350mm (91.7in) (1600) or 2300mm (89.7in) (1600S)
Track (front)	1,306mm (50.9in)
Track (rear)	1,272mm (49.6in)
MODELS AVAILABLE	Four-seat two-door sedan by Beutler
TOP SPEED	1600 = 90mph (145kph), 1600S = 100mph (160kph)

Another coachbuilder who tackled the four-seat option was also a company which had already had an association with Porsche in the past. That was Beutler of Thun, who had built probably the prettiest ever 356 cabriolet in the Gmünd days. In 1960, Beutler decided to venture into four-door Porsches, using the T-5 chassis and a number of body panels to create something that looked a bit like an Alvis from the side, though clearly a lot smaller. They made the front end remain broadly like a 356B, though the front grilles were extended a little. The tail featured two quite soft and rounded fins alongside; again, a structure which had been deliberately made to look like a rear luggage trunk. Twin grilles gave away the 'bootlid', but the car was otherwise a relatively straightforward three-box sedan.

What the Road Testers Said

A number of road testers observed that the headlamps and front end of the new 356B had been raised and there were mixed feelings about whether this change improved the appearance of the car. Most seemed to accept the change as 'progress' with neutral reactions, whilst some positively disliked it, saying that the redesign pandered to the Americans – which it did, but for all the right reasons. Firstly, the lamps had to be raised to comply with the requirements of all states in the United States; secondly, the United States was still the biggest export market for Porsche, so why not make your car more acceptable to that market? In any case, Porsche had enough commercial and styling good sense to ensure nothing outrageous was done.

By 1960, only the most entrenched road testers would not accept that the 356 was one of the finest European sports cars on the road. That said, most welcomed the technical changes of the 356B, as well as the practicalities of the revised bumpers and headlamps. *Autocar* in Great Britain was certainly impressed with the interior appointments of the 1600S (known in Britain as the 1600 Super 75), especially the facility to stow maps with ease, but thought that the rear demister was not very effective on short journeys. The reviewer also criticized the horn button in the centre boss of the steering wheel, preferring the horn ring which had been fitted to the 356A. Apart from that, his only other criticism was having to crawl underneath the car to change the spark plugs (he should have tried doing the job on a Carrera!).

Out on the road, the car was found to be reasonably viceless, except for its tendency to switch to sharp oversteer without notice when the driver had reached the limits of adhesion. Comfort on the road was reckoned to be good, as was general visibility, and the 0–60mph (96kph) time was very creditable, coming in at 11.4 seconds on the test. The best top speed that *Autocar*'s tester was able to extract was actually 110mph (176kph), ten miles an hour above Porsche's quoted speed. His overall fuel consumption in all conditions over a distance of 1,114 miles (1,782km) was 29.2 miles (46.7km) per Imperial gallon, which compared very favourably with such cars as the MGA 1600, although the Alfa Romeo Giulietta Sprint would top 35 miles (56km) and give 80bhp in 'Sprint' form, or 90bhp in 'Sprint Veloce' tune, both from a 1,300 engine.

Sports Cars Illustrated in the United States spoke very highly of the 1600 Super 90, but could not resist the comment that: 'old-line Porsche owners may bemoan the passing of the now-classic body style', but went on to point out that the raised bumper would enable the 356 to fend for itself in city streets. The tester also made the valid point that the raised headlamps would give better

From T-5 to T-6 and 356B to 356C

PORSCHE SUPER 75

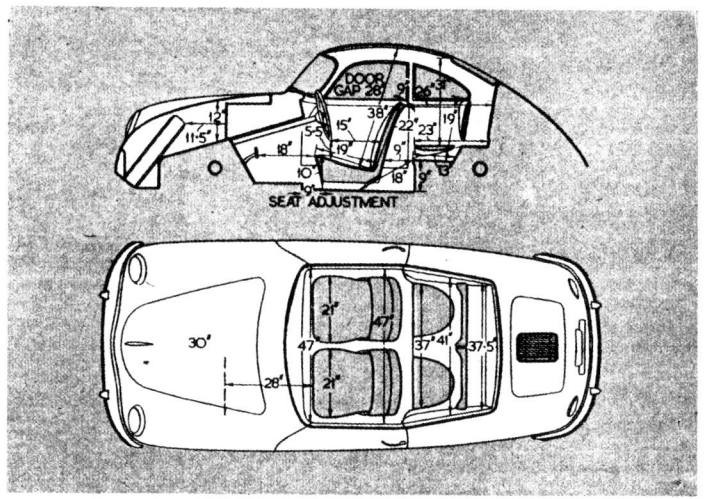

Scale ⅛in. to 1ft. Driving seat in central position. Cushions uncompressed.

PERFORMANCE

ACCELERATION TIMES (mean):

Speed range, M.p.h.	Gear Ratios and Time in Sec.			
	3.61 to 1	5.01 to 1	7.82 to 1	13.69 to 1
10—30	—	—	—	4.9
20—40	—	—	7.8	4.4
30—50	10.7	6.9	4.3	—
40—60	11.0	7.3	—	—
50—70	11.6	7.9	—	—
60—80	12.8	8.9	—	—
70—90	14.3	—	—	—
80—100	21.9	—	—	—

From rest through gears to:

30 m.p.h.	..	3.2 sec
40 "	..	5.6 "
50 "	..	7.8 "
60 "	..	11.4 "
70 "	..	15.6 "
80 "	..	20.6 "
90 "	..	28.8 "
100 "	..	41.7 "

Standing quarter mile 18.1 sec.

MAXIMUM SPEEDS ON GEARS:

Gear		M.p.h.	K.p.h.
Top	(mean)	108.8	175.2
	(best)	110.0	177.1
3rd		80	128.8
2nd		52	83.7
1st		29	46.7

TRACTIVE EFFORT (by Tapley meter):

	Pull (lb per ton)	Equivalent gradient
Top	210	1 in 10.6
Third	315	1 in 7.0
Second	470	1 in 4.7

SPEEDOMETER CORRECTION: M.P.H.

Car speedometer	10	20	30	40	50	60	70	80	90	100	110
True speed	10	18	28	39	50	59	68	73	81	90	100

BRAKES (at 30 m.p.h. in neutral):

Pedal load in lb	Retardation	Equiv. stopping distance in ft
25	0.20g	151
50	0.52g	58
75	0.85g	35.5
90	0.92g	32.8

FUEL CONSUMPTION (m.p.g. at steady speeds):

	Top Gear
30 m.p.h.	50.0
40 "	44.0
50 "	38.8
60 "	35.6
70 "	32.2
80 "	29.4
90 "	25.0

Overall fuel consumption for 1,114 miles, 29.2 m.p.g. (9.67 litres per 100 km).
Approximate normal range 27-35 m.p.g. (10.5-8.1 litres per 100 km).
Fuel: Premium grades.

TEST CONDITIONS: Weather: Dry, overcast. 0-5 m.p.h. wind.
Air temperature, 44 deg. F.
Model described in *The Autocar* of 11 September, 1959.

STEERING: Turning circle:
Between kerbs, L, 33ft 2in. R, 32ft 10in.
Between walls, L, 34ft 11in. R, 34ft 7in;
Turns of steering wheel from lock to lock, 2.2.

DATA

PRICE (basic), with coupé body, **£1,563**.
British purchase tax, £652 7s 6d.
Total (in Great Britain), £2,215 7s 6d.
Extras: Radio, £32 19s 3d (including tax).

ENGINE: Capacity, 1,582 c.c. (96.5 cu. in.).
Number of cylinders, 4.
Bore and stroke, 82.5 × 74 mm (3.25 × 2.91in.).
Valve gear, o.h.v., pushrods.
Compression ratio, 8.5 to 1.
B.h.p. 75 net at 5,000 r.p.m. (B.h.p. per ton laden, 74.1).
Torque, 88lb. ft. at 3,700 r.p.m.
M.p.h. per 1,000 r.p.m. in top gear, 20.0.

WEIGHT (with 5 gals fuel): 17.25 cwt (1,932 lb).
Weight distribution (per cent): F, 42.0; R, 58.0.
Laden as tested, 20.25 cwt (2,268lb).
Lb per c.c. (laden), 1.43.

BRAKES: Type: Porsche drum.
Method of operation, hydraulic.
Drum dimensions: F and R, 11in. dia., 1.57in. wide.
Swept area: F, 108.5 sq. in.; R, 108.5 sq. in. (214 sq. in. per ton laden).

TYRES: 5.60—15in. Michelin X.
Pressures (p.s.i.): F, 18.5; R, 23.0 (normal). F, 21.5; R, 25.5 (fast driving).

TANK CAPACITY: 11.5 Imperial gallons, including 1 reserve.
Oil sump, 8.8 pints, including filter.

DIMENSIONS: Wheelbase, 6ft 10.7in.
Track: F, 4ft 3.4in.; R, 4ft 2.1in.
Length (overall), 13ft 1.7in.
Width, 5ft 6.6in.
Height, 4ft 4.4in.
Ground clearance, 5.9 in.

ELECTRICAL SYSTEM: 6-volt; 75 ampère-hour battery.
Head lamps, double dip; 45-40 watt bulbs.

SUSPENSION: Front, independent, parallel trailing arms, transverse laminated torsion bars, anti-roll bar. Rear, independent swing axles with compensating transverse leaf spring, transverse round-section torsion bars.

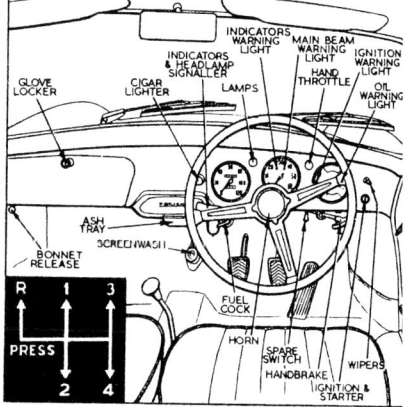

The Autocar road-test data panel from 15 April 1960.

From T-5 to T-6 and 356B to 356C

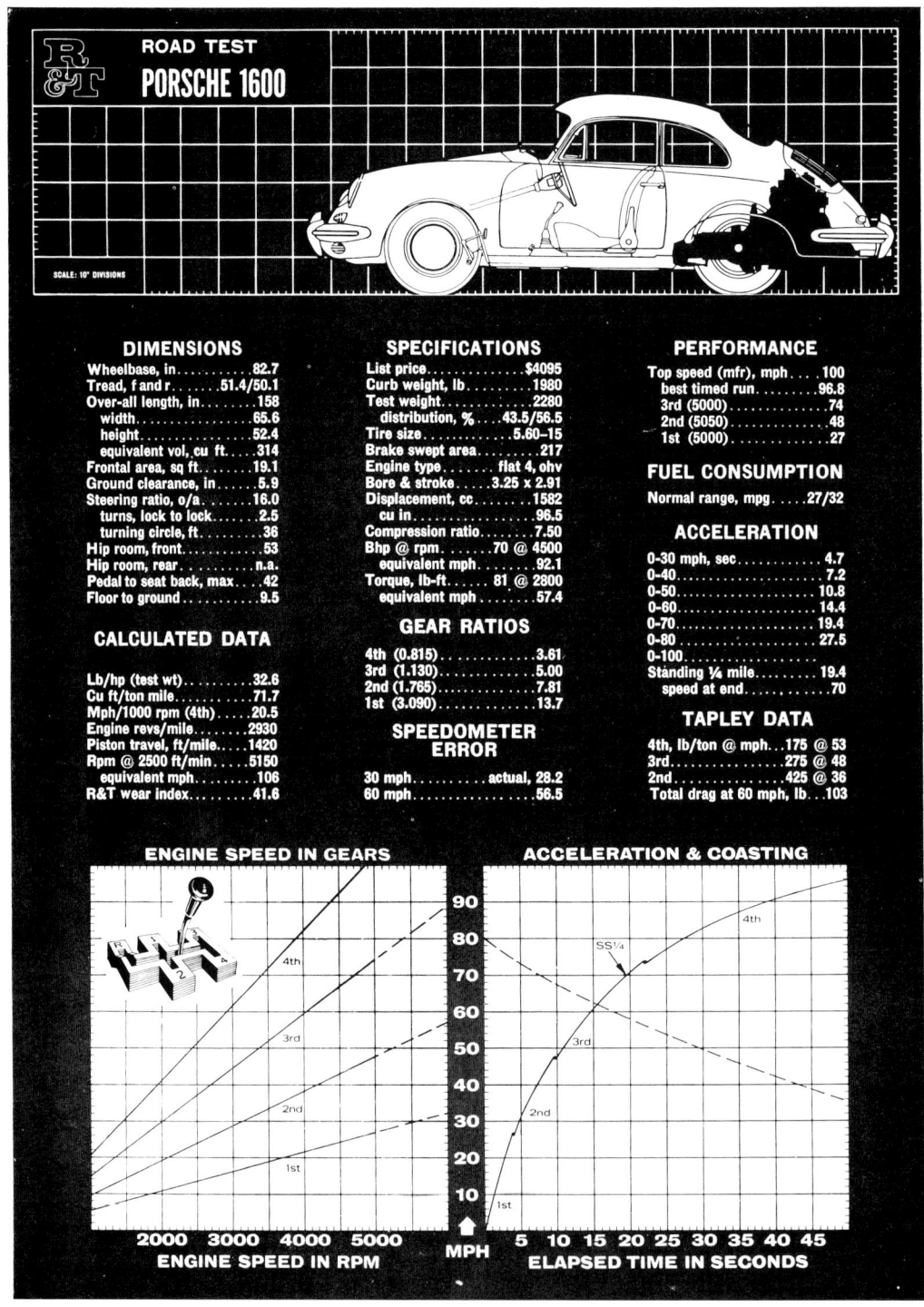

Road & Track *road-test data table from October 1961.*

illumination for high speed driving. He was critical, though, of the fact that the glovebox was too small to accept his Rolleiflex camera (Bill Boddy of *Motor Sport* always used to judge the 'worthiness' of a car's glovebox by its capacity to accommodate his Rolleiflex!). This road tester achieved 115mph (184kph) in a Super 90 and returned about 23 miles (37km) to the US gallon, which one has to say was not bad.

It seems that *Sports Car Illustrated* actually took two Porsches out on that road test run, the 1600 Super 90 and a standard 1,600 with the Normal, or Dame, engine. The lower powered car performed well, too, coming home with up to 29 miles (46km) per gallon and turning in a 98mph (157kph) top speed. Apart from comments about the styling of the car and its trim and equipment, the testers could not believe the astonishing roadholding of the 356B on the roughest of roads. The only safety-related criticism they could offer was about the interior heater controls, positioned on the inner faces of the sills just below the doors. The heater was reckoned to be very effective, but when one wanted to open or close the vents they could actually be too hot to touch with comfort. Other than that small point, *Sports Car Illustrated* praised both cars very highly.

Now, Australians have a reputation for being tough on cars, not least because of the terrain upon which they drive them – or did, back in the 1950s and 1960s, when Australian roads were not what they are today. A gruelling test was devised by the reviewer of *Sports Car World*, taking

A late T-5 Series 356B in an idyllic alpine setting.

From T-5 to T-6 and 356B to 356C

the Porsche 356A on a trip from Sydney to Wagga-Wagga, a distance of well over 200 miles (320km) going south-west into the Great Dividing Range, with four adults on board. Wagga-Wagga is west–south-west of Sydney and whilst the road was a main road, it was going to be a pretty arduous drive, especially with four-up. The idea was take two friends of the reviewer to their holiday location and then drive the car back with just two on board.

That the passengers even managed to get into the car in any degree of comfort is amazing enough, but our storyteller goes on to say that they fell asleep on the way to Wagga! Even more incredible was the fact that when they stopped to take on fuel, the front hood would not open, so they drove on, emptying the main fuel tank and switching to reserve. They reached Wagga and, with the aid of the local VW mechanic, managed to open the hood, so the car was filled up again. The staggering part about this particular road test is that the quoted average speed for the journey in both directions (four-up down and two-up back) was 108mph (173kph) and, even more incredible, they returned a fuel consumption of 34 miles (54km) per Imperial Gallon. What a road test!

THE T-6 BODIED 356B SERIES

As the 356B progressed through its life, a number of changes were implemented by Porsche. It was to be expected, as this manufacturer was not one to come up with calendar year models in order to maintain sales. They had no need to do that, because there was always a good market for their products and often a waiting list. During the life of the T-5, Karmann, who had a reputation for building exclusive cars and had bodied a Volkswagen as the Karmann-Ghia, had come up with a hard top version of the 356B, upon which the hard top was not removable, but welded into the body structure. Otherwise, it did not differ much in appearance from the factory hard top. Just over 1,000 examples were built in T-5 form and just under 700 in the new T-6 version.

So what was the new T-6? It moved still further away from the original shape by being higher and longer. Its width seemed to be immediately apparent by the fact that the front lid was squared off at its lower edge. In fact, this was illusory, because there was no actual width increase. Headlamps remained at about the same height as

This is the Karmann 356B hard top, with a fixed roof. Around 1,700 examples were built in total.

The T-6 Series 356B was immediately recognizable by the more squared-off bottom edge of the luggage compartment lid.

on the T-5, as did the bumpers, but a couple of features at the front end of the new body were certainly made very welcome. The first was a grille in the front cowl, just below the windscreen, which allowed fresh air into the car for the first time on a 356. The other feature, which eliminated a great deal of careless damage, was the removal of the fuel filler from under the hood to a position on the front right wing. This was a carefully designed flap, operated from inside the car, which opened to reveal a little rubber apron that folded out and protected the paintwork while a fuel nozzle was inserted into the filler neck.

Round the back, the more observant spotted immediately that the rear window was wider and deeper to give a better rear view, especially for reversing, as the view from inside left a little to be desired in that direction. The other change was a slightly larger engine cover with twin vertical grilles. Inside, other little touches improved the car, such as the dipping interior mirror for day and night use, an electric clock as standard and an optional petrol/electric interior heater, like that in the Carrera, which was welcomed by many. Other features anticipated by Porsche as in demand were the gearshift lock on all models and a zip-open rear window on the cabriolet.

Of course, the cabriolet had come through some changes and developments since the

Inside the luggage compartment, as the result of lowering the fuel tank, you could now place a reasonably sized suitcase (though you'll notice it was a soft one!).

From T-5 to T-6 and 356B to 356C

The T-6 Series 356B cabriolet.

Speedster days. Gone was the Speedster itself and now, in 1962, the Drause Convertible was also a thing of history, because a new cabriolet body, built by d'Ieteren Brothers in Belgium, had succeeded that. Both the Drause and the d'Ieteren bodies were built to Porsche designs and, when the decision was made to implement the T-6 programme, d'Ieteren, Karmann (who were making the hard top) and Reutter were all notified of the programme's implementation date. They had been kept aware of the design changes that would inevitably affect each of them, so had already tooled up for the changes in panel shapes that were to come. It was also important, of course, to maintain production continuity as far as possible during the transition.

It is only when one comes to examine the numbers of cars produced that one realizes how many 356Bs were produced in the two body forms in which it was offered. It seems that 15,354 T-5 356Bs were built, which alone outnumbered all the previous models (for example, 12,193 356As were produced), but then, perhaps surprisingly, there were over 16,000 356B T-6s manufactured, which means that the 356B almost outnumbers all the other variants of 356 in a ratio of two to one. But then, in 1963, came the last 356 in the line, the 356C.

LAST OF THE LINE – THE 356C

The first thing that separates the 356C from its immediate predecessor is the fact that the 'C' model was offered in only three variants. Gone was the Dame engine option, so there would now only be two pushrod engine choices, the 75bhp Type 616/15 and the 95bhp 616/16. Badging on the rear end of the car reflected these changes, with the

From T-5 to T-6 and 356B to 356C

A quick glance at the rear end of a 356B coupé told you whether it was a T-5 or a T-6, as the T-6 had a deeper rear window and twin air grilles.

75bhp version being known now as just the 356C, whilst the 95bhp version was called the 356SC.

There were several detail changes which came with the update to 'C', though the most significant functional alteration did not happen straight away. That was the change in the braking system. The first couple of hundred cars left the factory with drum brakes, but after that, the most significant difference between 'B' and 'C' took place. This was the installation of ATE disc brakes all round, which transformed the Porsche 356 by extending its performance envelope. These much more powerful brakes meant later braking, so raising average speeds on road or track.

Other features which distinguished the 356C from its predecessor included revised suspension tuning to improve riding comfort. Progressive rate rubber springs were introduced into the suspension, whilst the rear compensating spring used in the 'B' series cars was now dropped, except to special order. Also, the front anti-roll bar was stiffened, its diameter increased by an additional millimetre, then a Guibro coupling replaced the Hardy Spicer disc coupling between the steering box and the column. Then, the gearbox synchromesh was reinforced for the new model.

Inside the 356C, there were detail changes only. For example, a parking brake

The 356C coupé was little different from the T-6 Series 'B', as the body units were the same, but the giveaway is the wheels and flatter hub caps. All the other changes were on the inside.

Model: Porsche Type 356C 1600SC – 1963

Construction	Pressed steel fabricated and welded box-section chassis with unitary steel coupé or cabriolet bodywork
ENGINE	Type 616/16 (1600)
Crankcase	Light alloy with cylinders having Ferral (Biral from 1964) sliding surfaces
Cylinder head	Light alloy with inserted valve guides and seats
Cyls/Type	Four, horizontally opposed
Compression	9.5:1
Cooling system	Air, with finned cylinder barrels and belt-driven fan
Bore & Stroke	82.5mm × 74mm (3.2 × 2.9in)
Capacity	1,582cc (96.5cu in)
Main bearings	Plain bearings throughout
Valves	Two overhead per cylinder, pushrod actuation
Fuel supply	Mechanical pump/two Solex 40PJJ-4 carburettors
Power output	95bhp @ 5,800rpm
Ignition system	Coil and distributor with auto advance/retard
Lubrication	Wet sump, gear pump and oil cooling (magnetic filter)
BRAKES	
Type	ATE discs all round
TRANSMISSION	Porsche Type 741/2C four-speed synchro and reverse
Clutch type	Single dry plate
Gear ratios	1 = 13.682:1, 2 = 7.815:1, 3 = 5.003:1, 4 = 3.609:1 – R = 15.764:1
Final drive ratio	4.428:1 standard
SUSPENSION/STEERING	
Front suspension	Transverse torsion bars/trailing parallel links/telescopic shocks
Rear suspension	Transverse torsion bars/two trailing arms/telescopic shocks
Steering type	ZF Worm and stud, with divided tie rods and hydraulic damper
Wheels	Pressed steel 4.5J × 15
Tyres	165 × 15 radial

DIMENSIONS	**Cabriolet:**	**Coupé:**
Overall length	4,010mm	4,010mm (156.4in)
Overall width	1,670mm	1,670mm (65.1in)
Overall height	1,330mm	1,330mm (51.9in)
Wheelbase	2,100mm	2,100mm (81.9in)
Track (front)	1,306mm	1,306mm (50.9in)
Track (rear)	1,272mm	1,272mm (49.6in)

MODELS AVAILABLE	Cabriolet/coupé
TOP SPEED	115mph (185kph)

The 356SC carried the letters 'SC' in script just below the name over the registration plate.

warning light appeared on the instrument panel (though you would have thought a 356 driver would have known when the handbrake was on!), there were modified seats, giving better support and the rear flip-down seat backrests now had a lip at their upper edge on the back, so that when they were folded down and used as luggage space, the luggage had a natural stop at its foremost point (backrest retainers, to keep them in the vertical position when the seats were in use, had already been introduced as a safety measure). The passenger grab handle was now plastic covered, switches were relocated on the dashboard, a magnetic glovebox catch was introduced (though you still could not get a Rolleiflex inside), door armrests were now fitted and the interior lights were improved.

Two particular road tests of the 356SC stand out among the absolute host of praise heaped upon this little marvel. *The Motor* Sports Car Road Test of 11 July 1964 was headed up with the leader: 'One of the most solid one piece cars ever made ... for the connoisseur who pays and expects quite a lot.' What an accolade! The reviewer describes the acceleration of the 356SC as 'not the sort that jerks your head back. It is more the progressive kind that goes on a long time very uniformly in every gear, without the car feeling much faster or even getting much noisier ... Figures show the acceleration to be deceptively quick.' In fact, the 356SC seems to have had a slower 0–60mph (96kph) time than its predecessor, because *The Motor* records 13.2 seconds, whereas the 356B turned in 11.2. Perhaps it had something to do with the combination of state of tune on the day and the weight of the tester's right foot!

Did *The Motor* have criticisms of the 356SC? Indeed they did, and began with the total lack of luggage space for suitcases in the front trunk. That was a valid criticism, but not something most would-be Porsche buyers would have taken into account when contemplating their purchase. A 'two-up' situation was not a problem, because luggage could be thrown into the back of the car with the rear seats folded down. But the real success of long-distance travelling in a 356 was the use of soft bags, with one particular bag (placed inside the car) containing all the hard and knobbly bits of luggage. Small items could also be squeezed between the backrests and the squabs of the rear seats when folded down and still more small items could be slipped into the rear footwells.

The tester also did not particularly like the long clutch pedal travel or the heavy brake pedal. But Porsche never used any form of power assistance for their brakes, believing that the driver should 'feel' the braking effect all the way to a standstill. If you wanted more braking effort, then you simply pressed harder on the pedal – and it worked. *The Motor* reviewer also felt that the gear lever travel was a bit long, though praised the way in which the transfer from one gear to the next was so smoothly made. Overall, the opening accolade of his review stood and he was firmly impressed with the handling of the car, its surprising agility and its fuel consumption, which he recorded as between 26 and 28 miles (41.6–44.8km) per gallon.

We hop across to Australia once more for the next test review, this time from *Modern Motor*. Barry Cooke headlined his review thus: 'Fleet of foot, yet tough as nails, Porsche's 356SC gives new meaning to the words Grand Touring.' Another impressive opener! Mr Cooke found the cockpit completely functional and comfortable, though he thought the instrumentation a bit rudimentary. Nonetheless, the car came in for a lot of praise. There was the fact that the extra power of the 'SC' over the 75bhp 'C' seemed to transform the car. Torque, whilst very little more, was further up the engine speed band and so more effective for sustained high speed travel.

Contrary, however, to the *Sports Car World* review of the 356B, this road tester had little favourable comment about the rear seat accommodation in the 356, seeing it as child seating at best and extra luggage space as the most likely. Barry Cooke left no doubt about his view that this car was really a two-seater. After a preamble about the

The 356SC cabriolet was a superb 80–90mph (128–144kph) highway cruiser.

car's 'lumpiness' in traffic, in which he observed that top gear was best ignored, he went out of town and 'shook the dust off the Michelin Xs'.

Out on the open roads, the 'SC' was said to have an amazing capacity to lope along at 80–90mph (128–144kph) without effort and with power to spare. It was said to be the ultimate in sure-footedness on what Barry Cooke described as 'give-and-take' country roads, where anything resembling a corner was taken with a quick change-down and a sharp step on the throttle. Commenting on the 356's renowned understeer-to-neutral-to-oversteer characteristic as road speeds increased, Mr Cooke was apparently unable to provoke any loss of adhesion, demonstrating that the 356SC was certainly better behaved than its forebears.

Barry Cooke was clearly very impressed by what he experienced and again, as with the *Sports Car World* test, he came in with a very high fuel mileage, an amazing 32 miles (51km) per gallon. His 0–60 (96km) time was also 11.2 seconds, which suggests that Australian right feet are a little heavier and quicker than many an English right foot. Cooke concluded his review by saying that, unlike many cars in the GT category, the Porsche did not have the disadvantage of fragility. Thoroughly engineered in every way, it gave him the impression that it would last as long as a locomotive, while providing the comfort of a Pullman (for the front seat passengers anyway).

There was no doubt that the Porsche 356SC was the true pinnacle of pushrod Porsches in that series. But, as with all things, progress means change and the 356 could not forever represent the best in Porsche motoring. Indeed, Project 901 had reached fruition two years before the demise of the 356 in the form of the magnificent 911. But the price of the 911 was substantially more than that of the 356 and so, recognizing that a large sector of the original Porsche market still wanted a flat-four, the company continued to offer the 356 and then introduced a flat-four engined version of the 911 in the form of the 912. Another car for another time . . .

11 New Kids on the Block – The 912 and the 914

The year 1965 saw the final phase of the 356 draw to its close. It had been a remarkable chapter in motoring history, one in which a little car that had been the dream of its creator came into being on a shoestring under the most trying of conditions. But now, in 1965, with the 911 establishing its own market, Porsche had very wisely decided to keep a four-cylinder engined car in production. The argument in favour of such a decision was that, a year after the introduction in 1964 of the 911, when the old model should have been in serious decline, there were still just over 10,300 356s sold. Of course, the delay in bringing the 911 to full production must have helped, but there was clearly still a lot of faith in the Porsche flat-four.

So, when the development of the 911 was virtually complete, Porsche engineers took up the idea of examining the possibility of fitting a Type 616 engine instead of the normal Six. They decided that not only was it feasible, but even a good idea from a commercial standpoint, because a quick market survey suggested that an 'entry level' Porsche would be a very good idea. So began the programme 912, reinventing the flat-four Porsche – although even so, just under 1,700 356s were built in 1965, and even in 1966 ten 356 cabriolets were built. By then, the 356 really had reached the end of the line, the 912 had centre-stage.

Volkswagen, in the meantime, had come to the conclusion that their customers needed a little more excitement in their lives and so went to Porsche – who else? – to create it. The Karmann-Ghia body on the VW chassis platform was declining in sale, VW was under fire from all quarters for not being imaginative and failing to meet market demands, the Karmann-Ghia 2 was a commercial disaster, and so, in 1967, discussions began between Volkswagen and Porsche to produce something new. Porsche also needed a product to boost its market, as the 911 was very expensive and sales were not moving ahead as fast as had been hoped. By 1969, it had been revealed – the Type 914, engineered by Porsche and built at Wolfsburg by Volkswagen.

PROJECT 902 COMES TO LIFE

No, that's not a typographical error – Type 902 was the original number allocated by Porsche to the new four-cylinder variant of the 911, which in turn had originally been labelled 901. Unfortunately, Peugeot in France had been using three-digit model identification numbers for years with a zero in the middle, from 301, 401, 404 and so on. So, when they got wind of Porsche's new model having a zero in the middle of its type number, they promptly went off to the French copyright courts and secured a favourable ruling on their claim to exclusivity on the middle zero. Whilst Porsche could have retained '901' and '902' everywhere else in the world, it expected to sell cars in France too, and so changed the type numbers from '901' and '902' to '911' and '912'. Which is why we talk of Project 902.

So as not to 'muddy the waters' of project design and development, the idea of installing a four-cylinder engine was not even contemplated during the original creation and development to production of Project 901 – which, of course, became the legendary Porsche 911. It was as the six-cylinder car was going to production that the design team came back to the drawing board and looked at the prospect of fitting a Type 616 engine. They first examined the body weight of the 911 without an engine and compared that with the weight of the 356SC, and decided they could bring the weights of the two cars to within 100kg (220lb) of each other. Examining next the engine, it was concluded that a bit more torque could be squeezed out of it to assist the acceleration curve, as a result of which the idea was put to the Board of Directors.

The two most obvious market considerations offered in justification of the recommendation to the Board to go ahead with this idea were: retention of the existing four-cylinder car market; and provision, for the first time, of a lower cost 'entry-level' Porsche to lead potential buyers of a 911 into the Porsche fraternity at a price below that of the mainline model. However, there was also no escaping the fact that the company feared the possibility that existing Porsche buyers would not consider the newer model on the grounds that they felt 'it was not a true Porsche'. How many motor manufacturers have trodden that path in the past? So, a 'safety net' would be the 912, which would offer a body style that was up-to-the-minute in style and comfort, with the old familiar engine.

With approval from the Porsche Board of Directors, the production and engineering teams went to work and came up with a car

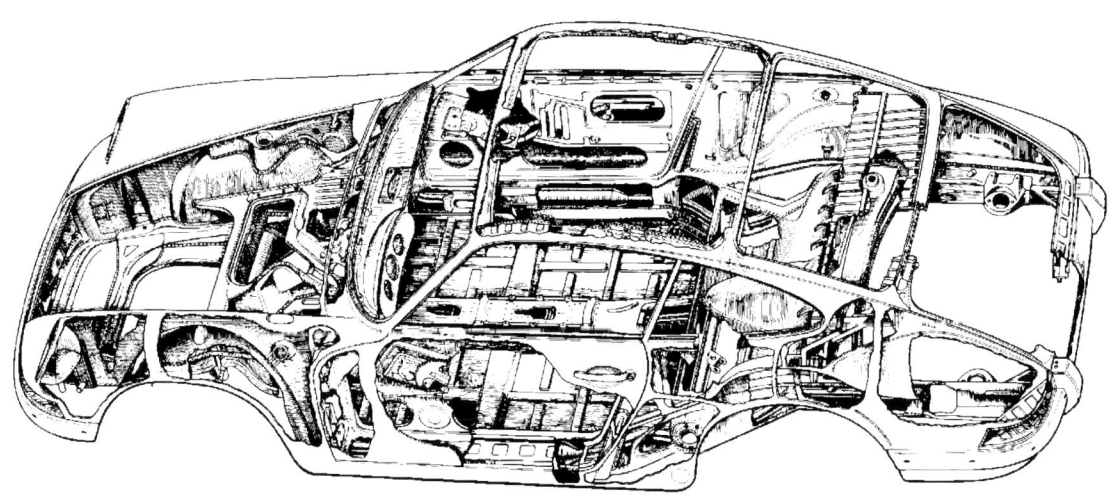

The bodyshell of the 912 in cutaway, showing the design of the structure. The rear end was adapted from the 911 to accommodate the four-cylinder engine.

that would weigh in at 2,138lb (just over 970kg). Its engine would yield 90bhp, give slightly better torque than the 356 and would enable the car to produce: a top speed of 115mph (184kph), a factory-predicted 0–60mph (96kph) time of 12.2 seconds and an estimated fuel consumption of 27.6 miles (44km) per US gallon (lifting the Imperial gallon fuel consumption to 34 miles (54km) per gallon on that basis). History tells us that this car really was capable of turning in that level of economy, not least because of the improved penetration qualities of its shape.

CREATING THE SUCCESSOR TO THE 356

One of the key marketing objectives of producing the 912 was to offer a car which was priced within easy reach of the 356SC, which it was ultimately to succeed. What was more, there was a body of opinion which claimed that the price of the 356 had risen out of proportion – one magazine reporter had even suggested that, through its price, the Porsche had now become a symbol of affluence rather than a car which was bought for its performance and handling, though that same reporter certainly criticized neither the performance nor the handling. In order to achieve the target price, the body specification of the 912 varied from that of the 911 in a number of ways.

Obviously, the first cost difference between the 911 and the 912 was the engine, the flat-six costing substantially more than the flat-four. Whilst the 911 featured the new five-speed gearbox, the 912 was offered with a four-speed gearbox as part of its standard specification, which was not detrimental to the car's market potential, as the 356 had always been sold with a four-speed. Then, inside the car, the seats were of a less expensive standard than the 911, the teak trim which was a feature of the 911 dashboard was replaced by an aluminium alloy trim and there were only three instead of five instruments on the panel. The steering wheel had a plastic rim instead of wood and, instead of the so-called 'butterfly wing' hornpush on the 911, a simple horn button was fitted in the 912.

Introduced to the market place in April 1965, the Porsche 912 quickly became Zuffenhausen's best seller, to the surprise of many. For example, in that year, only 3,390 911s were sold worldwide, whilst 1,688 356s were sold and 6,401 912s left the factory, bringing the total car production to 11,479 vehicles. This was a drop from the previous year, but a pretty significant achievement in the light of the traumatic change of introducing two entirely new models more or less at the same time, one of which was to cost around twenty-five per cent more than its immediate sibling and close to thirty per cent more than the 356, which, as has previously been noted, in the opinion of some was already expensive enough.

The engine of the new car would be a development of the now well-proven 616, designated Type 616/36, which retained the 1,582cc displacement, but with a slightly lower compression ratio than the 616 engine used in the 356SC. With a camshaft modified from the profiles of the earlier engine, this new version produced 90bhp, not 95, but gave 90 pounds feet of torque at 3,500rpm, whereas peak torque in the 1600SC came in at 4,200. The Solex 40PJJ carburettors were retained, though much larger air cleaners were fitted, partly to muffle engine noise on the intake side, whilst a single transverse silencer with a single outlet pipe dealt with exhaust noise.

In order to contain the selling price of the 912, Porsche offered the basic vehicle with

New Kids on the Block – The 912 and the 914

The dashboard of the 912 was a little more austere than the 911, with bright metal strips in place of woodwork, only three instrument dials and a central horn button.

only a four-speed gearbox. This did not create a problem, as 356 owners buying up to a 912 were already used to a four-speed, though in order to extract the best from the 616/36 engine, which was being asked to pull extra weight with the new body, it was felt that a five-speed would be a worthwhile option to offer. In fact, it seems the majority of 912 buyers did opt for the five-speed, recognizing that it gave better use of the power and torque available – and that it made the 912 more fun to drive. The ratios of the five-speed meant that a more constant engine speed could be maintained, as the four had quite wide gaps.

This elegant new Porsche was designed by Ferdinand ('Butzi') Porsche III, designer of Porsche's first 'plastic car', the 904GTS, described in an earlier Chapter. Not all of the 911/912 design was new, in that it carried over one feature of the 356 into the next generation. This was the rear torsion bar suspension, though there were a few changes. For example, the axle tubes of the early design were abandoned for open drive shafts. Then, the spring arm from the torsion bar acted as a trailing wishbone, whilst another link was a tapered tubular steel arm, the thick end carrying the hub and the thin end pivoted at the torsion bar end. The front suspension of the new body type employed a longitudinal torsion bar, positioned at the bottom of the suspension unit, with a wishbone attached which ran out to pick up at the bottom of a shock absorber strut and the hub carrier. The hub carrier also supported an ATE disc brake of the type used on the older 356.

The braking system of the 911/912 was virtually carried over wholesale from the 356. The ATE discs were now proven in service and had performed very well on the 356SC. So it made sense to bring this system over, incorporated into the new suspension, to the new models. In particular, the handbrake design on the ATE rear brake was especially effective. It was, in fact, a combined disc/drum brake. Many manufacturers of cars with disc brakes had experienced great trouble in making their handbrakes effective, particularly when it came to creating a brake that would not only hold the car on a slope, but would also pass annual testing standards throughout Europe. Creating a transverse linkage that would pull up enough to hold a car was difficult enough, to keep it reliable was proving near impossible. So Porsche went down

New Kids on the Block – The 912 and the 914

The 912 was identifiable from the rear by the '912' in diagonal script on the engine cover.

The rear torsion bar suspension of the 912 had round torsion bars instead of the earlier laminated spring type.

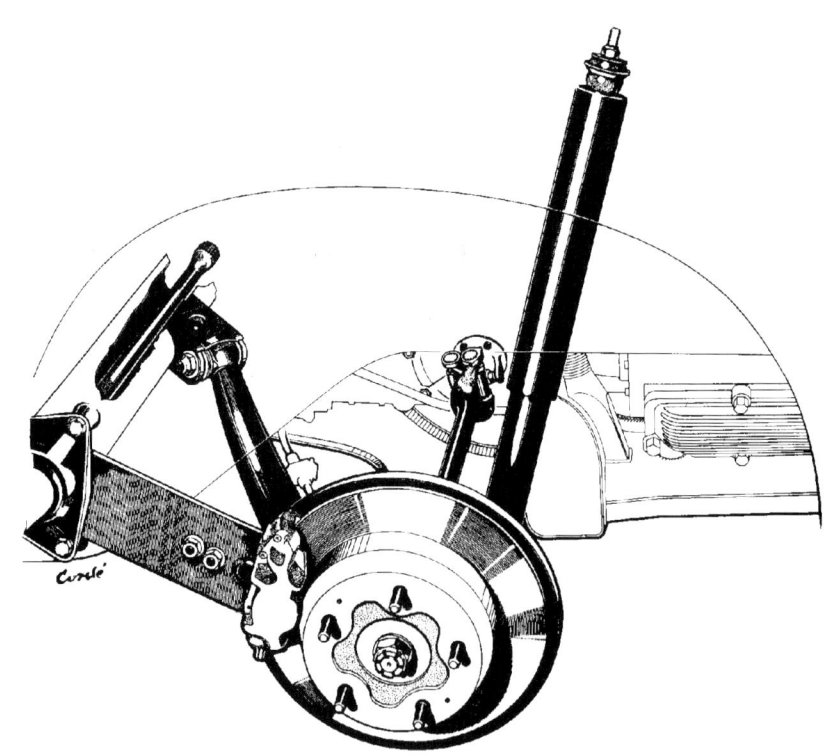

New Kids on the Block – The 912 and the 914

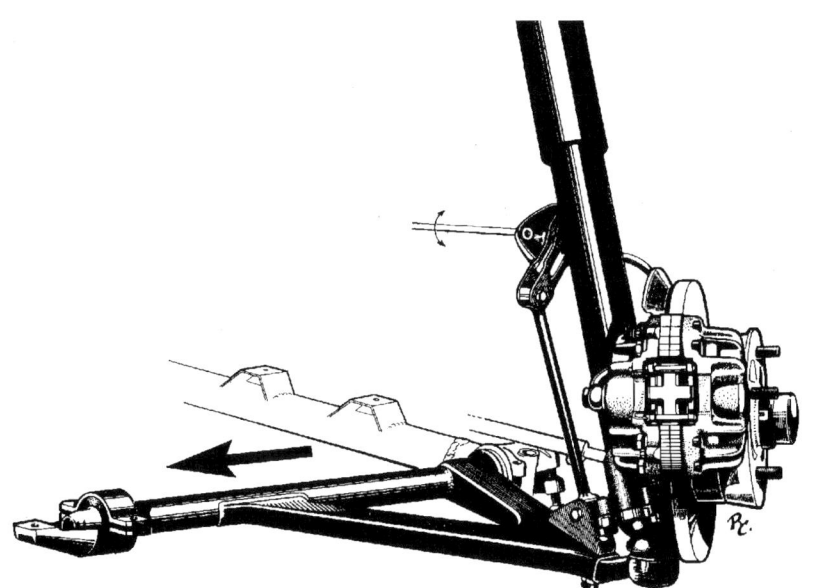

The front suspension, with its longitudinal torsion bar and disc brake assembly.

the road of persuading ATE to design and produce a rear disc brake with a central drum for the handbrake. It was a very effective system and, in use on the 356, had proved itself capable of passing the German annual road safety test with little difficulty.

The body design of the 911/912 followed the structural fundamentals of the 356, in that it had a substantial floorpan with strong peripheral sill members, but it was not a chassis with a body attached. This was a unitary construction design and, for its weight, was immensely strong. As experience showed, it did bring its own problems, like all the little nooks and crannies capable of retaining moisture, which led in the longer term to rust problems on a fairly serious scale, but more of that later. The appearance of the body brought accolades from far and wide. It certainly was a major step forward in Porsche styling and justifiably earned its stylist all the praise he received. Even thirty years later, the Porsche 911 was regarded as a symbol of brilliance in design.

Since the company had created a 'Targa' open-top car as a 911, it made sense to produce a similar version of the 912. So, as the production of the 356 was brought to its official end in September 1965, the Targa was announced at the Frankfurt Show, though it was another year before the car went into production as a 1967 model. The styling was quite ingenious, for it had to provide an open car, whilst compensating the structure for the lack of a roof. The solution came from the racing regulations in the United States, where rollover bars were called for in competition cars.

Butzi Porsche had originally wanted to change the whole back end, but was overruled on the grounds of cost. So, to substitute for a roof, a wide and substantial rollover bar was fitted, conferring considerable rigidity to the shoulders of the remainder of the car's structure. A rigid roof panel, clipped to the windscreen header at the front and to the rollover bar at its rear edge, together with a zip-out soft plastic rear window, was combined with wind-up

Model: Porsche Type 912 – 1965

Construction	Pressed steel fabricated and welded chassis platform with unitary steel coupé or 'Targa' bodywork
ENGINE	Type 616/36 (1600)
Crankcase	Light alloy with cylinders having Biral sliding surfaces
Cylinder head	Light alloy with inserted valve guides and seats
Cyls/Type	Four, horizontally opposed
Compression	9.3:1
Cooling system	Air, with finned cylinder barrels and belt-driven fan
Bore & Stroke	82.5mm × 74mm (3.2 × 2.9in)
Capacity	1,582cc (96.5cu in)
Main bearings	Plain bearings throughout
Valves	Two overhead per cylinder, pushrod actuation
Fuel supply	Mechanical pump/two Solex 40PJJ-4 carburettors
Power output	90bhp @ 5,800rpm
Ignition system	Coil and distributor with auto advance/retard
Lubrication	Wet sump, gear pump and oil cooling (magnetic filter)
BRAKES	
Type	ATE discs all round
TRANSMISSION	Porsche five-speed synchro and reverse (four-speed optional), ZF differential
Clutch type	Single dry plate
Gear ratios	1 = 13.682:1, 2 = 7.815:1, 3 = 5.003:1, 4 = 3.609:1 – R = 15.764:1
Final drive ratio	4.428:1 standard
SUSPENSION/STEERING	
Front suspension	McPherson Strut with longitudinal torsion bars and telescopic shocks
Rear suspension	Transverse torsion bars/two trailing arms/telescopic shocks
Steering type	ZF rack and pinion with centre-point connection
Wheels	Pressed steel 4.5J × 15
Tyres	165 × 15 radial
DIMENSIONS	**Coupé**: / **Targa**:
Overall length	4,163mm / 4,163mm (162.4in)
Overall width	1,610mm / 1,610mm (62.8in)
Overall height	1,320mm / 1,320mm (51.5in)
Wheelbase	2,211mm / 2,211mm (86.2in)
Track (front)	1,337mm / 1,337mm (52.1in)
Track (rear)	1,317mm / 1,317mm (51.4in)
MODELS AVAILABLE	Coupé/Targa
TOP SPEED	115mph (185kph)

New Kids on the Block – The 912 and the 914

There was also a cabriolet version of the 912.

windows in the doors to close the car against inclement weather. In fine weather, the driver simply zipped out the rear window and unclipped the roof panel which, when not in use, was placed in the trunk at the front of the car. Perhaps slightly ironically, the one-hundred thousandth Porsche to be built left the Zuffenhausen factory on 21 December 1966 with the blue lamp, sirens and loud hailer of those little white cars marked 'Polizei'.

The 912S Under Test

One of the first magazines to try out the 912 was *Car and Driver* in the United States. Its opening byline was: 'It's expensive and not very fast so what's it got to offer? Good grief, it's a Porsche!' Tongue-in-cheek or not, the article goes on to tell us what it has to offer. For example, it had Quality, Comfort, Engineering, Workmanship, Status and Mystique, plus the rare pleasure of driving a true 'Gran Turismo'. Whilst not a full road test, *C&D*'s review gave its author sufficient 'taste' of the car to establish that the handling of this lower-priced Porsche was impeccable and the steering precise. It was considered a fine car and, whilst lacking the performance of its six-cylinder sibling, was judged a fine grand tourer.

Soon afterwards, an American journal called *Auto Topics* looked at the 911 and 912 Targas. Outlining the differences between the 911 and 912, the four-cylinder car was described as 'slightly tamer' than its sister. It went on to describe the general specification, but gave little indication of an opinion in road-test terms. Nonetheless, the reviewer offered the view that the Targa would be a sure success with the sports-car minded on the American scene.

Ian Fraser was the test reviewer for Australia's *Modern Motor* in the July 1967 issue. Mr Fraser borrowed a 912 coupé from Porsche Distributors of Melbourne and drove around the city for a while, deciding that this was not a town car, as it did not like congestion, though it neither oiled up nor overheated. Like an earlier *Modern Motor* tester, he took a passenger out of town on his road test, though he only covered 75 miles (120km). His 'highly nervous' passenger dozed peacefully while Fraser 'put away 75 miles in an hour during our test over some of the stretches of the Hume Highway on the New South Wales side'. In these conditions, no vices were found, although again the over-long clutch pedal travel was criticized, as it kept the driver's left leg in the air for too long.

New Kids on the Block – The 912 and the 914

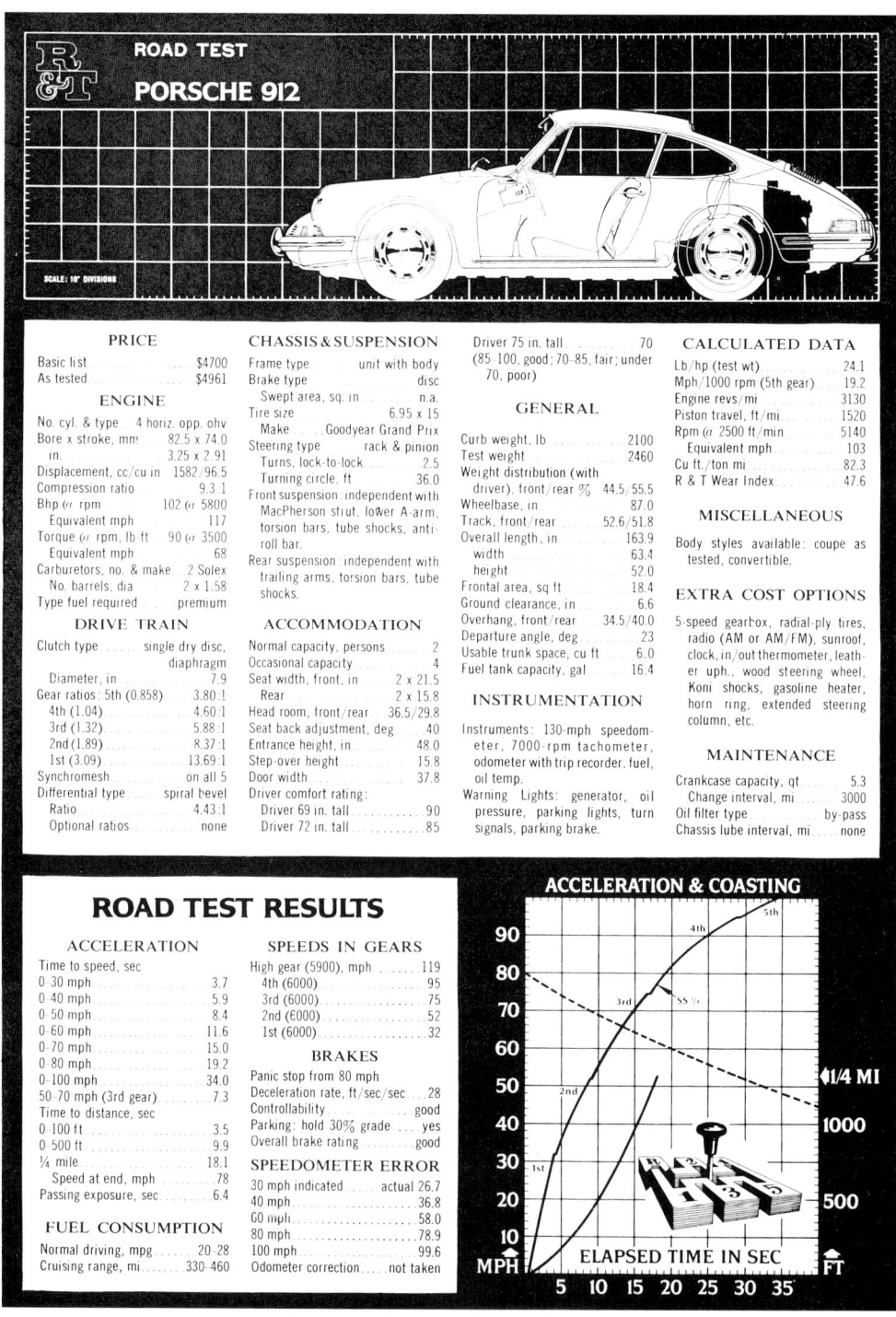

The Road & Track road-test data panel from February 1966.

New Kids on the Block – The 912 and the 914

Statistics of 22–30 miles (35–48km) per gallon combined with a 0–60mph (96khp) time of 11.2 seconds and a top speed of 116mph (186kph) made this car very attractive to its test driver. Whilst first gear was found to be a bit sticky and too far across the gate from the other four in the five-speed, Fraser found the ratios a delight and ideally suited to a Melbourne–to–Sydney at 80–90mph (128–144kph). It was found that a single stop sufficed for fuel, as the consumption neared 30 miles (48km) per gallon on that journey, even at the road speeds quoted. The tester's final quote was: 'At A$7,130, the Porsche 912 is not in the bargain price bracket, but good things rarely are!'

Finally, *Road Test* magazine took hold of a 912 and drove it out on road and track to conclude that the 912 was so superior in

By 1968, the '912' number on the engine cover had been lifted to a position just below the cooling grille and had changed to a block letter style. Inset is a view of the later, upgraded 912 interior.

the handling and cornering departments that it felt unlike a traditional Porsche at all. The tester did offer that the car would eventually reach the point of final, and conclusive, oversteer, but that point was so far beyond normal driving speeds that even the most enthusiastic Porsche driver would be unlikely ever to encounter it. *Road Test* was firm in its view that the 912 would outperform the Mercedes-Benz 250SL. Its style was described as like that of the 911 (naturally) and, with the five-speed gearbox, it was thought to be challenging and interesting to drive.

THE OTHER 'NEW KID', THE VW-PORSCHE 914

Sales of Volkswagen's Karmann-Ghia coupé had dropped and the VW company seemed to lack direction. Sales of Porsche cars were also dropping, because the 911 had proved to be a very expensive car. So Heinz Nordhoff, VW's chief executive, and Ferry Porsche, decided something had to be done. That 'something' was to introduce a sporty car into the VW/Porsche line-ups. It was a product of its time, in terms of technical specification and the business links which brought it about, for many companies in Europe were linking up to create a mid-engined sporting car after the huge success of Porsche's 904 Carrera GTS. In its time, that car had been the pinnacle of engineering and design technology, heralding the way ahead. Ferrari had then taken up the challenge and built the Dino 206GT, which had an engine manufactured by Fiat. Then, Lotus formed links with Renault for an engine to power its Europa. So Porsche and Volkswagen began their dialogue to create a volume-produced, mid-engined sporting car. That car was the 914.

The outcome of the early discussions was that Ferry Porsche and Heinz Nordhoff struck a deal in which Porsche would produce a mid-engined sports car to be sold through both manufacturers' dealer networks and to be powered by a version of the new Volkswagen engine developed for its 411 model. Essentially, this new model had to be able to be sold as a Volkswagen, yet not look like any Volkswagen built before, and also to be sold as a Porsche, while not resembling any previous Porsche in appearance either. So it was decided to approach a design studio named Gugelot Design GmbH, based at Neu-Ulm, about 80km (50 miles) from Stuttgart. Gugelot was not a car styling studio, but had already done some work in the field of reinforced plastic car bodywork with BMW.

Butzi Porsche stayed close to Gugelot as they progressed the design and, by early 1968, test examples were out on the road in both VW-engined and Porsche-engined forms. The shape of this new car was certainly different from anything either VW or Porsche had produced before. It had that squareness of style that bred such cars as the MGB, the Triumph TR4 and the Datsun Fairlady. It brought something of Porsche with it in the Targa top, though that feature was discreet enough not to scream 'Porsche' at everyone who looked at it. In size, it was shorter, wider and lower than the contemporary 911 and possessed a clean and simple line that could not offend either VW or Porsche enthusiasts.

Gugelot had concluded that a wheelbase of 2,450mm (95.5in) was essential to accommodate the mid-engined concept and to give adequate space for the 914's two occupants. Greater width gave better servicing access and more elbow room, whilst lower height improved the car's drag coefficient to very near that of Porsche's 911. Particular styling features included substantial

New Kids on the Block – The 912 and the 914

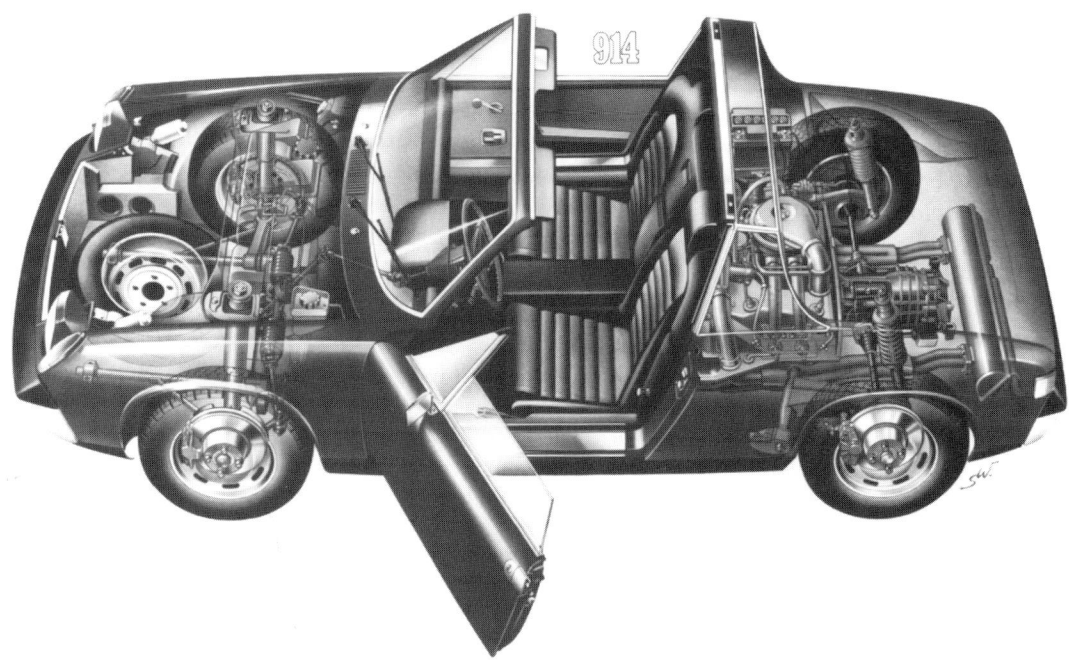

'Looking through' the VW-Porsche 914/4 in this view, you can see how the weight distribution was achieved, using the mid-engined configuration.

The twin luggage compartments of the 914 were really more of a novelty than practical facility.

New Kids on the Block – The 912 and the 914

The front and rear suspension of the 914 models. The front unit was 'borrowed' from the 912, except for the lack of an anti-roll bar.

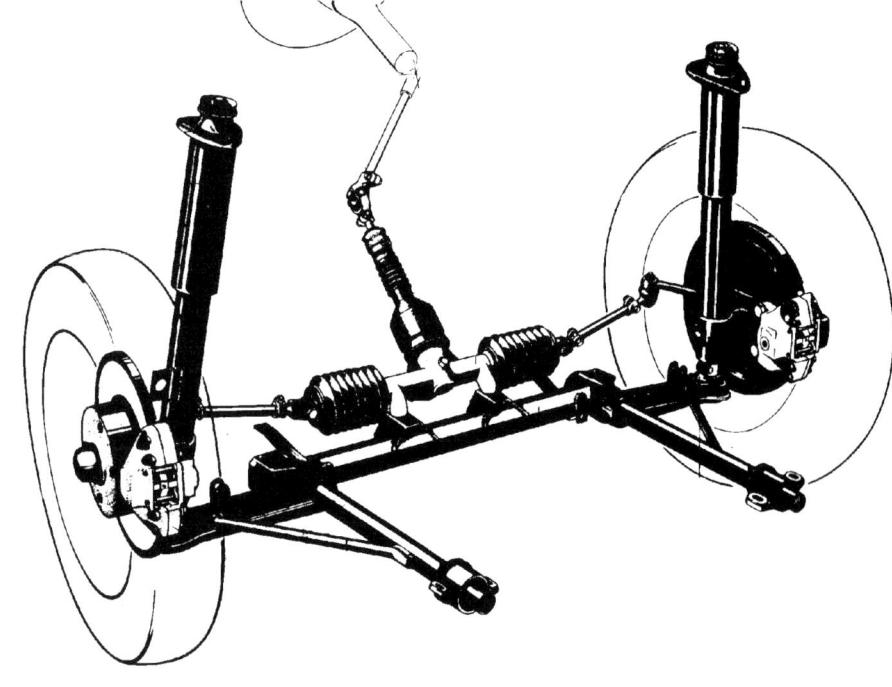

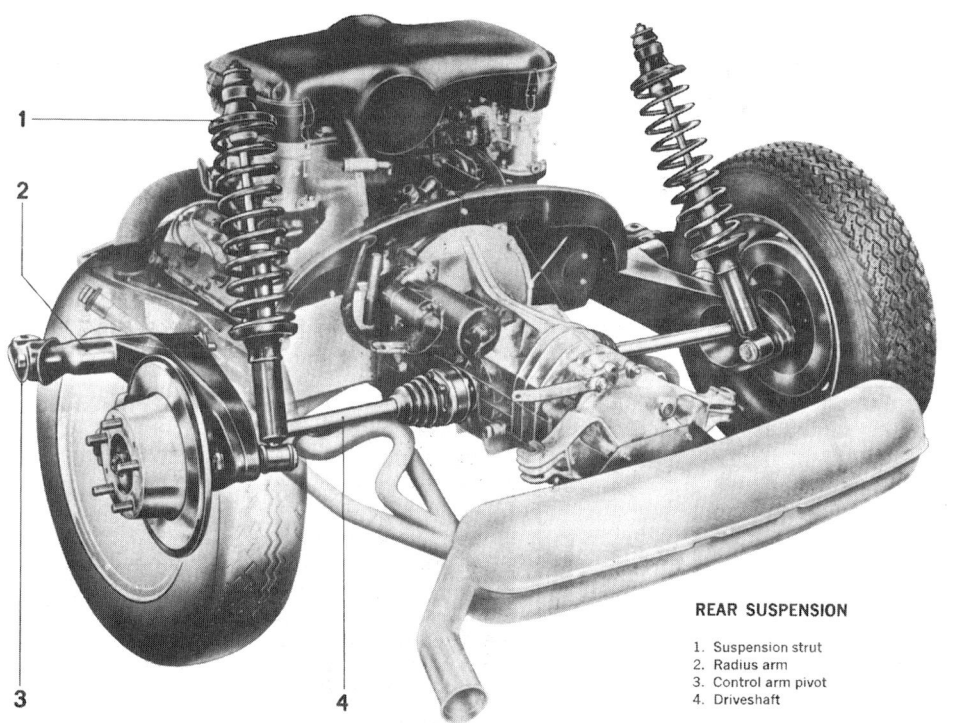

REAR SUSPENSION
1. Suspension strut
2. Radius arm
3. Control arm pivot
4. Driveshaft

Model: Porsche Type 914/4 – 1969

Construction	Pressed steel fabricated and welded chassis platform with unitary steel 'Targa' bodywork
ENGINE	Type W-80 mid-mounted
Crankcase	Light alloy with individual separate cylinders
Cylinder head	Light alloy with inserted valve guides and seats
Cyls/Type	Four, horizontally opposed
Compression	1700 = 8.2:1, 1800 = 7.3:1, 2000 = 7.6:1
Cooling system	Air, with finned cylinder barrels and belt-driven fan
Bore & Stroke	90mm × 66mm (3.5 × 2.6in)/93mm × 66mm (3.6 × 2.6in)/94mm × 71mm (3.7 × 2.7in)
Capacity	1,679cc/1,795cc/1,971cc (102.4/109.5/120.2cu in)
Main bearings	Plain bearings throughout
Valves	Two overhead per cylinder, pushrod actuation
Fuel supply	Mechanical pump/two Solex 40PJJ-4 carburettors
Power output	90bhp @ 5,800rpm/92bhp @ 5,800rpm/91bhp @ 4,900rpm
Ignition system	Coil and distributor with auto advance/retard
Lubrication	Wet sump, gear pump and oil cooling (magnetic filter)
BRAKES	
Type	Dual circuit discs all round
TRANSMISSION	Porsche Type 914/11 five-speed synchro and reverse (four-speed optional)
Clutch type	Single dry plate
Gear ratios	4sp: 1 = 10.627:1, 2 = 8.369:1, 3 = 4.605:1, 4 = 4.103:1 – R = 13.846:1
Final drive ratio	4.428:1 standard
SUSPENSION/STEERING	
Front suspension	Longitudinal torsion bars with triangulated links to telescopic shocks
Rear suspension	Oscillating wishbones with coil springs and telescopic shocks
Steering type	Centre-point rack and pinion
Wheels	Pressed steel 5.5J × 15
Tyres	155 × 15 or 165 × 15 radial
DIMENSIONS	**Roadster (Targa):**
Overall length	4,050mm (157.9in)
Overall width	1,650mm (64.4in)
Overall height	1,230mm (47.9in)
Wheelbase	2,450mm (95.6in)
Track (front)	1,337mm (52.1in)
Track (rear)	1,374mm (53.6in)
MODELS AVAILABLE	Roadster (Targa top)
TOP SPEED	110mph (177kph)

bumpers front and rear which were capped by large foam core self-skinning polyurethane to minimize the effects of impact. The vehicle's licence plate was carried on both bumpers and the front one also housed a pair of driving lamps. Porsche had never used pop-up headlamps, but this new car featured them, with individual motors to raise and lower them, even through a coating of ice if necessary.

There were two storage compartments on the 914, one at the rear of the car and one in front, in the traditional location for Porsche and VW. The detachable plastic roof panel was stored in the rear compartment when removed, whilst the front one housed the spare wheel, as well as the fuel tank, which was sandwiched between two bulkheads. A firewall behind the cockpit separated the passengers from the engine and another kept the contents of the rear trunk safe. The rear compartment was secured by an external lock and catch, whilst access to the front one was gained by a 'T' handle located under the dashboard. The 13-Imperial gallon (59 litre) fuel tank sat across the front trunk area and was filled by raising the front hood.

It has to be said from the outset that this new car was never intended to replace a Porsche in performance terms. It was intended to provide a lower entry level to the wonders of Porsche, as well as creating a new market level for Volkswagen. So it follows that the 1,679cc VW engine would be carefully prepared for the job it was about to undertake. Fuel-injected, the VW 411 unit produced 85bhp and 87 pounds feet of torque which, when coupled to the five-speed gearbox, ran up to 110mph (176kph). The 914's 0–60mph (96kph) time compared favourably with such cars as the MGB at 13 seconds, but of course was not up to the 912.

The suspension of the 914 was a case of 'something old and something new', with the front suspension borrowed directly from the 911, whilst the rear was a semi-trailing arm and coil spring set up. Road wheels were 4.5J × 15s and the tyres were 155 × SR15 radials. Stopping power was exceptional for such a car, with ATE discs all round, vented discs in front and solid to the rear. The handbrake was a clamping type caliper on the rear discs, unlike the 911/912 rear brakes with drums incorporated into the rear discs, but production cost was a consideration.

For Volkswagen, the 914 worked very well. It gave a lift to the failed Karmann-Ghia market and established a new model, the like of which had not previously been seen in the VW product range. It also opened up a whole new arena for the expansion of the Volkswagen product range. That expansion was to grow beyond all imagination, finally leaving behind the immortal 'Beetle' and even eventually the air-cooled engine.

THE 914 AND THE MOTORING PRESS

Once again, it was *Car and Driver* that got in first in the United States with a 'preview road test' of the 914 and its larger-engined sibling, the 914/6 (the 914/6 was powered by the 2-litre flat-six Porsche engine, so is not covered within these pages). David Phipps, of *C&D*, thought the 914 was not the finest example of automotive styling, though it clearly was able to perform. Handling was found to be remarkably even-handed, with little sign of Porsche's old breakaway habit on the limit. The front Macpherson struts did their job well and the weight distribution did a lot of the rest. The ride quality and braking performance were praised and Mr Phipps was satisfied that the more-than-

New Kids on the Block – The 912 and the 914

The rear quarter of the 914 presented a clean and contemporary line, giving little indication of its mid-engined layout

$1,500 price gap between the 914 and the lower echelon pure Porsche, the 912, gave very good value for money.

The ideal conclusion to the 914 section of this Chapter is to take a look at a road test conducted by *Road & Track* magazine in the United States. It reviewed the 914 and 914/6 as these cars entered the US market in 1969 and spoke highly of both, but with the experience of 50,000 miles (80,000km) under his belt, David S Engle was able to offer a much more objective view of this little roadster. Mr Engle sold his 50,000-mile Volvo in 1972 and bought a 914 from Jones Porsche in Springfield, Massachussets. He relates how he drove the car four blocks from the dealership and the engine died. But his dealer had a conscience and turned out to solve the problem which, it seems, was two corroded fuse contacts in the fuel injection system (how do you get two corroded fuses in a new car?).

Mr Engle explained that he sometimes changed plugs and oil himself and did the odd minor adjustment, too, which implied that he did not always take his car back to the dealership for regular servicing. That was probably after the warranty period had expired, for in 1972 the fuel injection gave up the ghost. Jones Porsche replaced the faulty part under the warranty (which they would not have done if the car had not been maintained according to the manufacturer's schedule. The problem had shown up as an idling fault which adjustment would not eliminate.

Over the 50,000-mile life, the 914 had turned in an average 30 miles (40km) per US gallon which, at almost 38 (60km) per Imperial gallon, was a pretty good average. Oil consumption after 30,000 miles (48,000km) was about half a pint per thousand miles (1,600km). Given that Mr Engle would have preferred the extra tread of 165 × 15 Michelins, the 155 ZXs apparently

New Kids on the Block – The 912 and the 914

gave excellent grip through the winter of 1970 without ever needing the additional confidence of chains in the snow. Having changed his tyres to 165s, no comment was offered about the effect on steering, which must have been heavier, but obviously not heavy enough to give a handling problem.

The two criticisms that arose were not serious. The first was the radio, which was dealer fitted and was not particularly happy on FM wavelength. A Blaupunkt would, in the opinion of Mr Engle, have been much better able to satisfy that problem. The other thing was the small panel which lay below the silencer at the rear of the car. In the winter, it acted as a snow shovel and became bent, so he removed it in the winter and replaced it after the snows cleared. One other fault which was frustrating but not a major problem was the nylon pulley around which the clutch cable travelled on its way from the pedal to the clutch withdrawal arm. It, being nylon, collected dirt and clogged up, causing the clutch pedal to be lumpy in action. But a clean up with kerosene soon solved the problem.

All in all, Mr Engle thought that Porsche service facilities were too remote to be convenient, especially after he moved to north Connecticut. Even so, his car had cost him an average seven cents a mile over the whole fifty thousand, which was a pretty satisfying level of cost for a sporty two-seater. It was a car which was easy and enjoyable to drive for reviewer and wife, and was strongly recommended to anyone who was looking for an economical two-seater sports car – certainly more than comparable with any of the other similar sized European sports cars on offer in the United States at that time.

The 912E bodyshell was externally identical to the 'H' Series 911s, except for the road wheels, and was the stop-gap between the 914/4 and the new 924 front-engined car that was to be the next four-cylinder Porsche.

Model: Porsche Type 912 E – 1975/76

Construction	Pressed steel fabricated and welded chassis platform with unitary steel coupé bodywork
ENGINE	Type 923 (2000)
Crankcase	Light alloy with individual separate cylinders
Cylinder head	Light alloy with inserted valve guides and seats
Cyls/Type	Four, horizontally opposed
Compression	7.6:1
Cooling system	Air, with finned cylinder barrels and belt-driven fan
Bore & Stroke	94mm × 71.1mm (3.7 × 2.8in)
Capacity	1,971cc (120.2cu in)
Main bearings	Plain bearings throughout
Valves	Two overhead per cylinder, pushrod actuation
Fuel supply	Electric pump, Bosch L-Jetronic fuel injection
Power output	90bhp @ 4,900rpm
Ignition system	Coil and distributor with auto advance/retard
Lubrication	Wet sump, gear pump and oil cooling (magnetic filter)
BRAKES	
Type	Self-vented discs all round
TRANSMISSION	Porsche 923/02 five-speed synchro and reverse (four-speed Sportomatic optional)
Clutch type	Single dry plate
Gear ratios	1 = 13.682:1, 2 = 7.815:1, 3 = 5.003:1, 4 = 3.609:1 – R = 15.764:1
Final drive ratio	4.428:1 standard
SUSPENSION/STEERING	
Front suspension	McPherson Strut with longitudinal torsion bars and telescopic shocks
Rear suspension	Transverse torsion bars/two trailing arms/telescopic shocks
Steering type	ZF rack and pinion with centre-point connection
Wheels	Pressed steel 4.5J × 15
Tyres	165HR × 15 radial
DIMENSIONS	Coupé:
Overall length	4,291mm (167.3in)
Overall width	1,610mm (62.8in)
Overall height	1,320mm (51.5in)
Wheelbase	2,211mm (86.2in)
Track (front)	1,337mm (52.1in)
Track (rear)	1,317mm (51.4in)
MODELS AVAILABLE	Coupé
TOP SPEED	119mph (192kph)

New Kids on the Block – The 912 and the 914

LAST OF A LINE – THE 912E, PORSCHE'S FINAL FLAT-FOUR

Production of the 914 came to an end in 1976 and the new generation four-cylinder Porsche, the front-engined 924, would not be ready for release for another year, which left a gap in Porsche's entry-level market. Fearful that this could cause damage to sales, the company took a most unexpected step by reintroducing a 912, the 912E. 'E' represented 'Einspritzmotor', or fuel-injection engine, that engine being essentially a 914 2-litre unit, but modified and developed by Porsche. The 912E was to be offered for the 1976 model year only and primarily to the US market.

The engine retained the 94mm × 71mm (3.7 × 2.8in) bore and stroke, the Volkswagen 411 engine much modified now to power a 'G' Series 911 chassis/body unit. The fuel-injection system used was the Bosch L-Jetronic, with a manifold sensor to provide additional monitoring of fuel feed and an air pump with two thermal reactors to control emissions. As with the 914 2-litre, compression was down to 7.6:1, but with a carefully profiled camshaft, this gave 90bhp at 4,900rpm and 93 pounds feet of torque at 4,000rpm. These figures endowed the 912E with a surprisingly good set of performance figures. For example, *Car and Driver* reported a 0–60mph (96kph) time of 9.6 seconds, and a top speed of their test car of 111mph (178kph), though other periodicals, including *Road & Track* came up with 115mph (184kph).

There were differences, of course, between the 912E and the 'G' Series 911, all aimed at keeping the price down to a realistic level for entry into the Porsche market. For example, the brakes had solid discs front and rear, the wheels were pressed steel discs, rather than the Fuchs cast alloys so familiar on the 911. Tyres were 165HR × 15 and there was no anti-roll bar at the rear. Inside, the seats, door trims and carpets were a little less plush and the rear quarter lights were fixed, opening types being available as an option. Critics were not too happy with the softer suspension, suggesting that pitch and roll were present, but generally the 912E was well received by the market and some 2,099 were built, commencing in 1975 for the 1976 model year. It was to be the least rust-prone flat-four Porsche ever built, but more of that in the next Chapter.

12 Enjoying a Flat-Four Porsche and Viewing its Competitors

Why in Heaven's name would you want to invest your hard-earned savings in an old rust-bucket of a 356 when you could buy a much newer 911 model for probably less money? Well, enthusiasts are a determined breed and if they decide they want to restore a rusting hulk just for the pleasure of sampling the dubious driving qualities of a car built forty-odd years ago, then they will spend their fortune and smile.

Quite often, the reason someone chooses a particular make of car as his or her favourite is the charisma generated by the maker in that car's original era. Certainly, the Porsche has a great deal of charisma. In the beginning, much of that came from a perception of the Porsche company having 'risen out of the ashes', something it almost literally experienced. The hardships and deprivation endured by both family and company in the early days at Gmünd took their toll, but there was a charisma to the emergence of the first 356 and, of course, it was immediately added to by Herbert Kaes' success in the Runt un dem Hofgarten. Without that Class win on the car's first competitive outing and the press it enjoyed, the name 'Porsche' may never have come to represent one of the world's greatest car manufacturers.

Nostalgia is, of course, the greatest driving force in most people's quest to own and enjoy an old car – or an old anything else, for that matter. There is a desire to enjoy something of the car's history, even past glory, that motivates the enthusiast. At the very least, it is a desire not to let that past glory die. And what is wrong with that? People spend millions on paintings, sculptures, books, items of jewellery and bric-a-brac, all in the name of preserving art, culture and history. In the approach to the twenty-first century, the automobile represents a larger part of our culture and history than perhaps any other single item – and it can be enjoyed in a living way. That's why you'd want to invest your hard-earned money into a 356, a 912 or a 914.

THE CASE FOR THE FLAT-FOUR

But be under no illusions. The flat-four Porsche first acquired a position in the classic market place because, like most other sporting cars, at a certain age the depreciation was such that it became a cheap car. At that point, it was often not the enthusiast for the make that bought it, but someone who wanted an inexpensive car as a daily runabout and thought this Porsche, a car they'd heard about but never driven, would be fun. The quirks of its driving habits would be learned about later, but for now it was seen as a reliable machine (how could it be anything else, as its mechanical bits were based on the VW

Enjoying a Flat-Four Porsche and Viewing its Competitors

Here we see an early application of underbody coating on a Porsche. The picture was actually taken at the Reutter body plant in the very early 1950s.

Beetle?) with a little 'something' about it. Isn't that how most of us came into the old car movement?

The case, then, for the flat-four Porsche is largely that it is a potentially reliable form of transport. Oily sometimes and perhaps a little noisy, but reliable – and different. Its reliability comes largely from the experience of the Volkswagens produced for military use in World War II. As this little car evolved, developments were always made with the preservation of that reliability in mind. Porsche knew well, from its earliest days, that a temperamental car would not contribute to their corporate growth, or even survival.

The next important aspect of owning and enjoying a flat-four Porsche is that it is fairly simple in most things (unless you acquire a quad-cam engined car, which is another experience altogether). It has a pushrod operated overhead valve system; it has individually detachable cylinder barrels; it does not suffer from all the usual faults of liquid-cooled engines, like cracked cylinder blocks in the winter because you forgot to put anti-freeze into the radiator – there is no radiator, except for the oil cooler. In fact, its only major foible is that most of its routine maintenance adjustments have to be done from underneath the car. This makes it a little more awkward than most conventional cars. But you did not buy a Porsche to be conventional, did you?

Porsche's synchromesh is internationally renowned and many other car makers have taken licences to use the blocking ring system in their gearboxes, recognizing that it not only makes for easier gear shifting, but helps to preserve the life of the gearbox itself. From the early 1950s, Porsches have had easier-to-use gearboxes than many more expensive cars. Indeed, they have been the envy of many other sporting cars down the years.

So what do you look for in your flat-four Porsche today? Chances are that most people reading this are looking at a 356 as their target purchase and the chassis area is the first place to look for trouble. Sadly, like almost all cars of the period, Classic Era Porsches are rust-boxes, because few manufacturers had spent much time considering the problems of corrosion resistance and body protection. Much of the reason for that was because the buying public had not yet made its presence felt and pressures had not been brought to bear to make cars last longer. Also, there was no particular interest on the part of many manufacturers in spending large sums of money on such research, as the process of making cars last longer might mean less cars were sold.

CHECKING YOUR CHOSEN PORSCHE

The 356 chassis was a well constructed unit, but it did have the capacity to collect moisture, and when Porsche began to apply an underbody coating to their cars it was done with the intention of preserving chassis life and to act as a sound deadener. However, unwittingly, it actually helped the decay process, as it dried out and cracked, then allowed water into the cracks and the resulting long-term moisture went to work on the oxidation process – rust to you and me – so corroding the structure. Therefore, take a very careful look underneath your prospective purchase to make sure there's enough metal left to repair, because there will almost certainly be some repair work to do.

After you've examined the chassis area, start checking over the body itself. It's very doubtful you'll be looking at one of the Gmünd cars, so the problems of alloy and steel corrosion at their interface is not an issue here. But rust in a 356 is a major issue. We have to remember that, whatever we do to stop the advancement of rust, we cannot convert the corroded metal back to strong metal. So the best we can hope to achieve with 'rust-proofers' or 'rust-killers' is to halt the process. Then we have to reinforce the decayed metal, which can be done by putting in new metal or using a substitute such as fibreglass. But beware of fibreglass, because the bond to metal is not going to be permanent, as even Porsche discovered with the 904GTS.

Floor panels rust, sills (or rocker panels) rust, battery boxes rust, door shut panels rust and so do the inner and outer wings (or fenders). The candidate for purchase of a 356 needs to check all these areas. Most can be repaired, but you need to be sure to clean out all the rust and weld in new parts to clean metal, then treat it with almost anything except a bitumen coating, because that is where a lot of these problems began. Another area that needs to be looked at is around the windscreen, the pillars in particular, but also across the top, as some cars display rust here, often when a windscreen has been replaced and the rubber seal has not been fitted back as it should, exposing

This was the author's 1965 356SC. A pretty car at first glance, but the slight blemish just to the right of the lower right quarter of the engine cover gives the game away. The rear wings (fenders) were rusting from the inside, though were caught in time. The other fault manifested in this car and not uncommon in others was the rusting of the windscreen header, just above the screen itself, caused by a badly fitted seal when the glassware was replaced.

metal to moisture. So, before parting with your money, recognize that there'll be work to do, often even on a quite sound-looking car, and check that the work you need to do can be carried out within a reasonable budget – or walk away and look for another car.

CHECKING THE BITS THAT ROTATE

The bits of a Porsche that rotate include, of course, the suspension. So we'll start there. Most suspension bits of a 356 are either replaceable or capable of renovation, but the first thing you need to look at is the mountings for them, including the torsion bars, because weak supports will do nothing to improve the handling of the car, even after you've reconditioned the parts. Also, if suspension mountings have weakened and flexed, then the chances are the components themselves have worn more than they otherwise might have. More cost, unless you're very careful. The problem is that a 356 can look almost concours from the outside and be pretty weak on the inside.

Remember that the torsion bar suspension was borrowed from the Volkswagen, so there are many components which will be interchangeable and, since the Beetle was in production long after the 356 was discontinued, you may well be able to find a number of components in the VW parts bin which, as a spin-off benefit, may cost you less than the equivalent component in a Porsche box (though there are not many of those left now, anyway). Of course, across the world where the flat-four Porsche is appreciated, there are also specialists and specialist parts suppliers/makers who can keep your 356 on the road for a lot longer than you would have been able to even twenty years ago. And there are VW motor component makers and suppliers who offer a service to air-cooled Porsche owners, too. To this day, there are many small items, such as seals and rubber boots, which can be bought off the VW parts shelf and will go straight on to a 356. So look at these possibilities, having bought your Porsche and discovered it was worse than you thought (isn't that always the case?).

Far be it for me to recommend the sacrilegious step of replacing major components of a Porsche with those from a Volkswagen, but I do remember that when the oil cooler split on my 912 – and I did not pick it up until the damage was done – the price of a set of cylinder barrels and pistons (you can't buy one without the other) for the original 1,582cc engine was substantially more than the price of an equal quality (and material specification) set made for converting VW engines to larger sizes. So, I increased the displacement of my 912 to 1,679cc by the expedient of increasing the bore to 85mm (3.3in). It had a minimal effect on the performance of the car, but it was just discernible and the fuel consumption was hardly affected.

The point to make is that it is possible to modify without taking anything away from the Porsche character of the car, and these days, if it proves to be a way to keep the car on the road, then why not do it? For not only can it prove expensive to 'stick to principles', it may, in some cases, simply prove impossible. If you want to keep your Porsche on the road, it may often be possible only by looking into other people's parts bins and if that's the case, your choice falls between continuing to enjoy your Porsche or giving up the fight.

There are many excellent, well-skilled and equipped enthusiast workshops which specialize in flat-four Porsches about the world. The newcomer would be well advised to single out one of these and ask advice

Enjoying a Flat-Four Porsche and Viewing its Competitors

A Porsche 616/36 cylinder barrel and piston, showing the chrome lining of the bore. The rings have been removed from the piston for clarity of illustration.

on doubtful aspects of the car. The owner might even know the individual vehicle. On the other hand, advice that's often given and not always taken up is to join your local Porsche club. Somebody there may also know the particular car you're eyeing up or have just bought.

LOOKING AT THE 912

Of course, when you come to the 912, it's a different story – or is it? Whilst the bodyshell of the 912 was structurally very well engineered, the car still suffered from rust. Sills, door shuts and door panels were vulnerable, as was the rear end of the body, inboard of the rear wings, again where it was often difficult to see. Check the Macpherson strut upper mountings to ensure they are solid and check that the front end is in line. With rack and pinion steering, the 912 was very vulnerable to poorly repaired front end shunts. So pull the carpet out of the trunk and check the steelwork for any ripples that should not be there. When you've satisfied yourself that the body is as good as you're going to get, buy the car, because the 912 is most of the fun of a 911 without the complication and horrifying cost (I know, I've had both).

The engine components of the 912 are much the same as those of the 356SC and so the comments about both engines apply equally. Most importantly, you need to ensure your oil cooler has no leaks. The most irritating aspect of owning any pushrod-engined Porsche is the awful little pool of oil that lies underneath the car to tell you that the pushrod tube oil seals have cooked so hard they no longer seal. You can ignore it for a while and tolerate the oil patch, while topping up the engine oil, or you can do something about it – and the latter step is the best one, because the problem will only get worse and one day you'll forget the oil and do serious damage.

In both the 912 and 356, one perennial problem is that virtually all your engine maintenance has to be done from underneath the car, but you can console yourself that at least you can see most of the problems as they occur, or simply turn over the maintenance to a specialist. In many places, Porsche dealers will still take pride in maintaining older cars, but you need to check your bank balance before you go there because, while there are published charges, they might well be quite a lot more than a genuinely skilled, probably ex-Porsche, mechanic can do for you in his little shop on the street corner.

Drive shafts on the earlier 912 are a potential problem. The originals were made by Nadella and have an extendable universal joint on their inner ends. As long as those universal joints are in good condition, they're fine, but when they fail, they fail quite quickly and are likely now to be much more difficult to recondition. Later cars were fitted with shafts that have Lohbro constant velocity joints in place of the older design. The CV joints are far more resilient than the Nadellas, but to convert from one

Enjoying a Flat-Four Porsche and Viewing its Competitors

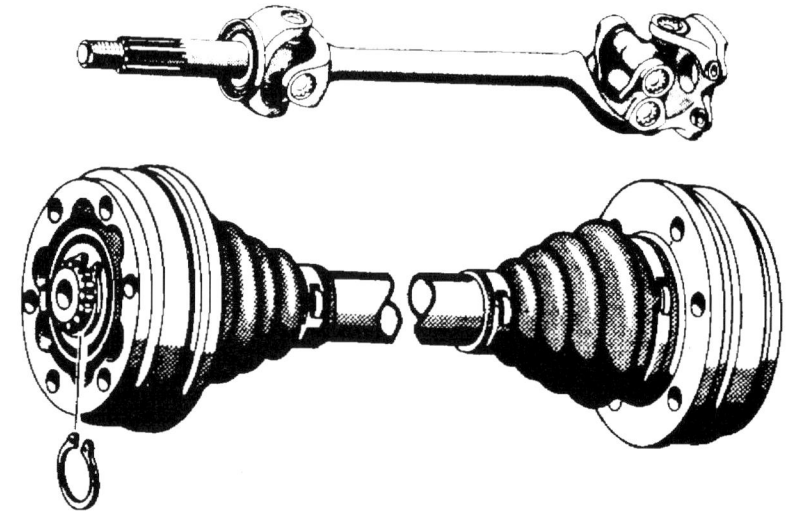

The Nadella drive shaft is the top one in this illustration. The Lohbro was fitted to later 912s and was by far the better choice.

type to the other means changing the hubs, a worthwhile expense if you intend to keep your 912 long term. One point about the Lohbro shafts, however, is that you absolutely must make regular inspections of the rubber boots at both ends of the Lohbro, as they hold in the grease to the joint and, if they split, will not only let out grease, but will let in grit and cause a failure. But if the boots are carefully checked and replaced immediately even the tiniest puncture is detected, the Lohbro shafts will last almost for ever.

For ride comfort and positive handling, it is most important to ensure that the Macpherson strut mounting bolts are checked for tightness and that the vertical movement of the strut is equal on both sides of the car. Check the rear shocks, too, because they can deteriorate and you won't know how badly until somebody takes a look at them. You probably will need professional help in making these checks, but it's an expense well worth incurring. One tip that was given to me many years ago was about front wheel balancing. With only 155 × 15 tyres on the road, well-balanced wheels can make a world of difference to the tyre's performance on the surface. If the wheel is out of balance, there is a constant lateral movement of the tyre which will wear it more quickly and reduce its adhesion to the road. For the minimal cost involved, it is worth having the wheels balanced in a proper wheel balancing shop on a regular basis. You may be surprised at the difference it will make to your enjoyment of your Porsche – to say nothing of prolonging the life of your tyres.

A LOOK OVER THE 914 AND THE 912E

The 914 was a different Porsche, with a VW engine and different rear suspension. The body of the 914 is, like all classic cars, the first place to look for damage from abuse and decay. Because the 914 was looked on as a 'cheap' Porsche, many found their way into the hands of 'young bloods' who would have bought any low-priced used sports car for a bit of fun and to impress the girls. Some bought old TRs, others old

MGs, or Alpines or Alfa Romeos. It often did not matter what the car was, as long as they could afford to buy it in the first place and as long as it was reasonably reliable and cheap to run. As reliability and low running cost were two features of the 914, so the car became very popular among the young.

Because the 914 was inexpensive to buy and run, it found itself the victim of some abuse, too. As a consequence, it can often be dents that need treatment as much as 'metal mouse' (rust). Those dents were quite frequently home-filled with body filler to save the effort, and higher cost, of pulling out the dents and finishing them properly. So, if you're going to do the restoration yourself, walk around the car with a magnet in your hand. If it clamps on to the bodywork, you're fine, but if it tries to grip but drops away, or fails to grip at all, look for filler and expect dents – or even filled holes. Checking for rust, look at the headlamp wells, the underbody (looking at floorboards), front and rear valances, lower edges of doors and the sills. All of these areas can be renovated and now there is a growing list of replacement panelwork being made by a number of specialists. These parts will seldom replace the originals directly and exactly, because they are made to a price and usually require a little careful 'working and fitting' to look right when they have been installed. But usually it's worth it.

The 912E is a slightly different animal, being the only flat-four Porsche to have had a seriously rust-inhibited body, in the 'H' Series 911-type bodyshell. These bodies were made from zinc-coated sheet metal, which enabled Porsche to offer a six-year rust penetration warranty in many parts of the world. So, whilst you can reasonably expect a 912E to be in potentially better shape than an earlier 912, you still need to take a careful look in the same areas as recommended for the original 912, because these cars today are over twenty years old and, with the best will in the world, Porsche's anti-corrosion warranty was not intended to cover twenty years!

THE MECHANICALS OF THE 914 AND THE 912E

The 'W-80' Series of Volkswagen flat-four engine, despite being a Porsche development of the 411 engine, remains relatively inexpensive to buy parts for and renovate. All three engine sizes were available in the 914: 1,700, 1,800 and 2,000, whilst only the 2,000 (Type 923) was installed in the 912E. The smaller displacement engines both used the same crankshaft of 66mm (2.6in) stroke, the bores of 90mm (3.5in) and 93mm (3.6in) providing the differences in size. The 2,000 had the largest, 94mm (3.66in), bore and 5mm (0.2in) more in the stroke, bringing it to 71mm (2.8in). Quite often, not-very-wealthy sporting types would take an 1,800 914 and put a few extra cubic centimetres into it by installing maximum oversize 2-litre pistons, bringing the bore to 95mm (3.7in) which, combining with the original 66mm stroke, brought the engine up to 1,871cc without the expense of a new crankshaft.

Talking of new crankshafts, there was one outfit in the United States a few years ago which offered a conversion crankshaft made by Okrasa, a drop-forged item fully machined and balanced, which increased the stroke of a 2-litre W80 engine to 80mm (3.1in). Combining this with a set of Mahle-made cylinder barrels and pistons which gave a bore of 97mm (3.78in) would raise the displacement to 2,365cc and, according to *VW & Porsche* magazine, would put the power up to around 180bhp with a few other modifications. These include reprofiling the camshaft, lightening, magnafluxing, polishing and balancing the connecting rods and fitting new big end bolts and nuts. A small addition was the inclusion of Allison electronic ignition. Alternatively, if you wanted to develop your engine on a smaller budget, you could use the 97mm Mahle pistons and barrels in combination with the standard crankshaft (remachined and balanced), standard con-rods suitably balanced and fitted with the replacement bolts and a milder cam profile to produce an engine of 2,187cc and probably 130–140bhp.

Imagine applying either of these treatments to the Type 923 engine of a 912E! The result would be an engine that provided, in 2,365cc form, a power curve quite similar to that of the 2.7–litre 911 as offered in the United States, with better weight distribution. The handling would have been startling, though reliability would have to be proven. But even the milder form of work on increasing to 2,187cc and using otherwise standard components in company with the Allison ignition and a replacement chip for the fuel-injection system would have made for an exciting car on a forty to fifty per cent increase in power. There is no doubt that the Porsche gearbox would have taken the extra strain and the Lohbro drive shafts were designed for 2.7 Carrera power (210bhp). Talking of Lohbro drive shafts brings to mind the suspension of the 912E which is, of course, essentially the same as the 912, so there is little point in by covering it all again.

The rear suspension of the 914 is a relatively orthodox trailing arm/coil spring Macpherson strut-type design. The arm needs to be checked for play at the pivot end and, if the bushings are worn, you're in for some replacement costs. It used to be that you would replace the whole arm, but these days you're looking at reconditioners. On the trailing end, where the hub is mounted, there is a taper roller bearing carrying the hub assembly. Regular maintenance and relatively low mileage will mean there's not much to be concerned about, but it's still worth a check. The drive shafts are Lohbro on the 914 and so relatively trouble-free, as long as the rubber boots are all right. Finally, park the car on level ground and check that the body sits parallel to the ground. If it doesn't, the chances are you have a weak spring, or shock absorber or both, so get them professionally checked and replace as necessary for the best ride. The

The MG TF Midget carried the banner for Abingdon's until 1955, though its successor, the MGA, was clearly the better adversary for the 356.

front suspension is much the same as that on the 912, with a Macpherson strut connected to an 'A' arm rotating on a longitudinal torsion bar, whilst steering is also like the 912, with centre-point rack and pinion steering.

LOOKING AT THE ADVERSARIES

Back in 1948, the Porsches, father and son, were not especially concerned with their potential competitors in a commercial sense, only in a sporting sense. Their prime target in those days was to build a car which met their own demanding criteria. The most popular small sports car around then was the MG TC Midget and a lot of pre-war small sports cars being brought back into use. Then came the MG TD and the Triumph TR2 from Britain, whilst Italy brought out the Alfa Romeo Giulietta and the Lancia Ardea and Aprilia. But by the 1950s, the picture had changed, as Europe awoke to a post-war prosperity and to the realization that the United States was a market just waiting to be supplied.

As Porsche developed the 1,300 and 1,500, so Great Britain brought forth the MG TF Midget, soon to be followed by the most exciting looking British sports car of the Fifties – the MGA. Elsewhere, Alfa Romeo brought out the Giulietta Sprint and Spyder as the 1,900 went into decline, Triumph had the TR2 and TR3 (though these were not 1,500s, they were inexpensive British sports cars). Lotus was beginning to appear, though its early sports cars, the Six and Seven, were crude and spartan. It was only when the Lotus Elite came on to the scene that they presented any real competition and then with an under 1,300 engine, though the performance was up to the Porsche, for as long as the early Elites could be kept going. And the Morgan Plus-Four was another potential competitor for the 1950s Porsche cabriolet, although not for the Speedster in anything but price.

By 1958, the Lotus Elite was the closest competitor to the 356 from Britain in terms of performance, with the MGA Twin Cam and Italy's Alfa Romeo Giulietta following up behind. The 2-litre Triumph TR3 cost less than the MGA and was more reliable, but the MGA's superb styling put it

Milan's answer to the Porsche line was the Alfa Romeo Sprint.

The Lotus Elite was a startling performer and could match the 356 with ease, but only on a good day, as it was not always as reliable as it might have been.

comfortably in contention, along with the Giulietta and the quite pretty Elite. However, only the Alfa Romeo was a match for the reliability of the Porsche, even though the German car cost so much more in Britain (the gap not being so wide in the US).

A couple of years later, the contest was hotting up, as the Sunbeam Alpine came on to the scene to take some of the lower end of the market share, whilst MG now had the MGA 1600, which was immensely more reliable than the Twin Cam and quite a bit cheaper, although not so quick, losing six mph (9.6kph) in the transition back to a pushrod engine. But it still had its good looks and it competed well on the track, and cost a lot less than the Porsche. The Lotus Elite, with its Climax FWE engine, had improved and was selling quite well by now, but Porsche had established its niche and its market was getting stronger.

MG recovered some of the Twin Cam's lost speed when it introduced the MGA 1600 Mark II, with 105mph (168kph) as its top, with a price tag roughly half that of the Porsche 356 Super 90 Cabriolet 1600. Alfa Romeo in the meantime had brought in the Giulia 1600 to replace the Giulietta, producing 109mph (174kph) against the Porsche's 115 (184), with a pretty comparable performance table on the way to that top speed. From Britain, Elva had entered the fray with their Courier, which was a fairly spartan, but quite rapid, sports car with few concessions to comfort (Elva, of course, was to try Porsche engines in their quest for performance on the track). Then Triumph came in with the TR4, still a 2-litre, but now capable of 110mph (176kph) on a budget. Lotus had, by this time, introduced the Elite Special Equipment (S/E) and lifted the top speed to 120mph (192kph) with a blistering set of times on the way.

As the 1970s unfolded, Porsche's four-cylinder machine was the 914/4, which did not quite have the performance of the last 356s or the 912. Triumph's GT6 was a nifty little car with good looks and a 100 plus (160 plus) top speed, a six-cylinder engine that was willing and reasonably economical and a price tag that was a snip. Datsun was, of course, now knocking at the door with the

Enjoying a Flat-Four Porsche and Viewing its Competitors

The MGA 1600 was an elegantly styled and much less expensive alternative to the Porsche 356 and though it did not quite have the same performance, it did have its own following.

240Z, though a much larger engine for its roughly $3,000. Alfa Romeo was now up to the 2000, in GTV and Spyder forms, whilst MG had fallen back with the slab-like MGB. Even so, both MG and Porsche had strong followings, but Lotus was building theirs and the new Europa was out, a mid-engined two-seater coupé of 1,558cc

Heir to the 'flat-four' heritage, and never a competitor to the Porsche line, was the Alfa Romeo Sprint. Developed along similar lines under the influence of an ex-Porsche engineer (Rudolf Hruska), the Alfa came from 1,300cc two-cam to 1,700cc quad-cam, though it was front engined and liquid cooled. Nonetheless, in its class one of the finest performers on the road, the Sprint was withdrawn from sale in 1989 and is itself now much sought after.

tweaked Renault power, turning in 117mph (187kph) for a lump less than the price of a 914/4.

1976 was the year and 912E was the car – in the States. The Datsun 280Z was a much bigger car for engine and car weight, but the price tag was well below the Porsche 912E. The Datsun was quicker, but did not match the fuel consumption and, of course, Porsche aficionados were not about to buy the new Nippon invader. The Triumph TR7 was a shadow of its predecessors, the Jensen Healey was quick, economical and relatively cheap, but was not going to beat a Porsche for image, weather-proofing or long-distance touring. Which left you with the Ford-engined TVR 3000M for performance and not too high a price tag (and not such good looks as the 912E), or the Lotus Esprit, another fibreglass-bodied fiery animal from Norfolk, which had a similar price tag to the 912E. It was reasonably comfortable, it had a very striking performance, up to 138mph (220kph) and up to 30 miles (48km) to the gallon, and was developing a following.

But, at the end of the day, you buy a Porsche for its unique qualities. The rear engine, the reliability and the sheer pleasure of owning something significantly different from the rest of the crowd. There really were only two other European cars that came anywhere near it for charisma and fun. They were the Alfa Romeo Giulietta (and Giulia) and the MGA. But if you want the engine behind you, not in front, then your choice is made. So enjoy it.

APPENDIX 1: THE FOUR-CYLINDER PORSCHE CHASSIS NUMBERS

This Appendix gives the Chassis Number groups in which all the flat-four Porsches were built, where possible. Information has come from the archives of Dr Ing h.c. F. Porsche GmbH & Co (with the kind help of Jurgen Barth) and from Porsche Cars Great Britain Limited (with the kind help of Angela Stacey). No absolute guarantee can be given as to the accuracy of these numbers, but they are as precise as the information available allows.

Model/type	Year	Chassis batch
356/001 (Gmünd) Roadster	1948	001
356/2 (Gmünd) coupé/cabriolet	1948	2.001 – 2.050 & 2.052
356-Alu (Gmünd) Aluminium coupé	1949	2.053 – 2.055
356 1100 coupé/cabriolet/sports coupé	1950	5001 – 5600
356 1100 coupé/sports coupé	1951	10001 – 10170
	1952	11126 – 12084
356 1300 coupé	1952	50001 – 50098
	1953	50099 – 53008
540 American Roadster	1951	No numbers available
356 1300 cabriolet	1951	10350 – 10432
356 1500 cabriolet	1951	10433 – 10469
	1951	10531 – 11125
	1952	12301 – 12387
356 1500S cabriolet	1952	15001 – 15116
356 1300/1300S cabriolet	1953	60001 – 61000
356 1500/1500S cabriolet	1953	
356 1300/1300A/1300S Speedster	1954	80001 – 80200
550–1500RS Spyder	1954	5500001 – 5500090
356A 1500GS de Luxe coupé	1955	12235 – 12387
	1955	53456 – 59090
	1955	55001 – 55390
356 1300 coupé	1955	53009 – 55000
356 1500/1500S Speedster	1955	80201 – 81900
356A 1300 coupé/1300S sports coupé	1955	55001 – 59090
356A 1600S sports coupé	1955	55001 – 55390
356A 1300S cabriolet/sports cabriolet	1955	61001 – 61499
356A 1500GS cabriolet	1955	61001 – 61892
356A 1600S cabriolet	1955	61001 – 61982
356A 1600/1600S Speedster	1955	81901 – 83691
	1957	83792 – 84922
Type 550A-1500RS Spyder	1956	550A0101 – 550A0144
356A 1300S coupé	1957	100001 – 101692
356A 1600 coupé	1957	101693 – 108917
356A 1500GS/1500GS-GT coupé	1957	58312 – 59090
356A 1600S/1600 cabriolet	1957	61500 – 61892
356A 1600GS/1600GS-GT Speedster	1958	84938 – 85886
356A 1600S/1600 cabriolet	1958	150001 – 152475
356A 1600GS/1600GS-GT cabriolet	1958	104524 – 106174
356B 1600GS-GT coupé		
356A 1600S convertible	1958	85501 – 86830
356A 1600GS/1600GS-GT coupé	1958	150001 – 153334
Formula Two Type 718 single seater	1958	718201 – 718204
Type 718-1500RSK Spyder	1958	718001 – 718034
356B 1600/1600S-90 Roadster	1959	86831 – 89483
Type 718 RS 60/718 RS 61 Spyder	1959	718051 – 718078
356B 1600 coupé	1959	108916 – 117476
	1961	118951 – 125239
356B 1600S cabriolet	1959	152476 – 155569
Formula Two Type 718/787 single seater	1960	718205
Monoposto Formula Two Type 787	1960	78701 – 78702
356B 1600GTL Abarth coupé	1960	11001 – 11021
Type 718 RS 61 coupé Le Mans/718 (62) Spyder	1961	718044 – 718047
356B 1600S coupé	1961	117601 – 118950
356B 2000GS coupé	1961	119289 – 121099
356B 1600/1600-90/1600S-90 cabriolet	1961	155601 – 158700
	1961	89601 – 89849
356B 1600S-90 K-hard top	1961	200001 – 201048
356B 1600S/1600-90 K-hard top	1961	201601 – 202299
Formula One Grand Prix Type 804	1961	80401 – 80404
3568 1600S/1600-90 K-hard top	1961	201601 – 202299
3668 1600S-90 K-coupé	1962	210001 – 214400
356C 1600C coupé	1963	126001 – 131930
356C 1600C K-coupé	1963	215001 – 222579
356C 1600SC cabriolet	1963	159001 – 162165
356C 2000GS coupé	1963	119289 – 125239
	1963	156566 – 158700
904-6/904-8 competition coupé	1964	904001 – 904006
904GTS competition coupé	1964	904007 – 904106
912 1600 coupé	1965	350001 – 351970
912 16QQ K-coupé	1965	450001 – 461140
912 1600 coupé	1966	351971 – 354000
	1966	354001 – 354970
912 1600K-coupé	1966	454470 – 458100
	1966	458101 – 461140
912 1600 K-coupé	1967	461141 – 463204
912 1600 coupé	1967	354971 – 355601
912 1600 Targa	1967	550001 – 550544
912 1600 K-coupé	1968	12800001 – 12805598
	1968	129020001 – 129023450
912 1600 coupé	1968	12820001 – 12820427
	1968	12900001 – 12900428
912 1600 Targa	1968	12870001 – 12871217
	1968	129010001 – 129010801
914.4 1.7 coupé	1969	4702900001 – 4702913312
914.4 1.7 coupé	1970	4712900001 – 4712916231
914.4 1.7 coupé	1971	4722900140 – 4722921580
914.6 2.0 coupé	1971	9142430001 – 9142430240
914.4 1.7 coupé	1972	4732900001 – 4732927660
914.4 1.7 coupé	1973	4742900001 – onwards
912E 2.0 coupé	1975	9126000001 – 9126002099

APPENDIX 2: PORSCHE TYPE NUMBERS

Type	Year	Design item	Type	Year	Design item
7	1930/31	Wanderer 1.86-litre chassis (first Porsche office design)	116	1938/39	KdF-backed 1.5-litre racing car with Type 114 components
8	1930/31	Wanderer 3.25-litre chassis	120	1940	Volkswagen engine as generator power unit
9	1930/31	Supercharged version of Type 8	121	1940	Volkswagen stationary engine
12	1932	Zundapp 'People's Car' prototype	122	1940	Volkswagen stationary engine with battery ignition
22	1932/37	Auto Union GP car			
30	1933	Prototype for Volkswagen 'Beetle' – 30 built	124	1940/41	Modification of Kübelwagen for use on railway tracks
32	1933	NSU prototype 'People's Car'			
38	1938	Second Series pre-production 'People's Car (Volkswagen) – 30 built	125	1940	Wind-powered generator feasibility study
52	1934	Auto Union sports car Design	126	1940/41	Fully synchronized power transmission for KdF wagen
60	1934/41	KdF small car – Volkswagen ('KdF' = *Kraft durch Freude* or 'Strength through Joy')	128	1940/41	KdF-based amphibian prototype Schwimmwagen
60K10	1939	KdF sports coupé for Berlin–Rome race	129	1940	Short chassis version of Type 128
			133	1940/41	Carburettor design
62	1936	KdF cross country: open-sided body	135	1940/41	Wind power generator 130 watt
64	1937/38	Sports car 1.1-litre: based on KdF components	136	1940/41	Wind power generator 736 watt
			137	1940/41	Wind power generator 4500 watt
66	1938	KdF right-hand drive	138	1940/41	Amphibian Schwimmwagen: alternate design
67	1939	KdF ambulance			
68	1939	KdF panel van	139	1941	Variation of Type 138 without central chassis spine
70	1936	'X'-form 32-cylinder 17.7-litre liquid-cooled aero engine			
72	1936	V-16 19.7-litre liquid-cooled aero engine	151	1941	KdF-Volkswagen 'Plus' power transmission system
			152	1941	'Steiber' power transmission system for Volkswagen
76	1936	Laboratory unit			
78	1937	Sleeve valve aero engine	153	1941	Skoda 'Ostrad' traction engine with air-cooled six cylinder engine
80	1938/39	Mercedes-Benz land speed record car			
81	1939	Volkswagen van chassis	155	1941	Half-track version of Type 82 Kübelwagen
82	1939/40	KdF-based military Kübelwagen			
83	1939/40	Volkswagen with 'Kreis' power transmission system	156	1941	Modification of Type 166 for use on rail
84	1939/40	Volkswagen with 'Dr Hering' power transmission system	157	1941	Railway conversions of Types 82/87
85	1939/40	Volkswagen four-wheel drive study	158	1941	Wood gas generator for automotive use
86	1949	Kübelwagen four-wheel drive feasibility study			
87	1939/41	Kübelwagen with four-wheel drive	160	1941	Self supporting body feasibility study for Volkswagen
88	1949	Bus body on Kübelwagen chassis			
89	1940	Beier automatic transmission system for Volkswagen	162	1941	Experimental Kübelwagen with self-supporting body
92	1940	Cross-country adaptation of Kübelwagen	164	1941/42	Three axle experimental cross-country truck with dual engines
93	1940	Limited slip differential	166	1942	Production version of amphibious Schwimmwagen
94	1937	W-24 Daimler-Benz Grand Prix racing engine	170	1942	Marine Landing Craft (*Sturmboot*) power unit: version I
95	1940	Buss chassis and suspension	171	1942	Marine Landing-Craft (*Sturmboot*) power unit: version II
96	1940	Hydraulic power transmission system			
97	1940	Daimler-Benz heavy truck	174	1942	Marine Landing-Craft (*Sturmboot*) power unit using normal KdF engine
98	1940	Volkswagen amphibious car with Type 62 body	175	1942	Steel-wheeled military tractor Ostradschlepper
100	1939/41	Leopard tank prototype			
101	1942	Tiger battle tank with 88mm gun	177	1942	Five-speed gearbox for Type 82 Kübelwagen
102	1942	Type 101 with hydraulic transmission			
103	1942	Tiger tank with Voith electric transmission	179	1942	Fuel injection system for KdF-Volkswagen engine
106	1939	Volkswagen Type 60 with PIM experimental power transmission	180	1942	Tank design with electric transmission
107	1939	Volkswagen supercharged engine	181	1942	Tank design with hydraulic transmission
108	1938	2-stage supercharger for Mercedes-Benz	182	1942	High-chassis, sand tyred & tropicalized 'Kübelwagen'
109	1939	Motorcycle engine			
110	1938/39	Small tractor Volkspflug	187	1942	Type 182 Tropical Kübelwagen four-wheel-drive
111	1939/40	Small tractor: new design			
112	1940/41	Larger-engined small tractor	198	1942	Tank starter gear mounted on to Type 82 Kübelwagen
113	1941	Small tractor: version III			
114	1938/39	F-Wagen: 1.5-litre Porsche sports car design	200	1942	10-litre air-cooled diesel engine
			205	1942	180-ton tank Maus
115	1939	Supercharged 1.1-litre KdF engine overhead camshafts	209	1942	Daimler-Benz 44.5-litre air-cooled diesel engine

Appendix 2

Type	Year	Design item	Type	Year	Design item
212	1942	Air-cooled 16-cylinder diesel tank engine			5-speed gearbox
220	1942/43	Air-cooled V-16 36.8-litre super-charged diesel engine	383	1948	Porsche synchromesh system for VW gearbox
225	1942/43	Brown Bouverie electric power transmission for Volkswagen	384	1948	Alternative synchromesh gearbox for Volkswagen
230	1942/43	Wood/gas generator for Volkswagen	385	1948	Cisitilia water turbine
231	1942	Acetylene system for Volkswagen	425	1948	20hp diesel tractor
235	1942/43	Electric transmission for Volkswagen	502	1950/51	1.5-litre sports engine for Type 356 car
236	1942/43	Grating for use with wood/gas generator Type 230	506	1950/51	1.3-litre engine for Type 356 car
			506/2	1954/55	Type 506 with 3-piece crankcase
238	1942/43	Cable hoist for use on Volkswagen/Kübelwagen	509	1951	1.3-litre prototype engine, developed from Type 506 unit
239	1942/43	Wood/gas generator for Type 82 Kübelwagen	514	1951	Le Mans cars for 1951 (Type 356 SL)
			519	1951/52	Synchromesh gearbox for Type 356
240	1942/43	Propane gas conversion for VW/Kübelwagen engine	522	1952	Volkswagen design proposal with strut-type front suspension
245	1942	18-ton multi-purpose tank	527	1951/52	1.5-litre production engine for Type 356: 60 bhp
247	1943	VW-based aero engine			
250	1942/43	Turretless tank with 105 mm gun	528	1952/53	1.5-litre sports engine for Type 356: 1500S or Super
252	1943	Volkswagen 'PIV' power transmission	528/2	1954/55	Type 528 with 3-piece crankcase
261	1943	Interior heating for Panther tank	530	1951/52	Experimental four-seat Porsche: 2400 mm wheelbase
276	1943	Pintle towing hook for Type 82 Kübelwagen	531	1952	1.3-litre engine with revised camshaft
283	1943	Modified wood/gas generator for Type 82 Kübelwagen	532	1952	Single carburetter for Type 369 engine
285	1944/45	Water turbine: 3.5hp: experimental version	533	1952	1.1-litre racing engine
			534	1952/53	Porsche/Volkswagen small sports car prototype
287	1944	Command car on 4-wheel-drive chassis	535	1953	Porsche-Allgaier plantation tractor
288	1944/45	Water turbine 13hp	539	1953	1.5-litre engine for 356
289	1944/45	Water turbine 15hp	540	1952	America Roadster and Speedster bodies
291	1945	Through-flow water turbine (up to 40hp)	541	1952	Special sporting version of 356
292	1945	Through-flow water turbine (65hp)	542	1952/53	Studebaker V-6 Sedan
293	1944	Tracked personnel carrier (also modified for rail use)	543	1952	Industrial version of 1.5-litre flat-four engine
294	1944	Ski rack	544	1952	Industrial version of 1.5-litre flat-four engine
298	1944/45	Radio receiver for Volkswagen			
307	1945	Dense-medium carburettor	546	1952/53	Plain-bearing version of Type 527: 1500 or Normal
309	1945	2-stroke diesel engine for VW or tractor	546/2	1954/55	Type 546 with 3-piece crankcase
312	1945	Petrol-engined tractor	547	1952/53	1.5-litre four-camshaft racing engine
313	1945	Diesel tractor	547/1	1955	Production version 1.5-litre Type 547
315	1945	Ski cable for VW engine power	547/3	1958	Developed 1.5-litre racing engine for Type 718 and 718/2
323	1946	11hp diesel tractor			
328	1946	28hp tractor	547/4	1957	1.6-litre racing engine for Type 718
335	1946	Drum winch	547/5	1957	1.7-litre racing engine for Type 718
336	1946	Capstan winch	550	1953	Mid-engined 2-seat sports-racing car
339	1946	Conveyor belt	550A	1956	Redesigned Type 550 with tubular space frame
340	1946	Two-wheel whellbarrow			
352	1947	Saloon car study for von Senger	555	1956	Prototype for Volkswagen
355	1947	Delivery van based on Volkswagen	557	1956	1.5-litre Porsche flat-four engine for USA
356	1947	2-seater sports car on VW basis: first production Porsche	559	1957	Power transmission study
356/2	1947/48	Porsche sports car: built in Gmünd	568	1957	Exhaust induced cooling system for Fletcher Aviation (USA)
356A	1955/56	T-2 bodied Porsche:1600cc engines	574	1957	Electric clutch design for 356A
356B	1959/60	T-5 bodied Porsche	575	1958	Support bracket
356C	1963/64	Final version of 356 Porsche: T-6 body:disc brakes	577	1958	Porsche/Dunlop disc brake design for 356
356 SL	1951	Racing version of Type 356/2 coupe	587	1961	2.0-litre racing engine for Type 718
360	1947/48	Cisitalia Grand Prix car	587/1	1961/62	Production version of Type 587 for Carrera 2
361	1947	Single-cylinder test engine for Type 360 Grand Prix car	587/2	1963	Racing version of Type 587/1 engine
362	1948	2-litre unsupercharged version of Type 360 Grand Prix car	587/3	1963/64	Improved 2.0-litre racing engine for Type 904
369	1949/50	1.1-litre engine for Type 356/2 and 356 cars	589	1953/54	1.3-litre sports engine for Type 356: 1300S
370	1947	Cisitalia 1.5-litre sports-touring car	589/2	1954/55	Type 589 with 3-piece crankcase
372	1947	Cisitalia 2-litre sports car with air-cooled V-8 100bhp engine with	592	1955	2-litre experimental engine

Appendix 2

Type	Year	Design item
593	1955	Reinforced four-speed gearbox
596	1956	Two-cylinder industrial engine
597	1954/55	Jagdwagen (Hunter) 4-×4 on-off road vehicle
606	1955	Underfloor engine design for Volkswagen
616/1	1955/56	1.6-litre engine for Type 356A 1600
616/2	1955/56	1.6-litre sports engine for Type 356A 1600S
616/3	1956	Industrial version of Type 616/1
616/7	1960	90hp engine for Type 356B/1600S-90 or Super 90
616/12	1961/62	Type 616/2 with cast iron cylinders for Type 356B
616/15	1963/64	1.6-litre engine for Type 356C 1600C
616/16	1963/64	1.6-litre sports engine for Type 356C 1600SC
616/36	1965	1.6-litre engine for Type 912
616/39	1967/68	Type 616/36 with U.S. emission control
619	1957	Volkswagen diesel engine study
621	1957	Porsche/Allgaier single cylinder engined tractor
622	1957	Porsche/Allgaier two-cylinder engined tractor
623	1957	Porsche/Allgaier three-cylinder engined tractor
624	1957	Porsche/Allgaier four-cylinder engined tractor
627	1957/58	Volkswagen swing-axle
628	1957/58	Volkswagen interior heating system
631	1957/58	Porsche diesel engine study
632	1957	Development studies for 356
633	1957	Revision of Studebaker saloon design
638	1958	Volkswagen engine studies – 1.2- and 1.6-litre flat six underfloor units
643	1956	Four-speed gearbox for 356
644	1957	4-speed tunnel-case gearbox for Type 356B
645	1956	Experimental sports-racing car 'Mickey Mouse'
654	1956	Motor boat design study
655	1956	Single cylinder 49.8cc air-cooled moped engine
672	1956/57	Volkswagen mini-car design study, using underfloor engine
673	1956/57	Volkswagen 1.2- and 1.6-litre six-cylinder engine design studies
675	1958	Volkswagen small car design study
678	1959	1.6-litre aero engine
678/1	1959	65hp aero engine with reduction gear
678/3	1959	52hp aero engine direct drive
678/4	1959	75hp aero engine with reduction gear
690	1958	5-speed tunnel-case transmission for Type 718
691	1956	Type designation for Type 550RS Spyder for 1956
692	1958	Improved 4-camshaft engine for Carrera
692/0	1958	1.5-litre Type 692 with roller bearings
692/1	1958	1.5-litre Type 692 with plain bearings
692/2	1958/59	1.6-litre plain-bearing Type 692 for touring Carrera
692/3	1959	GT racing version of Type 692/3
692/3A	1961	Improved Type 692/3 with *Schleifsteine*
693	1958	1.3-litre version of engine Type 547
694	1958	Civilianized cross-country development of Type 597 *Jagdwagen*
695	1959	Porsche disc brake design
700	1959	Large family car design study for Volkswagen
702	1961	75hp aero engine for helicopter use (Gyrodyne)
703	1959	Design developments for 1.6-litre engine
704	1959	Porsche diesel engine design study
709	1959	Porsche gearbox investigative design studies
710	1959	Improved synchromesh gearbox for 356
715	1959	Test-bed gearbox
716	1959	4-speed gearbox for Type 356A with improved synchromesh
718	1957	Mid-engined sports-racing car
718/2	1959	1.5-litre single-seater racing car
719	1959	Fuel injected racing engine for RSK
722	1959	Flat underfloor-mounted engine design for Volkswagen
724	1959	1.4-litre flat-four Volkswagen engine
726	1959	Body on VW chassis for Volkswagen
728	1959	Development of Type 675 for Volkswagen
729	1958	Inboard-mounted flat-four marine engine
737	1959/60	Porsche outboard motor
741	1959/60	4-speed gearbox for Type 356B
741/A	1961/62	4-speed gearbox for Type 356B and 356C
751	1960	Gearbox with automatic clutch for Volkswagen
752	1960	Volkswagen flat-four engine of 1,000cc
756	1959	Body and chassis design for Carrera Abarth GTL
759	1959	Porsche drive four-speed gearbox
763	1959	Production seat design
764	1959	Volkswagen six-seat saloon car design
768	1959	1.6-litre fuel injection flat-four engine
769	1959	Porsche differential design
775	1959	Six-speed gearbox for coupling to diesel engine
787	1961	Grand Prix car
792	1960	Inboard boat engine
798	1962	Chassis and transmission for 2000GS/GT
801	1961	1.6–1.8-litre flat four engine
802	1961	Fuel injected flat-four engine (Michael May engine)
804	1962	Grand Prix car
902/0	1965/66	4-speed gearbox for Type 912 and 911
902/01	1967/68	4-speed gearbox for Type 912
902/02	1967/68	5-speed gearbox for Type 912
902/1	1965/66	5-speed gearbox for Type 912 and 911
903	1963	Automatic clutch for sports car
904	1963/64	4-cylinder mid-engined GT competition coupe
912	1965	4-cylinder engined version of Type 911
912E	1975/76	Fuel-injected four-cylinder engined version of Type 911
914	1969/70	Mid-4-cylinder-engined Volkswagen/Porsche
914/11	1969/70	5-speed gearbox for Type 914 and 914/6
914/12	1972/73	5-speed gearbox for Type 914
923	1975/76	2.0-litre engine for Type 912E
966	1970/71	Projected mid-engined production Volkswagen

APPENDIX 3: PORSCHE FLAT-FOURS AND THEIR ADVERSARIES

1955

Car and model	Engine Type and Size	Gearbox	Road-Test Speed	Consumption	GB Price*
Porsche Super 356 Spyder	Flat-4 air-cooled 1,488cc	4-speed	110.6mph (177kph)	27/30mpg (43/48kpg)	£1,320/00s
Alfa Romeo Giulietta Spyder	In-line 4 cyl w/c dohc 1,290cc	4-speed	105.0mph (168kph)	30/35mpg (48/56kpg)	£1,300/00s
MGA 1500	In-line 4 cyl w/cooled 1,489cc	4-speed	96.7mph (155kph)	26/29mpg (42/46kpg)	£595/00s
Morgan Plus Four	In-line 4 cyl w/cooled 1,991cc	4-speed	95.3mph (152kph)	27/32mpg (43/51kpg)	£795/00s
Triumph TR3	In-line 4 cyl w/cooled 1,991cc	4-speed	104.7mph (167kph)	26/32mpg (42/51kpg)	£765/00s

1958

Car and model	Engine Type and Size	Gearbox	Road-Test Speed	Consumption	GB Price*
Porsche 356A Carrera Cabriolet 1600	Flat-4 air-cooled dohc 1,587cc	4-speed	124mph (200kph)	25/30mpg (40/48kpg)	£1950/00s
Alfa Romeo Giulietta Spyder	In-line 4 cyl w/c dohc 1,290cc	4-speed	105mph (168kph)	30/35mpg (48/56kpg)	£1,300/00s
Lotus Elite Coupé	In-line 4 cyl w/c sohc 1,216cc	4-speed	112mph (179kph)	30/35mpg (48/56kpg)	£1,299/00s
MGA Twin-Cam	In-line 4 cyl w/c dohc 1,588cc	4-speed	107mph (171kph)	22/28mpg (35/45kpg)	£842/10s
Morgan Plus Four	In-line 4 cyl w/cooled 1,991cc	4-speed	95.3mph (152kph)	27/32mpg (43/51kpg)	£732/00s
Triumph TR3A	In-line 4 cyl w/cooled 1,991cc	4-speed	105mph (168kph)	25/31mpg (40/50kpg)	£793/00s

*Above prices do not include taxes

1960

Car and model	Engine Type and Size	Gearbox	Road-Test Speed	Consumption	GB Price*
Porsche 356B 1600S-90	Flat-4 air-cooled 1,582cc	4-speed	115mph (185kph)	29/38mpg (46/61kpg)	£1,330/00s
Alfa Romeo Giulietta Spyder	In-line 4 cyl w/c dohc 1,290cc	4-speed	105mph (168kph)	30/35mpg (48/56kpg)	£1,300/00s
Lotus Elite coupé	In-line 4 cyl w/c sohc 1,216cc	4-speed	112mph (179kph)	30/35mpg (48/56kpg)	£1,299/00s
MGA 1600 Mk I	In-line 4 cyl w/cooled 1,588cc	4-speed	100.9mph (161kph)	24/31mpg (38/50kpg)	£663/00s
Morgan Plus Four	In-line 4 cyl w/cooled 1,991cc	4-speed	95.3mph (152kph)	27/32mpg (43/51kpg)	£732/00s
Sunbeam Alpine	In-line 4 cyl w/cooled 1,494cc	4sp + o/drive	99mph (158kph)	25/28mpg (40/45kpg)	£685/00s
Triumph TR3A	In-line 4 cyl w/cooled 1,991cc	4-speed	105mph (168kph)	25/31mpg (40/50kpg)	£793/00s

1962

Car and model	Engine Type and Size	Gearbox	Road-Test Speed	Consumption	GB Price*
Porsche 356B 1600S-90 cabriolet/coupé	Flat-4 air-cooled 1,582cc	4-speed	115mph (185kph)	28/36mpg (45/58kpg)	£1,707/00s
Alfa Romeo Giulia Spyder	In-line 4 cyl w/c dohc 1,570cc	5-speed	109mph (174kph)	28/34mpg (45/54kpg)	£1,470/00s
Elva Courier Sports	In-line 4 cyl w/cooled 1,622cc	4-speed	105mph (168kph)	27/33mpg (43/54kpg)	£702/00s
Lotus Elite S/E	In-line 4 cyl w/c sohc 1,216cc	4-speed	120mph (192kph)	28/35mpg (45/56kpg)	£1,495/00s
MGA 1600 Mk II	In-line 4 cyl w/cooled 1,622cc	4-speed	105mph (168kph)	25/31mpg (40/50kpg)	£663/00s
Morgan Plus Four	In-line 4 cyl w/cooled 1,991cc	4-speed	95.3mph (152kph)	27/32mpg (43/51kpg)	£815/00s
Sunbeam Alpine	In-line 4 cyl w/cooled 1,592cc	4sp + o/drive	101mph (162kph)	25/28mpg (40/45kpg)	£712/00s
Triumph TR4	In-line 4 cyl w/cooled 1,991cc	4-speed	110mph (176kph)	25/30mpg (40/48kpg)	£825/00s

*Above prices do not include taxes

1972/73

Car and model	Engine Type, Size and Power	Gearbox	Road-Test Speed	Consumption	GB Price*
Alfa Romeo 2000GTV	4 in-line water cooled dohc 1,962cc, 124bhp	5-speed	110mph (176kph)	23/27mpg (37/43kpg)	£4,009.00
Alfa Romeo 2000 Spyder	4 in-line water cooled dohc 1,962cc, 124bhp	5-speed	121mph (193kph)	20/24mpg (32/38kpg)	£2,195.00
Lotus Europa	4 in-line water cooled ohv 1,558cc, 106bhp	4-speed	117mph (187kph)	26/30mpg (42/48kpg)	£2,224.00
Porsche 914/4	Flat-4 air-cooled pushrod ohv 1,795cc, 92bhp	5 speed	110mph (176kph)	23/28mpg (37/45kpg)	£3,596.00
Triumph GT6 coupé	6 cylinder in-line water cooled ohv 1,998cc, 104bhp	4-speed	107mph (171kph)	26/28mpg (42/45kpg)	£1,469.00
MGB GT coupé	4 in-line water cooled ohv 1,798cc, 95bhp	4-speed	103mph (165kph)	25/27mpg (40/43kpg)	£1,570.00

1976

Car and model	Engine Type, Size and Power	Gearbox	Road-Test Speed	Consumption	GB Price*
Porsche 912E	Flat-4 air-cooled pushrod ohv 1,971cc, 90bhp	5 speed	115mph (184kph)	28/34mpg (45/54kpg)	£7,350.00 (est)*
Datsun 280Z	6 cylinder in-line water cooled ohc 2,753cc, 162bhp	4/5-speed	127mph (203kph)	24/26mpg (38/42kpg)	£3,900.00 (est)*
Lotus Esprit	4 in-line water cooled dohc 1,973cc, 155bhp	5-speed	138mph (220kph)	28/30mpg (45/48kpg)	£7,883.00
Triumph TR7	4 in-line water cooled ohc 1,998cc, 90bhp	4-speed	108mph (173kph)	25/29mpg (40/46kpg)	£3,146.00
TVR 3000M	V-6 water cooled ohv 2,994cc, 142bhp	4-speed	125mph (200kph)	23/27mpg (37/43kpg)	£3,990.00
Jensen Healey	4 in-line water cooled dohc 1,973cc, 140bhp	4-speed	120mph (192kph)	28/30mpg (45/48kpg)	£2,190.00

*Price converted to Sterling and adjusted to allow for import duties and taxes. Car actually not available in GB

INDEX

Numbers in **bold** identify illustrations.

Abarth 26, 135, 139, 145
AFN Limited 54, 55
Aldington brothers 54
Alfa Romeo 26, 52, 63, 64, 102, 115, 117, 137, 145, **145**, 146, 158, **197**, 198, **199**, 200
Austrian-Daimler 7, 8, **9**, **10**, 11
Auto-Union 13, **14**, 16, 17, 28, 59, 115
Autocar 158, 159
Avus (Berlin) 84

Baden-Baden Rally 61
Barth, Edgar 88, **94**, 97, 144
Behra, Jean **87**, 88
Benz 5, 12
Berlin-Rome-Berlin 17
Bertone, Nuccio 137
Beutler 40, 42, 156, 157, 158
Blocking Synchromesh 153
Bonnier, Jo 90, 92, **92**, 94, 95, 97, 144
Brabham, Jack 92
Brussels Motor Show 77

Car & Driver 177, 184
Caracciola, Rudolf **12**, 50
Carrera Panamericana **64**, 65, 74, 77
Chassis Number groups 201
Cisitalia Grand Prix car 26, 27, **27**, 57, 66, 113

Daimler, Gottlieb 5
de Beaufort, Carel 95, 133
Dean, James 53
Donington Park 16, 26
Drive shafts, Type 912 194
Dusio, Piero 26

Earls Court Motor Show 53
El Alamein, Battle of 21
Engine assembly **46**
Engine comparisons 57

Ferdinand anti-tank cannon 23, **23**, 24
Fletcher Aviation 74
Frankfurt Motor Show 105, 108, 116
Franz-Ferdinand, Archduke 7, 8, 8
French GP 95, 97
Frere, Paul 74, 88
Front suspension 356 **69**
Fuhrmann, Ernst 60, 75, 77

Gendebein, Olivier 92
Ginther, Ritchie 94

Glockler, Helm 74, 75, **81**
Glockler, Walter 62, **63**, 72, **72**, 74
Glockler-Porsche 62, 63, 72, **72**, 73
Gmünd 17, 23, **24**, 28, 30, 32, 34, 37, 42, 158
Gmünd Porsches 60, **60**, **61**, 62, 63
Goetze, Rolf 123, **123**
Gregory, Masten 89
Gugelot Karrosserie 180
Gurney, Dan 89, 94, 95, **95**, 97
Gyrodyne Corporation 52, 109, **109**

Heinkel Flugzeugbau 144, **145**
Henry, Prince of Prussia (Trial) 8, 10
Henschel, Dr Ernst 37
Herrmann, Hans 74, **74**, 77, 79, 83, 90, 94, 95
Hill, Graham 92
Hill, Phil 94, 144
Hindenburg, Count von 13
Hirth, Albert 57
Hitler, Adolf 13, 16, 20, 24
Hockenheim 92
Hoffman, Max 50, 53, 66, 133
Holbert, Bob 89
Hruska, Rudolf 37, 135, 136, **136**
Hungarian Grand Prix 14

Jaguar 51, 51, 79

Komenda, Erwin 19, 20, 75, 102
Kubelwagen 21, 21, 22, **22**, 52, 109, 111

Landwehr **10**
Lautenschlager, Christian 11
Le Mans 24 Hrs Race 50, 59, 60, **60**, 61, **61**, 65, **73**, 74, 77, 78, **81**, 84, 87, 89, 140, **140**, 141, 149,
Leopard tank 22
Liege-Rome-Liege Rally 62, **63**, 66, 133
Linge, Herbert 88, 144
Lohner, Ludwig 6
Lohner-Porsche 7, 7
Lotus 146, 147, 149, 197, **198**
Lurani, Count "Johnny" 64

Maffersdorf 5, **5**
Maglioli, Umberto 83, 88, 123
Mahle pistons 47
Masaryk Race 13

May, Michael **82**, 83, 97
Meisl, Charles 53, 54
Mercedes 7, 11, **11**, 12, **12**
Mercedes-Benz 16, 28, 64, 65, 156
MG 198, 196, **199**, 200
Mille Miglia 63, 64, 65, 77, 87, 123, 126, 132, 135
Modern Motor 177
Monaco GP 90
Monte Carlo Rally 134, **134**, 149, 151, **151**
Montlhery 62, 63, 72
Monza Autodrome 79, 84
Moss, Stirling 89, 90, 92, **94**
Mussolini, Benito 16

Neuebauer, Alfred 11
Nordhoff, Heinz 28, 66, 98
NSU 12, 13
Nurburgring 74, 77, 83, 87, 134

Olympic Games 16

Paris Salon 50, 77
Piech, Anton 25
Piech, Louise 25
Polenski, Helmut 79, 81
Pomigliano d'Arco 37
Porsche
 Diesel Motorenbau 109
 Flat Four adversaries 206
 Type 52 115, **116**
 Type 60-K10 (T64) 17, **17**, 18
 Type 70 (Aero engine) 15
 Type 80 (LSR car) 15
 Type 111 Tractor 109, **109**
 Type 114, 17, 18, 19
 Type 136 22
 Type 174 23, **23**
 Type 356 "Ferdinand" 41
 Type 356 "Windhund" 41
 Type 356 (1952) 68
 Type 356 189
 Type 356 1100/1300 44
 Type 356 1300 46, **47**
 Type 356 1500 45
Porsche
 Type 356 America 99
 Type 356 Beutler 41, 42, **43**
 Type 356 Cabriolet **55**
 Type 356 Carrera 1500 115, 117, 124
 Type 356 Carrera 1600 123, 125, 126, **126**
 Type 356 Carrera 2000 129, 130, 131, 132, **132**
 Type 356 Carrera Speedster 116, 117, **121**, 123, **123**, 131

207

Index

Type 356 Continental 104, **104**
Type 356 Convertible D 114, **114**
Type 356 dashboard **56**
Type 356 Gmünd models 35, **36**, 37, 38, **38**, **39**
Type 356 prototype 28, 29, **31**, 33, 33, **33**, 34
Type 356 Speedster 53
Type 356 Speedster 98, 101, 102, **102**, **103**, 104
Type 356, 5000th 99, **99**
Type 356A 105, **105**, 106, 107, **107**, 108, **108**
Type 356A Carrera GS 118, 119, **119**, 122
Type 356A Carrera GT 120
Type 356A Speedster 105, 114
Type 356A/S 70, 100, 114, **114**
Type 356B 153, **153**, 154, **154**, 155, 160, **161**
Type 356B 2000GS-GT 135, 141, 142, 143, **143**, 144
Type 356B Carrera 1600 **127**, 128
Type 356B Carrera GTL 135, 137, **137**, 138, 139, **139**, **140**
Type 356B Karmann Hardtop 162, **162**
Type 356B Super 75 159
Type 356B T-6 162, 163, **163**, 164, **164**, **165**
Type 356C 164, 165, **165**, 166, 167, **167**, **168**, 172, 173, **191**
Type 360
Type 369 engine 30
Type 519 gearbox **69**, 71
Type 527 engine 71
Type 528 engine 71
Type 530 52, **52**
Type 540 America 65, **65**, 66, 67
Type 540 America Roadster 98
Type 546 engine 71, **71**
Type 547 Engine 75, 77, **77**, 117, **117**, 121
Type 550 72, **73**, 74
Type 550/1500RS 75, 76, 77, 78, **78**, 79, **79**
Type 550A/1500RS 80, 81, **82**
Type 587 Engine **127**, 131, 140
Type 589 Engine 99, **101**
Type 597 4x4 109, 110, 111, **111**, 112, 113, **113**
Type 616 Engine 172, **193**
Type 644 Gearbox 108
Type 645 (*Mickey Mouse*) 83, **83**, 84
Type 678 Engine 111, **111**

Type 718 84, **84**, 85, 86, 87, **87**, 88, **88**, 89, **89**, 91
Type 718 F2 car 90, 92, **92**, 93, 94, **94**, **95**
Type 787/1 97
Type 902 170, 171
Type 904GTS 144, **144**, 145, **145**, 146, **146**, 147, **147**, 148, 149, **149**, 150, 151, **151**, 191
Type 912 171, **171**, 172, 173, **173**, **174**, **175**, 176, 177, **177**, **178**, 179, **179**, 189, 193
Type 912E 186, **186**, 187, 188, 194
Type 914-4 180, 181, **182**, 183, **185**, 189, 194, 196
Type F1-804/4 96, 97, **97**
Type Numbers 202-205
Anton 6
Professor Dr Ferry 28, **33**, 48, **48**, 50, 52, 54, 55, 62, 66, 69, 72, 83, 90, 98, 107, 102, 115
Professor Ferdinand 5, 6, **6**, 7, **8**, 8, 9, **9**, 11, 12, 13, 16, 22, 23, 24, 25, 26, **26**, 32, **33**, 33, 37, 59, 60, 84
Ferdinand Alexander (Butzi) 144, 175, 180
-Allgaier 109
-VW Engine Type W80 182, 195
Prinzing, Albert 38, 39, 54, 109

Rabe, Karl-Peter 47, 71
RAC Rally **54**
Reimspriess, Franz Xavier 137, 139
Reutter 38, 40, 43, 55
Rheims 84, 90, 132
Riley 9, **9**, 104
Ringenberg, Walter 79
Road & Track **178**, 185
Road Test 179, 180
Roller bearing crankshaft 57, 58, 58
Rosemeyer, Berndt 16
Rucker, Klaus 123

Sailer, Karl 11
Sascha **10**
Sauter, Heinrich 65, 66
Scania-Vabis 42
Schmidt, Karl coachworks 40
Schwimmwagen 22
Sebring 12 Hours Race 149
Semmering 6, 7
Senger, Rupprecht von 32, 33, 34
Skoda, Baron 9
Speer, Albert **23**

Sports Car World 161, 162, 168, 169
Sports Cars Illustrated 161
Steyr 12
Storez, Claude 123
Strahle/Linge 126
Stuck, Hans, 13, **14**
Studebaker 52
Stuttgart 356, 40, 45, **45**
Suspension, Type 356 **40**
Sweden 42
Swiss Grand Prix 13

Targa Florio 11, 83, 84, 88, 134, 143, **143**, 149
Thompson, Richard 101
Tiger tank 22
Tomala, Hans 97
Triumph 102, 198, 200

Underbody coating, Type 356 190, **190**
US Army 37, 45, 107
US Marine Corps 52, 109

Veuillet, Auguste 59, 61,
Volkswagen 13, **14**, 16, 17, 18, 20, 38, 56, 57, 59, 66, 98, 107, 109, 111, 152, 170, 180, 184
Volkswagen Type 62 20, **21**
Volkswagen Type 64 20, 28,
Volkswagen Type 82 20
Volkswagen Type 82A 20, 22, **22**
Volkswagen Type 86 20
Volkswagen Type 87 20
Volkswagen Type 128 22
Volkswagen Type 166 22
von Frankenberg, Richard 62, **73**, 74, 77, 79, **81**, 83, 84
von Hanstein, Huschke 54, 62, 72, 133,
von Neumann, Johnny 53, 103, 133
von Trips, Wolfgang 83, 90, 94

Walker, Rob 94
Weber, Friedrich 30, 32
Weidenhausen coachworks 72
Wendler coachwork 156
Werner, Christian 11
Wiener-Neustadt 9
Wolfsburg 20, 28, 66, 170, 180
World War 2 20, 34, 42, 50, 51, 104, 115

Zagato, Carrozzeria 137
Zuffenhausen 37
Zundapp 12, 13, **13**

208